After state regulators forced Binion to give up his interests in the Horseshoe Club, Binion kept up his spirits, but he took the news hard. He returned to a life of alcohol and drugs, further straining his relationship with Murphy, who had grown accustomed to spending $5,000 a month, sometimes much more, of his money on clothes and dining at gourmet restaurants.

Anticipating a breakup, Murphy was looking to profit financially from the three years she had invested in the relationship so she could continue to lead a life of luxury. She knew that she had signed a cohabitation agreement and that Binion had not put her in the will.

Tabish, meanwhile, was deep in debt and saw Binion's wealth as a quick way to ease his financial troubles. And Murphy had the kind of charm and sexually expressive personality that played up to Tabish's virility. Even better, Murphy was close to Binion, his potential cash cow.

And so began the plot to kill the wealthy fifty-five-year-old gambling figure.

THE DEATH OF A
LAS VEGAS CASINO BOSS

MURDER
IN
SIN
CITY

JEFF GERMAN

AVON BOOKS
An Imprint of HarperCollinsPublishers

MURDER IN SIN CITY is a journalistic account of the actual murder investigation of Rick Tabish and Sandy Murphy for the 1998 killing of Ted Binion in Las Vegas, Nevada. The events recounted in this book are true. The personalities, events, actions, and conversations portrayed in this book have been constructed using court documents, including trial transcripts, extensive interviews, letters, personal papers, research, and press accounts. Quoted testimony has been taken verbatim from court transcripts and other sworn statements.

AVON BOOKS
An Imprint of HarperCollins*Publishers*
10 East 53rd Street
New York, New York 10022-5299

Copyright © 2001 by Jeff German
ISBN: 0-380-81873-6
www.avonbooks.com

First Avon Books paperback printing: August 2001

Avon Trademark Reg. U.S. Pat. Off. and in Other Countries, Marca Registrada, Hecho en U.S.A.
HarperCollins ® is a trademark of HarperCollins Publishers Inc.

Printed in the U.S.A.

10 9 8 7

*To the memory of June German,
my mother, my inspiration, my forever valentine*

Contents

······················
Author's Note
······················

THIS BOOK IS the result of more than three years of covering the troubled life and death of Ted Binion for the *Las Vegas Sun*. I have written more than 350 stories and columns on the subject and have spent countless additional hours doing research.

The story of Binion's demise has been pulled together from newspaper articles, secret and public court transcripts, confidential law enforcement documents and fresh interviews with key players in the homicide investigation.

I was not one of Binion's favorite reporters his last months alive. My stories disclosing his underworld ties led to the revocation of his gaming license, his downward spiral in life and, of course, his final betrayal. In the push to bring his killers to justice, I came to know Binion better in death than in life, and I learned to admire his uniqueness as the last of a dying breed of colorful casino bosses.

As with any project of this magnitude, there are many people to thank. I would like to start with my friends at the *Las Vegas Sun*. I owe a debt of gratitude to Publisher Barbara Greenspun and her astute sons, Brian and Danny Greenspun, for giving me the freedom to pursue this book. The Greenspuns have been like family to me over the years, and I am proud to have had a chance to sharpen my journalistic skills under the tutelage of the legendary Hank Greenspun.

Executive Editor Mike O'Callaghan, whom I regard as a second father, was always there for me on this project with the kind of solid advice that only he could give. And Managing Editor Michael J. Kelley, who has become a valued asset to the Las Vegas community in only a few short years, gave me the benefit of his insight and patience as I sometimes struggled to put this book together. Thanks also go out to Metro Editor Warren Johnston, who provided me with much encouragement and motivation. Johnston is what all big-city newspaper editors should strive to be. Photo Editor Marsh Starks was a huge help in assembling most of the pictures for this book that were taken by the newspaper's award-winning photographers, Steve Marcus, Lori Cain, Sam Morris, Aaron Mayes and Ethan Miller. And librarian Rebecca Clifford assisted with research. I also wish to thank my fellow reporters at the paper for carrying the load in my absence, as well as office manager Gail Perry and my other editors and copy editors, who I'm sure missed my smiling face on many occasions in the morning. Special thanks also to Stacy Willis and Martin Kuz for their well-done profiles of Sandy Murphy and Rick Tabish. Those stories were very helpful.

There are many people outside the *Las Vegas Sun* who deserve thanks, too.

I never really had a chance to get acquainted with Bonnie Binion, but I want to thank her for handling the tragedy of her father's death with grace and dignity. You'll see excerpts here later from a moving letter Bonnie wrote expressing sorrow over losing her father. I didn't come across the letter until the book was nearly completed, but it gave me comfort—as I'm sure it will give others—in dealing with the loss of a cherished parent.

Thanks also go out to Becky Behnen, who gave me the benefit of her keen sense of perception on a regular basis. Becky always was there to answer my questions. More than anyone, she was responsible for lighting a fire under investigators to uncover the truth about her brother's death. I also owe much gratitude to David Roger, who with this case has become one of the premier prosecutors in Las Vegas and probably the nation. I could not have written this book without his wisdom and assistance.

Tom Dillard earned a much-deserved reputation as the city's top private investigator during this case. Thank you, Tom, for putting up with my phone calls for more than two years. One of the many unsung heroes of this case was homicide detective James Buczek, who is as professional and dedicated as they come. Buczek was a tremendous help. So were David Wall, Wayne Petersen, James J. Brown, Richard Wright, Harry Claiborne, Joseph Bonaventure, Al Lasso, Nick Behnen, Stewart Bell, Bill Koot, Ron Flud and Bob Stoldal.

There were many others who provided me with inside information on both sides of this case, but wished to remain anonymous. Thanks to you, as well. You know who you are.

These acknowledgments would not be complete without expressing appreciation to Sarah Durand, a first-rate editor who made this first-time experience enjoyable for me.

I also wish to thank my group of close friends—among them Art Nadler, Frank Fertado, George McCabe, Rob Powers and Will Kemp—who put up with me for months while I was busy writing. Over drinks and coffee, they kept my spirits high and, once in a while, gave me good advice. I also had many consoling conversations with my brother-in-law Mike Smith, the *Sun*'s award-winning cartoonist.

My family members were especially supportive and understanding. I wasn't always there for them when they needed me during a difficult family time. Thanks to my father, Max German, sisters Julie Smith and Jill Zwerg, brother Jay German, and my other brother-in-law Fredric Zwerg. I love you all.

Finally, I wish to thank my mother, June German, who like many Las Vegans was enthralled with this story. Mom never missed reading one of my articles. She was my inspiration, always believing, even when I had my doubts, that I was capable of writing this book. She passed away six weeks before I signed my book deal and never got a chance to see the trial. You will always be in my heart, Mom. This is for you.

PART

I

The Death

CHAPTER 1

• • • • • • • • • • • • • • • • • • •

The Death Scene

• • • • • • • • • • • • • • • • • • •

STEVEN REINCKE, a veteran fire department paramedic, and his crew were the first to arrive at Ted Binion's posh ranch-style home in Las Vegas about 3:57 P.M. on September 17, 1998.

As they hurried past the opened steel security gates, they ran into Sandy Murphy, the wealthy gambling figure's beautiful twenty-six-year-old girlfriend, sobbing on the steps of the front door. Minutes earlier, the frantic former topless dancer had telephoned police to report that her "husband" had stopped breathing.

Hysterical and screaming, Murphy led the paramedics inside. They rushed along the white marble floors of the spacious sunken living room and passed the dining room on the right to Binion's den, his favorite place in the 8,000-square-foot home, where they found his lifeless body on a blue sleeping mat in the middle of the moth-colored carpeted floor. Clad only in a half-buttoned long-sleeve shirt and Calvin Klein briefs, the fifty-five-year-old Binion's arms were at his sides and his legs were straight and covered with a quilt. He was lying alongside his favorite piece of furniture, a plum-colored sofa that was worn out and spattered with cigarette burns on its left side, where Binion had often smoked and watched television on his thirty-two-inch console across the modest-sized room. Next to his body were a

3

pair of black jeans, some loafers, three disposable lighters, an opened package of Vantage cigarettes, a television remote control and, most intriguing of all, an empty bottle of the prescription sedative Xanax that the former casino executive had obtained a day earlier. Binion, the second son of the late gaming pioneer Benny Binion, who founded the downtown Horseshoe Club, one of the most popular gambling joints in Las Vegas, was known to take Xanax to ease himself off heroin, a drug he had been addicted to for years.

It didn't take long for Reincke to discover that Binion had been dead for some time. His face looked ashen and there were signs of rigor mortis in his jaw. As Reincke examined the body, Murphy, an athletically built bottle blonde, returned to the den in an excited state.

"She came running into the room and just about fell on the body," Reincke later testified.

As his partners escorted Murphy out of the den, a twenty-foot-by-thirty-foot room with a low ten-foot-high ceiling, Reincke determined that Binion had no pulse and wasn't breathing. His pupils were dilated. Turning Binion over onto his right side, the paramedic saw large purple bruises on his back, which meant his blood had not been circulating for some time. No attempts were made to revive Binion.

Once it was clear that the casino boss was dead, police and crime-scene analysts were called to the home. Michael Perkins, a seasoned crime lab supervisor, took charge of surveying the death scene. Upon entering the house, Perkins found it odd to see a Halloween decoration, a white skeleton with "R.I P." in large black letters, hanging over a light fixture above the doorway. Halloween, he thought, was six weeks away.

By now, word about Binion's death had spread throughout his upscale neighborhood. Reporters, friends, family members and neighbors began congregating outside his 2408 Palomino Lane home as a steady stream of plainclothes and uniformed officers made their way inside what quickly became a chaotic scene. The phone was ringing constantly in the den while Reincke attended to Binion's body. Messages from well-wishers were pouring into a recorder.

Perkins and his crime analysts scoured the den, taking photographs and looking for more clues to Binion's death. The room was filled with mementos from Binion's colorful life. On one glass end table on which Binion usually sat was a large glass ashtray, a pair of reading glasses and a photo of Binion as a teenager at his father's ranch in Montana, standing next to a bobcat that had been hunted down. There also was an empty envelope from Peter Ribaste, a reputed Kansas City mob associate who had been sending Binion monthly checks to repay a $100,000 loan. There was the book *Players: The Men Who Made Las Vegas,* written by local author Jack Sheehan. It contained a chapter on Benny Binion. Also on the end table was an invitation to the Las Vegas premiere of the documentary *Mob Law,* the life story of criminal defense attorney Oscar Goodman before he was elected mayor of Las Vegas in June 1999.

Across the wallpapered room were Civil War, fishing and gun books, as well as various Western knickknacks, scattered on large white bookshelves and cabinets that took up the entire wall. In the middle was his television console. And on one end near the entrance to the den was a thirteen-inch split-screen surveillance monitor attached to video cameras outside his home. On a padded bench on the other side of the room, next to a door that led to one of Binion's garages, was a Victoria's Secret magazine addressed to Murphy. There also was a note from Murphy written on a large white envelope. It read: "Teddy, I went to the gym. I couldn't sleep this morning. Love you, Sandy."

In the bathroom inside the den, crime-scene experts found heroin paraphernalia and a large knife with a small amount of black tar heroin on it. The items were on top of a gold-colored plastic stand next to the toilet. That discovery, along with the empty bottle of pills and the fact that there were no signs of violence inside the house, was enough to persuade police to go on the evening news and suggest that Binion had died of a drug overdose. It was no secret, after all, that Binion had returned to using heroin in March after Nevada gaming regulators kicked him out of the casino industry because of his ties to underworld figures.

Like his legendary father, Binion was a man of many vices and temptations. He became hooked on heroin in 1980 and later wound up arrested for possessing the street drug in 1987. His arrest led to the suspension of his gaming license as part owner and casino manager of his family's storied Horseshoe Club.

Following his separation from his wife and longtime companion, Doris, in 1995, Binion had found happiness prowling the adult nightclub scene with the likes of Herbert "Fat Herbie" Blitzstein, a confidant of slain Chicago mob kingpin Anthony Spilotro. Binion liked hanging out with wise guys and being with beautiful women. But he also was a homebody, an intelligent, well-read man regarded as an expert on many subjects, especially history and politics. His intellect, good-old-boy Texas drawl and gregarious personality enabled him to hobnob with the city's social elite whenever he chose to, affording him a varied lifestyle. On any given night, Binion could be seen escorting the outgoing Murphy around town to a $1,000-a-plate charity dinner with the movers and shakers, and then carousing at the topless clubs with the Blitzstein crowd the next evening.

In the world of business, Binion was regarded as a throwback to the old Las Vegas, when agreements were struck with a handshake on the street instead of a written contract inside a stuffy boardroom. He didn't like banks. He was known to carry a wad of $100 bills in his pocket, hide hundreds of thousands in cash and jewels inside his home and even bury valuables at his 125-acre ranch in nearby Pahrump, Nevada.

Gripped by paranoia his last months alive, Binion never went anywhere without a gun strapped to his body. At his home and his ranch, a wide range of weapons was kept within arm's reach in every room. The day of his death, however, there was not a firearm in sight in the den. Also missing were his prized antique coin and currency collections worth hundreds of thousands of dollars. Cash was nowhere to be found, and his safe had been cleaned out.

Murphy, who had charmed her way into Binion's life while dancing topless at Cheetah's, a local adult nightclub, in March 1995, remained in a highly emotional state inside the home that day. She appeared so distraught that paramedics had to transport her to a hospital. Once she was there, however, nurses trained in observing such patients found her hysterics to be "almost theatrical."

Binion's sister, Horseshoe Club president Becky Behnen, never trusted Murphy, a beauty queen from Southern California with an eye for men with money and a penchant for living in the fast lane. Loud and hot-tempered, Murphy had made it clear to Behnen that she was living with Binion and having sex with him solely for his money. The evening of her brother's death, Behnen was the first to publicly voice concerns that he had met with foul play.

When Binion's estate lawyer, James J. Brown, was informed of Binion's death that evening, he had good reason to be suspicious as well. A day earlier, Binion had telephoned his longtime friend Brown and instructed him to remove Murphy from his will. Murphy had persuaded Binion in July to give her his $900,000 home, its contents and $300,000 in cash upon his death.

"Take Sandy out of the will if she doesn't kill me tonight," Brown recalled Binion saying. "If I'm dead, you'll know what happened."

It later was learned that Binion had cut off Murphy's $5,000-a-month credit-card habit a week earlier, and on the same day of his conversation with Brown, he had frantically looked for a private investigator to put a tail on Murphy. He had come to learn that Murphy was having an affair with one of his friends, Rick Tabish, a thirty-three-year-old Montana contractor who always seemed to be looking to involve him in crazy business ventures.

Tabish, the son of a wealthy Missoula, Montana, businessman, was among the horde of onlookers milling around the white front gate of Binion's house as police collected evidence of his death inside. A two-time convicted felon who liked partying with Binion and Murphy, Tabish ran trucking companies in Missoula and Las Vegas. One of his clients was Binion, who had hired him to transport $6 million in silver bars and coins from his family's Horseshoe Club two months earlier and bury it in an underground vault in Pahrump, a small town sixty miles outside Las Vegas. Tabish told reporters he'd been on his way to the airport to head back to Missoula when he heard the news of Binion's death and decided to turn around and stop by the home.

"I never had any bad dealings with the man," he said. "What a tragedy. I know he was trying real hard to change his life."

Records later showed Tabish did not have an airline reservation for Missoula that day.

Eventually, paramedics wheeled the screaming Murphy out of Binion's home on a stretcher and took her to nearby Valley Hospital. She had been "choking" and "vomiting," detective Pat Franks reported. Tabish immediately jumped into his black four-door Mercedes and followed the ambulance to the hospital. Once there, he learned that another detective was interviewing Murphy about Binion's death, and he quickly drove back to Binion's house. There he cornered Richard Wright, a well-known criminal defense attorney who had represented Binion during his epic battle with state gaming regulators. He told Wright police were interrogating Murphy, and he persuaded the lawyer to go to the hospital with him to stop it.

After they arrived, however, the two men learned that detective James Mitchell already had concluded his thirteen-minute interview with Murphy. In his report, Mitchell said Murphy told him that Binion had returned to using drugs after losing his gaming license in March . She described him as suicidal, saying she once saw him stick a gun in his mouth while under the influence of drugs. At the home, Murphy told detective Franks that her boyfriend had planned to enter a drug rehabilitation center. She later informed Mitchell that Binion had obtained the prescription for Xanax from his neighbor, Dr. Enrique Lacayo, a day earlier.

"My neighbor's a doctor," she said as she wept and spoke in choppy sentences. "And my neighbor used to give him that shit before, when we were . . . and I told him if you ever give him that stuff again . . . And he gave him some more last night."

Then she said Binion had gotten "other pills" from another physician a couple of weeks earlier.

"He told me this was the last time, and he wasn't gonna ever do it again," she said.

Police later would learn that Binion had scored twelve balloons of black tar heroin the night before as well.

As Mitchell struggled to interview Murphy, she said she last saw Binion alive in the morning. Binion, she said, had awakened her in the middle of the night and asked her to watch him sleep because he was concerned he might have a seizure. After he had fallen asleep, Murphy left the house and returned a short time later. She sat on the sofa in the den and watched him some more, but then left the house again to run some errands.

Then, in a hysterical voice, she described what she saw when she found him on the floor of his den shortly before 4 P.M. on September 17, 1998.

"I thought he was alive," she said. "He looked like he was sleeping. I thought he was sleeping, and he wouldn't wake up. He wouldn't wake up. He wouldn't wake up. Oh, God! Oh, God! Oh, God!"

Ultimately, Wright arranged for Murphy's release on the condition she stay the night at the home of Janis Tanno, another longtime Binion neighbor.

At Binion's home, meanwhile, as his body was transported to the coroner's office, police were wrapping up their investigation. Detective Franks reported that the residence appeared "clean and neat" and that there were no signs of a struggle around the body or anywhere else in the residence.

Months later, however, police would come to a different conclusion. Following one of the most intense murder investigations of all time in Las Vegas, a probe that was encouraged by the wealthy Binion estate, police would conclude that the death scene was staged on September 17, 1998, and that Binion's home, including the large safe in his garage, had been looted. Police also would conclude that Murphy was acting at the hospital. The day after Binion's death, she had given a videotaped tour of the casino man's sprawling home in which her demeanor changed from grieving girlfriend to greedy, foul-mouthed heir looking to grab whatever she could from Binion's estate. Hours later, Tabish was caught digging up Binion's $6 million silver fortune in Pahrump. In his briefcase were love notes from Murphy. Six months after that, Las Vegas police would arrest Murphy and Tabish and charge them with having murdered the casino boss.

The hanging of the "R.I.P." Halloween sign above the front doorway to Binion's home would later be cited by investigators as an example of the gruesome sense of humor of his accused killers.

CHAPTER 2

....

A Father's Legend

....

ONE CHILLY NIGHT in November 1987, the roar was deafening inside the Thomas & Mack Center, an arena made famous by the nationally ranked UNLV basketball team.

But the more than 18,000 Las Vegans chanting, "Benny, Benny, Benny," weren't there to watch the Runnin' Rebels run up the score on another overmatched opponent. They had come for free beer and hot dogs and good country music, courtesy of legendary Las Vegas gaming mogul Benny Binion, who was celebrating his eighty-third birthday. Country entertainers Willie Nelson, Reba McEntire and Hank Williams Jr., all good friends of Binion, were among those performing. Dale Robertson and Gene Autry also made an appearance to honor the man who once had served as the best man at the wedding of Roy Rogers and Dale Evans.

It was a bizarre scene even for Las Vegas. Most of the revelers weren't even born when Binion was in his prime forty years earlier, running the illegal gambling rackets in Dallas.

One month prior to the big bash, the Binion name in Las Vegas had been besmirched. Word leaked out that the Justice Department's Organized Crime Strike Force had launched a racketeering investigation aimed at taking away Binion's beloved Horseshoe Club, a popular, free-spirited casino he had run since 1951 after fleeing Dallas for the upstart legal gambling business in Las Vegas. No one cared about that investigation that night. Binion wouldn't let them.

The backslapping Binion, patriarch of one the most politically connected families in Las Vegas, had come a long way from his notorious days in Texas, where he had developed a reputation for being a killer, a tax cheat and an illegal gambling kingpin. He had poured hundreds of thousands of dollars into Las Vegas charities and political races and, for the most part, had stayed out of trouble with the law to earn everyone's respect. And now Las Vegas was giving him its ultimate embrace.

In January 1947, Binion left his lucrative and sometimes violent gambling empire in Dallas and moved his wife, Teddy Jane, and five young children—Barbara, Jack, Ted, Brenda and Becky—to Las Vegas. He arrived, some say, with $2 million in cash stuffed in suitcases, one step ahead of Texas authorities. This was during the same month that colorful mobster Benjamin "Bugsy" Siegel had opened the Flamingo Hotel and Casino on what later became the world-famous Las Vegas Strip. Four years later, Binion bought the old Eldorado Club on Fremont Street and renamed it the Horseshoe Club, a local joint that still flourishes today.

Binion was born on November 20, 1904, on a farm near the small town of Pilot Grove, Texas, just north of Dallas. His father, Lonnie Binion, was a horse trader and a gambler who drank heavily. In his childhood days, Benny punched cows and helped his father sell horses. At fourteen, he picked up on his father's knack for gambling when he moved in with relatives in El Paso. He was exposed for the first time to the numbers game. While there, he met his idol, the legendary Mexican hero Pancho Villa, who was a regular customer in the horse-trading business. In his twenties, a restless Binion began to look for greater opportunities on the streets, so he moved to Dallas, where he took up with a group of bootleggers. He married Teddy Jane in 1931 and started his own numbers racket, which thrived in post-Depression Dallas. He also introduced the game of craps to

Dallas. At one point, Binion was said to be doing as much as $1 million a year in business in the back rooms there. In those days, Dallas police were lax in their enforcement of illegal gambling operations. Binion paid a weekly fine to stay in business. Among his customers were the likes of Howard Hughes and Texas oilman H. L. Hunt, both of whom would go on to be listed among the richest men in the world.

"Eventually, Daddy took a piece of everybody who opened up an operation," said Becky Behnen, his younger daughter who now runs the Horseshoe. "He owned the town."

While in Dallas, Binion was a suspect in several slayings, but he was charged in only two. In 1933, he shot to death bootlegger Frank Bolding behind his Dallas home after Bolding came at him with a knife. Binion called it self-defense, and his friendship with the district attorney resulted in a mere two-year suspended sentence for the killing. Then in 1936, Binion was charged with murder in the slaying of Dallas racketeer Ben Frieden following a shootout in Binion's neighborhood. The charge was dismissed three years later.

"I try to keep anybody from doing anything to me where it'll cause any trouble," Binion told the *Houston Chronicle* in a rare 1989 interview months before his death. "But if anybody does anything to me, he's got trouble."

By 1946, Binion had worn out his welcome in Dallas. A new law-and-order district attorney was elected, and on New Year's Eve in 1946, the gambling halls and casinos were shut down. Binion headed for Las Vegas a month later.

"He thought this was only going to be a temporary stay until the political climate changed in Dallas," Behnen said. "But things changed here."

In 1953, two years after Binion had opened the Horseshoe Club, his stormy days in Dallas caught up with him. He was convicted of tax evasion. He received a five-year prison term, a $20,000 fine, and was ordered to pay $750,000 in back taxes. Binion served a little more than three years in the federal penitentiary at Leavenworth, Kansas, before being released on parole in March 1957.

Once he returned to Las Vegas, Binion no longer could hold a gaming license as an ex-felon. Officially, his older son, Jack, ran the Horseshoe Club, but it was Binion who remained the brains behind the operation—which earned a reputation as a place where locals could gamble without any limits and dine at reasonable prices on the best food in town, including beef from the Binion family ranch in Montana.

In 1970, Binion started the World Series of Poker, an event that has become an international tradition in Las Vegas. The winner of today's high-stakes Texas Hold'em series can easily walk away with $1 million, about as much as Binion used to make in a year on the streets.

Binion remained a colorful figure throughout his years in Las Vegas. He could be seen daily holding court during lunch at his favorite table in the back of the Horseshoe's crowded downstairs coffee shop. Lawyers, politicians, friends and even reporters would drop by to pay their respects. On top of the stairs to the restaurant, Binion kept $1 million in $10,000 bills on display inside a bulletproof case, in front of which patrons could pose for photos. In the wintertime, Binion would run around town wearing a full-length buffalo coat. He had a knack for remembering faces, especially those of people he thought could help him.

For years, the Horseshoe developed a reputation as the friendliest casino in town. But the one thing you didn't want to do was cross the Binion family. The Horseshoe also was known for taking care of its problems with its own brand of frontier justice. The federal strike force investigation focused on the November 22, 1985, beating of two card counters who had won about $4,500 at blackjack. The two men were taken to a security office and beaten, both suffering a number of broken ribs. One of those later charged in state court in the beating was one of Binion's grandsons. But the strike force was said to be looking at dozens of other such incidents that had occurred at the Horseshoe over the years. One involved Ted Binion, the Horseshoe founder's younger son. In 1979, Binion and a security officer chased a gambler who had thrown a chair through a window. When the gambler was caught, he was shot and killed. The two men then ran back to the Horseshoe and locked themselves in the casino cage. Ultimately, Ted Binion was charged with obstructing a police officer, but the charge was later dropped. The security guard pleaded guilty to manslaughter and was given probation.

As the years went by, Benny Binion became obsessed with obtaining a presidential pardon for his tax conviction, primarily, he used to say, for the sake of his grandchildren. But Presidents Richard Nixon, Jimmy Carter and Ronald Reagan all refused to oblige him. He never asked John Kennedy and Gerald Ford. Binion blamed Jimmy "the Weasel" Fratianno, a Mafia hit man turned FBI witness, and partly himself for mouthing off for his failure. Fratianno wrote a book in 1981 in which he acknowledged participating in a Binion-ordered 1953 hit on Louis "Russian Louie" Strauss, an old-time Las Vegas gambler who had crossed the Horseshoe Club founder. Binion always denied killing Strauss, but when pressed about the slaying by a reporter, he responded: "Listen, go back and tell them FBI [agents] I'm still able to do my own killings." Later, Binion would tell the *Houston Chronicle,* "Goddamn, I made a mistake, I did set 'em off." He went to his grave in 1989 without a pardon.

Despite his hardened, hoodlumlike image, Binion was a loving father and described by many in Las Vegas, including the late *Las Vegas Sun* publisher Hank Greenspun, as a "family man" with "few peers."

Behnen called her father and mother the "best parents" in the world. "There's nothing I couldn't tell them," she said. She claimed her father had a unique way of making you feel at ease during a conversation. "He could talk about anything," she said.

Behnen said her brother Ted resembled her father the most out of all of his children. The elder Binion put his son to work as casino manager of the Horseshoe at the young age of twenty-two in 1964. Like his father, Ted had a nose for gambling and proved to be a sharp boss on the floor. But his personal demons began to take control of his life and threaten his promising career in gaming. By 1980, after dabbling in marijuana and other drugs, he had become hooked on heroin. In April 1987, Binion was arrested by Las Vegas police for possessing what was thought to be heroin. It set off an epic battle with Nevada gaming regulators, who ultimately forced him out of the casino industry in March 1998.

Besieged by his drug problems and having become a central figure in the federal government's racketeering probe at the Horseshoe Club, Binion was unusually quiet the night Las Vegans came out to help his legendary father celebrate his eighty-third birthday. He knew Benny was saddened by his drug use.

Months before his death, Benny Binion had vowed to stay alive to straighten out his younger son. Barbara, his oldest daughter, had died of a drug overdose in 1983, and Binion couldn't stand to let that happen to Ted. But keeping his son away from drugs might have been the one promise the elder Binion failed to keep in his life. Binion died on Christmas Day in 1989. After eighty-five years of his living life to its fullest, his heart finally gave out. At his funeral, his good friend, former Mirage Resorts chairman Steve Wynn, was among the hundreds of mourners.

"He was either the toughest gentleman I ever knew or the gentlest tough person I ever met," Wynn said in his eulogy.

The strike force investigation of Benny Binion and the Horseshoe died with him. But troubles for his son Ted were just beginning.

CHAPTER 3

• • • • • • • • • • • • • • • • • • • •

Life's Troubles

• • • • • • • • • • • • • • • • • • • •

ON MAY 22, 1997, Ted Binion stood before the five-member Nevada Gaming Commission and made a rare public plea to keep his casino license as co-owner of his family's Horseshoe Club.

"This is my life," he told the stern-faced commissioners at the hearing packed with spectators and reporters. "I've got nowhere else to go."

Binion's plea appeared to be coming from the heart. Flanked by a battery of high-priced lawyers, he looked uncomfortable at the witness table in his charcoal-gray business suit, beads of sweat accumulating on his balding forehead. But he spoke candidly, acknowledging that he had made mistakes in his life. He said he felt as if he had been living in "purgatory" during his decade-long fight to hold onto his license. Though his troubles with regulators had begun in 1987 with his drug arrest, Binion had struggled with a heroin addiction since 1980, the same year of his marriage to longtime companion Doris and of the birth of his daughter, Bonnie. This time, however, Binion wasn't in hot water over his drug use. Regulators had charged him with violating a 1994 agreement to stay out of the Horseshoe Club's operations, and he was being accused of palling around with reputed mob figures while his license was suspended.

What hurt Binion the most that day in front of the Gaming Commission was an affidavit from his sister Brenda Michael, who alleged that he had threatened her life and tried to cut off her daughter's salary at the Horseshoe. One of Binion's lawyers, Mark Ferrario, told the commissioners that Binion merely was "spouting off" because he was angry that his late mother had left Brenda the family's ranch in Montana in her will.

"They don't relate to one another like most people do," Ferrario said of the Binion clan.

At the time, the family was battling for control of the Horseshoe Club. Binion's other sister, Becky Behnen, had made it clear she wanted to buy out her siblings and take over the casino that her father had made famous. The civil war escalated in court when Behnen filed a lawsuit against her older brother Jack Binion, who had been running the Horseshoe since 1964, accusing him of mismanagement. Ted was taking sides with his brother.

Though they listened intently for hours, the commissioners had no sympathy for Binion that day. They voted to keep him under suspension indefinitely in order to give the Nevada Gaming Control Board, the law enforcement agency that monitors the casino industry on a daily basis, time to investigate Binion's mob ties. A week earlier, the Control Board had filed a new complaint against Binion over his relationship with two underworld figures, Herbert Blitzstein, a reputed Chicago mob associate, and Peter Ribaste, who lawmen suspected had the ear of Kansas City Mafia bosses.

Blitzstein, a tall, heavyset man with an array of physical problems, including a heart condition and diabetes, was killed gangland style on January 7, 1997, as part of a scheme by the Los Angeles and Buffalo crime families to take over street rackets in Las Vegas. Blitzstein, nicknamed "Fat Herbie," had been the right-hand man of slain mob kingpin Anthony Spilotro, who ran the Las Vegas rackets for the Chicago mob. FBI agents once had probed Binion's ties to the much-feared Spilotro, who was killed outside Chicago in

1986 following a wave of federal indictments that cracked down on the mob's hidden influence at Las Vegas casinos. Spilotro's slaying was never solved, but investigators believed he was killed by his own crime family members.

In the aftermath of Spilotro's death, the Chicago mob had relinquished its traditional control of the streets of Las Vegas, allowing other crime syndicates to move in. Los Angeles and Buffalo were looking to assert their dominance. Blitzstein, who had spent time in federal prison on wire fraud and tax charges after Spilotro's death, no longer had the same protection on the streets that he had enjoyed during Spilotro's reign.

One evening, as he was walking inside his modest home in southeast Las Vegas, two men armed with .22-caliber handguns with silencers shot him in the back of the head. As he was falling to his death on the floor, he was heard asking, "Why me? Why me?" Earlier, other participants in the murder plot had broken into Blitzstein's home and cleaned it out of its valuables, including a gold watch Binion had given Blitzstein as a gift. The hit occurred in the middle of a massive FBI racketeering investigation into the Mafia takeover scheme, but the FBI was unable to stop it. Shortly after the killing, agents learned how the Los Angeles and Buffalo mob families planned to divvy up Blitzstein's loan-sharking and insurance fraud operations.

About the same time, authorities informed Binion of a plot to murder him in similar fashion. Blitzstein's killers, it turned out, had heard rumors that Binion liked to hide millions in cash at his home.

FBI agents had learned of the scheme from John Branco, a longtime wise guy they had enlisted to work undercover during the racketeering probe. Having been caught off guard by Blitzstein's shooting, John Plunkett, supervisor of the FBI's organized crime squad at the time, decided Binion needed to be told of the contract on his life. But the FBI couldn't make the call because Blitzstein's killers were still at large, and agents didn't want to compromise Branco's role in the investigation. So Plunkett telephoned homicide detective Mike Franks and handed off the task to him.

In a February 1, 1997 memo, Franks said he had contacted Horseshoe Club security the previous morning to get word to Binion that they needed to talk. Later that day, the detective met with Binion and two of his lawyers, Richard Wright and Harry Claiborne, at Wright's downtown office.

"Inquiries were made into Binion's knowledge of Blitzstein with little information received," Franks wrote. "Binion was then informed of the possible threat to him. He was told to be cautious and very careful in his wanderings."

The casino man then surprised Franks.

"Binion did not seem fazed by the information of a possible death threat," Franks said. "He possibly already had the information."

What Franks didn't know was that Binion's friend Tony Musso, one of those ultimately arrested in the FBI racketeering investigation, had indeed told Binion of the murder plot.

The subject had come up at a local social club, where the underworld figures, including Branco, had been hanging out.

Musso later told detectives that he didn't believe the mob figures were serious.

"None of them had the balls to go over there and do it, because Ted, he'd kill every one of them. Nobody would have a chance," he said.

Musso described Binion as a sharpshooter.

"He could hit a fly a hundred yards away or so," he said.

When detectives asked Russo about Binion's reaction to being told of the death threat, he said Ted replied: "Fuck 'em. Let them try to come over."

Did he take any other precautions? Was he starting to carry more guns? the detectives asked.

"Oh, Ted always had a gun," Musso responded. "He carried a gun to the bathroom, for God's sake. So it was like this is nothing new. He slept with a shotgun by his bed . . .

It was never uncommon to see Ted with one of those forty-fives with a little rawhide strap on his shoulder and another one on his belt."

Musso said Binion always answered his door with weapons strapped to his body, even when Blitzstein came over.

Binion and Blitzstein had become pals in 1995 while Binion carried on his fight with gaming regulators. They would have lunch and dinner with each other, and frequently they were seen in public making the adult nightclub scene together. The two men had become so close that Blitzstein once helped Binion arrange an abortion for his girlfriend, Sandy Murphy, at a local hospital.

"Teddy had a lot of superficial friends who always wanted something from him," said attorney John Momot, a longtime Binion friend and Blitzstein lawyer. "I think he was a lonely guy. That's why he developed a friendship with Herbie, who was a very charismatic type of guy.

"Their relationship developed absolutely against my advice. I told them it wasn't wise to associate with each other because this was a TNT mixture. It was definitely going to cause Teddy problems with gaming regulators. But neither one of them listened to me. They were both bullheaded. They were going to do what they wanted to do.

"Teddy was a man's-man type of guy, a cowboy, gambler," Momot added. "He was a great guy to be around. He was what Las Vegas was all about. And Herbie, he was a gambler, a product of Chicago. He knew all the wise guys. The relationship was headed for disaster."

In an April 2, 1996, interview with the *Las Vegas Sun,* Binion acknowledged publicly for the first time that he was friends with Blitzstein.

"I'm nice to the guy, and he was never anything but nice to me," he said.

Two weeks earlier, Blitzstein had asserted his Fifth Amendment right against self-incrimination and refused to answer questions about his ties to Binion at a hearing before the Gaming Control Board. Momot was there at Blitzstein's side. Among other things, gaming agents were interested in how Blitzstein was able to cash $11,500 in checks at the Horseshoe on New Year's Day with Binion's help. Horseshoe records showed that Murphy had approved the transactions. But like Blitzstein, Murphy ended up ducking questions under oath about the checks.

Binion defended his girlfriend in the *Las Vegas Sun* interview, saying she was "not the bad person she's made out to be. She's not a lowlife."

About the same time, a loud and obnoxious Murphy had gotten into an argument at the upscale Aristocrat restaurant with Mike O'Callaghan, a former two-term Nevada governor and the executive editor of the *Sun,* over his newspaper's aggressive coverage of Binion's bitter fight with gaming regulators.

Then, at an April 10, 1996, Control Board hearing, Binion was forced to publicly acknowledge that Murphy regularly had smoked marijuana in his presence since moving into his home a year earlier. He also testified under oath that he suspected she had been snorting cocaine.

The admissions did not go over well with regulators, particularly then Chairman Bill Bible.

"How does that reflect upon Mr. Binion's suitability where he's cohabitating with an individual who is using controlled substances, marijuana and apparently cocaine, in his house and he doesn't report it to the proper authorities?" Bible asked at the end of the hearing.

Two weeks later, at a Gaming Commission hearing, Binion, under questioning from Ferrario, his own lawyer, again was forced to acknowledge that his girlfriend was using drugs.

"Did she use marijuana?" the lawyer asked.

"Yes," a nervous Binion responded.

"And was she a regular marijuana user?"

"Not at first, but later, yes."

"On approximately how many occasions did you see her using marijuana in your presence?"

"About five times."

"And were there other occasions where you did not see her using marijuana, but you smelled marijuana smoke in your home?"

"Yes."

"On how many occasions did that occur?"

"Approximately twenty."

"Now, did there come a point in time where Miss Murphy admitted to you that she used cocaine in your home?"

"Yes."

"When did that occur?"

"In early December."

"Did you ever see her use cocaine in your home?"

"No."

"Did you ever see any indication in your home that you thought she might be using cocaine?"

"Yes."

"Why don't you tell me what you saw in your home that gave you an indication that you thought she might be using cocaine."

"I saw on about three occasions rolled-up $100 bills and on about two occasions papers that looked like they contained possibly cocaine. It looked like there was some powder residue in them. Then on two occasions on some marble tile, there was some remnants of powder, like white powder."

"And where did you find these materials?"

"In her bathroom and bedroom."

Murphy's drug use, however, would turn out to be the least of Binion's problems with regulators.

At the April 10, 1996, Control Board hearing, Binion also acknowledged that he had associated with Blitzstein more than two dozen times over the past year. He described Blitzstein as a "dying, old ex-felon who was lonely." Board members, however, suspected Binion's ties to the mob were deeper, and they pressed on with the investigation. At the same time, rumors were circulating within the gaming industry that Binion had become a street informant for the FBI. The rumors were never confirmed. But some wondered how the FBI's racketeering investigation at the Horseshoe Club, which focused heavily on Binion, had quietly disappeared a few years earlier.

Transcripts of secret FBI electronic surveillance during the racketeering investigation of the Los Angeles mob later revealed that Branco had befriended Binion and Murphy while Branco was working undercover for the bureau. A February 2, 1997, transcript showed that Branco had talked about getting money from Binion to buy Club Paradise, a popular topless nightclub across the street from the Hard Rock Hotel & Casino. Branco and one of the targets of the racketeering probe, Peter Caruso, were to get a piece of the club after Binion had bought it. The club was long rumored to be controlled by associates of the Chicago mob.

During an April 14, 1997, conversation secretly recorded by Branco, the undercover informant discussed a plan with a ranking Los Angeles mob member to get people in key positions at the Horseshoe Club to wield hidden influence there. The subject came up while Branco was talking about his relationship with Blitzstein and Binion.

In its May 1997 complaint, meanwhile, the Control Board accused Binion of bringing discredit upon Nevada's casino industry by doing business with another reputed mob figure, Peter Ribaste, a forty-two-year-old convicted felon who lawmen alleged ran an illegal gambling operation for the Kansas City mob in the 1980s. Ribaste, once married to the daughter of well-known Las Vegas gambler Lem Banker, was said to have answered directly to the hierarchy of the Kansas City crime family. Earlier in 1997, Ribaste had been indicted on tax evasion charges stemming from an IRS probe into his hidden interests in Kansas City topless clubs.

Just days before the Control Board complaint was filed, Binion acknowledged at a public hearing that he had loaned Ribaste $100,000 to help him invest in a Las Vegas used-car dealership. He said he had written him two $50,000 checks in December 1996 and that Ribaste promised to pay him $4,700 until he got his investment back and then $2,350 a month for the next sixty months. Gaming agents, in the middle of a crackdown on the Kansas City mob's presence in Las Vegas, had stumbled onto Ribaste's ties to Binion while making a case to nominate Ribaste for Nevada's Black Book of undesirables banned from casinos.

Telephone records subpoenaed during the Black Book probe found a large number of calls from Ribaste to Binion's home. Binion told the Control Board at the hearing that he had found Ribaste to be a "pretty good fella" and became comfortable dealing with him after learning that the respected Banker was Ribaste's father-in-law.

But gaming agents clearly had lost patience with Binion. They stepped up their efforts to nail down his mob ties.

In early June 1997, in the middle of those efforts, Binion's home was sprayed with bullets in a drive-by shooting. One bullet went through the front door, and others struck his Dodge pickup, which had been parked in his circular driveway. No one was hurt, but police intelligence detectives knowledgeable about organized crime immediately launched an investigation. As the probe proceeded, attention quickly turned to Behnen's twenty-one-year-old son, Benny, and his friends. Relations at the time were not good between Binion and the Behnens, who knew they would have a much easier time taking over the Horseshoe if regulators forced Binion to sell his 20 percent interest. Becky's husband, Nick, was arguing constantly with Binion over the telephone. Each made regular threats against the other. Murphy was weighing in as well. At one point, Murphy telephoned Becky's secretary, Lynn Saladino, to warn Nick to keep his mouth shut or he'd wind up "dead on the streets."

Police, meanwhile, were never able to pin the drive-by shooting on Binion's nephew, and Becky insisted her son was not involved. She said Murphy made up the accusation because she was mad that Ted had been invited to Benny's twenty-first birthday party days earlier and she wasn't.

Then, on July 14, 1997, FBI agents Charles Maurer and Michael Howey, who were investigating Herbie Blitzstein's slaying, paid a jailhouse visit to Ron Mortensen, a disgraced Las Vegas police officer convicted of killing a twenty-one-year-old Hispanic man in a drive-by shooting. Mortensen turned over twenty-three pages of handwritten notes he had surreptitiously taken from jailhouse conversations with Antone Davi, one of the men later convicted of shooting Blitzstein. Davi and Mortensen were cellmates for several weeks. The FBI agents were so impressed with Mortensen's work that they planned to call him as a witness at Davi's trial, but Davi ended up pleading guilty and Mortensen wasn't needed.

"Mortensen said Davi almost immediately began to trust him and thereafter told Mortensen about his, Davi's, criminal activities," Maurer and Howey wrote in a two-page report obtained by the *Las Vegas Sun.* "Mortensen would subsequently write down the things that Davi told him when Davi was not around or when he could disguise his activities as if he were writing a letter."

Among the explosive tidbits Davi revealed was a plan by a New York Mafia family to authorize Alfred Mauriello, the reputed Los Angeles underworld associate who had hired Davi to shoot Blitzstein, to arrange a hit on the son of jailed Gambino crime boss, John Gotti. Davi also provided Mortensen with information about the mob's infiltration of the topless nightclub scene in Las Vegas.

But most intriguing to the agents was Davi's insistence that Mauriello was also planning to arrange a hit on Binion. Then there was another surprise. Mortensen said Davi told him that Binion originally had approached Mauriello about a contract to kill his sister Becky Behnen. But the mob figures, believing Binion had been stashing as much as $12 million in cash at his home, planned to turn the hit around and kill Binion instead in anticipation of a much more lucrative payday. Davi told Mortensen that Binion was offering Mauriello only $50,000 to kill his sister. Both Davi and another man later convicted of shooting Blitzstein, Richard Friedman, were to draw the assignment of taking out Binion. The casino boss never knew that a double cross was in the works. Months later, after pleading guilty to killing Blitzstein and agreeing to cooperate with the government, Davi told FBI agents that Friedman, who boasted of his ties to the Russian Mafia, had come up with a plan to use a stun gun on Binion at his home and then overdose him on heroin. Agents had found a stun gun in Friedman's apartment when they arrested him for Blitzstein's slaying.

Though Binion's mob ties clearly were dominating the state's investigation in 1997, talk of his drug use remained on the minds of many, including the casino man himself. Binion insisted he had been free of drugs since his 1987 arrest, even though recent hair tests had turned up positive for marijuana and cocaine. Binion contended the hair tests weren't reliable. He said the marijuana likely had gotten into his hair as a result of Murphy's drug use. The presence of cocaine, he insisted, probably was the result of residue from others snorting it around him while he was prowling the topless nightclub scene.

"I've had over 300 urine tests since 1987," Binion said in a secret deposition in Behnen's lawsuit against his brother, Jack. "They are the only tests that work, and I've never failed one of those."

At the May 22, 1997, Gaming Commission hearing, Richard Wright complained that the Control Board had targeted Binion unfairly.

"He could have been the Pope, and they would have recommended against him," Wright said. "He's the most tested man in America."

By March, 23, 1998, Binion's drug use became moot. The Control Board had accumulated enough evidence of his underworld ties to persuade the Gaming Commission to revoke his license.

"It's not the end of the world," a smiling Binion told reporters afterward.

Six months later, he was dead.

CHAPTER 4

....

Meeting Sandy

....

CHEETAH'S WAS ONE of the most popular topless night-clubs in Las Vegas. On most nights, there were two hundred scantily clad young women working their way through this noisy and crowded adult playland, soliciting $20 lap dances from drunken male gawkers with lots of money to spend.

Beautiful girls, many down on their luck like twenty-three-year-old Sandy Murphy in March 1995, would flock to Cheetah's from all over the country to dance topless in the shadow of its famous red-and-blue neon lights and mirrored walls, all in hopes of making some quick bucks.

Murphy, still stinging from a drunken-driving arrest in Orange County, and her friend Linda Carroll had decided to come to Las Vegas for a weekend gambling trip to relieve some stress. Carroll, several years older than Murphy, had been in the "City of Glitz" before, selling costumes to top-less dancers. She had a work card as a cocktail waitress at Cheetah's. The two women spent most of their time at Caesars Palace, where Murphy ended up losing her life savings of $13,000 at the blackjack tables. Comforting her girlfriend over her losses, Carroll persuaded Murphy to go to Cheetah's with her on a costume run.

Murphy, with her good looks and outgoing personality, took a stab at peddling costumes for a couple days but didn't earn much money. While struggling as a pitch woman, she saw how easily the other young women working the crowd around the long, granite-trimmed bar were picking up cash just for taking off their tops and dancing to the blare of music from the high-powered speakers above. She saw girls with $20 bills stuffed in their G-strings and strapped to their ankles leaving the lap-dance room off to the side of the bar. It looked like easy work to her. Then Carroll got a great idea. She telephoned some wealthy friends in Texas and asked them to pay a visit to Cheetah's. In a matter of days, Murphy and Carroll had struck it rich. The Texans, though, weren't interested in their costumes, but rather their bodies.

"We went to the VIP room and danced for them and drank Dom Perignon, made lots of money," Murphy would later explain in a sworn deposition in Binion's divorce case. "They were handing us $100 bills. We made thousands, like $3,000 in probably three hours."

Carroll denied that she danced at the club. But Murphy said in her deposition that in less than two weeks she went on to win back more than the $13,000 she had lost at Caesars Palace before returning to Southern California. Tall, lean and athletic, Murphy had a perfect body to match a beautiful face with high cheekbones, pouty lips and big brown eyes. Her shoulder-length hair was naturally brown, but she had dyed it blond.

The trip, it turned out, was more lucrative for Murphy than she could have imagined. One night while dancing in her adult version of a Dallas Cowboys cheerleader's outfit, she ran into Ted Binion, who was feeling depressed because of troubles with his wife, Doris.

"A friend came over and introduced us," Murphy said in her 1996 deposition. "I was having a hard time with my boyfriend. We had just broken up. He [the friend] says Ted wants some company, but he is, you know, his wife just ran off tonight. He was drunk, and I was drunk. We just sat and visited, and then I went back to California to face my DUI charges."

Murphy and Binion, however, didn't get along at first.

"It wasn't like we met, then had this great affair, because we just—we really didn't like each other," she said.

Then she recalled a conversation with Binion that night: "I said 'I can't believe I'm doing this. If my dad ever found out, it would embarrass my family and everybody else' . . . and he tried to hand me a wad of money, almost like $1,700, and I gave it back to him. I said, 'I don't want your money.' "

A short time later, Murphy returned to Las Vegas and telephoned Binion, who promptly invited her to a dinner party at his sprawling home on Palomino Lane. Picked up in a Horseshoe Club limousine, Murphy arrived at Binion's house to find him with another woman he had been dating. Infuriated, Murphy told Binion never to embarrass her like that again and persuaded him to stop seeing the other woman. Within days, she was asked to move into his home and share his life of luxury.

"Sandra just simply took over and said, 'What the hell are you doing?' " Binion's divorce lawyer, Thomas Standish, said in court documents. " 'You're not going to see this woman if you're going to date me.' And that was kind of the beginning of their relationship. She just sort of planted herself in Ted's life and never . . . uh . . . never was out of it."

Standish recalled that Binion was impressed with Murphy's svelte body and her aggressiveness with him during their short time together.

Doris Binion testified in court that she had left her husband and sought a divorce after overhearing Binion and Murphy planning a picnic at Binion's 125-acre ranch in nearby Pahrump, Nevada, one day in April 1995.

Sid Lewis, a longtime Binion friend and Horseshoe Club pit boss, told investigators that Murphy appeared to move into Binion's home with very little belongings.

"I don't think she even had a car, to tell you the truth," Lewis said, adding he had come to the conclusion that Murphy was only out "to get her grips" into Binion. He said Binion let her manipulate him because she was "good in bed."

Murphy had arrived on the Las Vegas social scene in

style. It was a long way from her high school days in
Downey and Bellflower, two blue-collar suburbs of south
central Los Angeles. She lived a relatively normal childhood
in the home of her father, Kenneth, who ran an auto repos-
session business, and her stepmother, Sandra, who loved
her like her own child. Murphy excelled in elementary
school and junior high school. She was popular with her
schoolmates—serving on the student council—and was active in sports, especially swimming.

At fourteen she experienced a downturn, however, when
she was raped by a classmate one day after school. Her stepmother would later recall that she was never the same after
that traumatic event. She suffered from recurring nightmares
and her grades declined. Still, Murphy's good looks and engaging personality landed her, at age seventeen, a runner-up
spot in the Miss Bellflower pageant. Friends described her
as smart and outgoing. But, darkened by the rape experience, she never graduated from high school and eventually
left home. She moved in with a wealthy older man who
owned a beach house, and she learned the finance side of the
car business. Within two years of leaving high school, she
was seen driving a new Corvette.

Horror crept back into her life in early 1994, when her car
broke down while she was driving on the interstate. Two
young men stopped to check her out. They dragged her off
the interstate into a strawberry field and took turns sexually
assaulting her. Before leaving, they urinated on her and
threw her into a Dumpster.

Soon afterward, Murphy's troubles with the law began
when she was arrested in Orange County for driving with a
suspended license and impersonating someone else to a police officer. A year later, she was arrested again, this time for
driving under the influence of alcohol. She received a forty-
five-day jail sentence, which she never completed, and lost
her driving privileges. By then, Murphy was ready to leave
Southern California and start a new life.

After she moved in with Binion in April 1995, he paid

$15,000 to send her to Sober Living, a substance-abuse rehabilitation program in Newport Beach, California, to fulfill the obligations of her DUI sentence. She spent about a month there.

Murphy made her presence felt within weeks of starting her life with Binion at his $900,000 home. She completely remodeled Doris Binion's bedroom. She got rid of the bedroom furniture and replaced it with a handmade set from Italy, and she ripped out the carpet and put in white marble floors.

"She spent a lot of time bragging about how she was fixing up her house and how [Binion] was going to put the house in her name," the former casino executive's eighteen-year-old daughter, Bonnie, later told investigators.

Bonnie, the chief heir to Binion's $55 million estate, said she rarely got along with Murphy, who Bonnie said once pulled a gun on her and threatened to shoot her.

"I actually told my dad that she would have to change her behavior and the way she dressed and acted to move into our house, because I wasn't going to have that . . . basically a whore living in our house," she said.

Becky Behnen recalled that her brother had asked her to take Murphy shopping one day to buy her more conservative clothes.

Murphy, meanwhile, had made it clear to Behnen and to Binion's friends that she was with the casino boss solely for his money.

"She was a young, spoiled, immature, greedy young lady," Standish said.

Murphy, he said, was determined to marry Binion to ensure that she would share his wealth. She used to go around town calling herself Sandy Binion, even during the height of Binion's bitter divorce with his wife.

Binion, however, told his friends he would never marry "that bitch," and it was Standish who persuaded him to force her to sign a cohabitation agreement. Upon their breakup, the agreement said, Murphy would get only the Mercedes sports coupe that Binion had bought her and half of a six-figure stock deal the two had invested in at the Rio Suite Hotel & Casino. When Murphy became pregnant in 1996, Binion made her get an abortion.

Behnen said her son, Benny, told her that her brother had left little doubt about his true feelings for Murphy early in their relationship. Following a wild argument between Binion and Murphy that Benny had observed, Binion decided to leave the house.

"Where are we going to go?" the younger Behnen asked.

"Let's go back to Cheetah's and get another one," Binion replied.

For a while, early in her relationship with Binion, Murphy toned down her appearance. But it didn't last long.

Thomas Loveday, who did gardening for Binion, recalled that Murphy used to hang out with dancers and "big-busted girls who didn't mind showing it" to strangers.

"They'd be walking around the house in tiny T-shirts with no bras," he said. "These girls got everything done—plastic surgery—I remember seeing her girlfriends in there with Band-Aids over their noses after having their noses done."

Word spread throughout the Binion family that Murphy would often hold parties with the neighborhood youths while Binion was spending time riding horses at his Pahrump ranch.

Murphy did other things with those boys as well, Bonnie Binion later said.

"She'd, um . . . They'd smoke a lot of weed and snort a lot of coke together," Binion's daughter told investigators.

Becky Behnen said that after one of the more conservative parties she had chaperoned for her brother, one of Murphy's girlfriends left with a sixteen-year-old youth and didn't return with him for two days.

"She took him off like he was a toy or something," Behnen said. "Who knows what they did? I felt so bad. I had no idea this kind of thing would happen."

The father of the youth was a prominent Las Vegas attorney and a former federal prosecutor, Behnen said.

Murphy also liked to do the Las Vegas nightclub scene without Binion. She even made appearances in public with celebrities, such as NBA bad-boy Dennis Rodman, whom Binion hated. She was seen being chauffeured around town with Rodman in Benny Binion's old Rolls-Royce limousine, which was under his son's care. Murphy even kept a risqué photo of her and Rodman in the living room of Binion's house. Behnen described the photo as offensive to her. It made little secret of the fact that Rodman wasn't wearing any underwear. One night Behnen recalled receiving a phone call from Rodman, looking for Murphy after she had become involved in a violent fight with Binion.

"They went out on the town," Behnen said. "You'd have to use your imagination to figure out what they did, because she was a real groupie for black ballplayers."

Murphy even bragged to Behnen that she used to hang out with another NBA superstar, Magic Johnson, while she was in high school. Behnen said she never tried to confirm that story.

In their early days, Loveday, the gardener, said, Ted Binion and Murphy loved to smoke marijuana and party with each other. "Sex," he explained, "was the thing with them, big-time at first."

Murphy often flaunted her attractive body around the house, many times in the presence of the teenage neighborhood boys. It was not uncommon for her to answer the door nude or draped only in a skimpy towel, or to play the piano in a negligee in front of Binion's friends.

In return for sex and picking up after him, Binion provided Murphy with all of the cash and amenities she needed. She had her Mercedes sports coupe, and he gave her a credit card with a $10,000 limit that was paid off every month. Murphy often would be seen at the finer clothing stores in Las Vegas buying a $5,000 designer outfit on a whim. And Murphy and Binion often dined at posh restaurants and rubbed elbows with the movers and shakers of Las Vegas.

But living a life of luxury had its price. Murphy later would complain that Binion regularly beat her. Still, maybe

because of the past trauma in her life or the financial benefits Binion had provided her, Murphy seemed to accept the
punishment in her role as his partner. Tom Martinet, another
old Binion friend, said he once saw Murphy with a bruised
face and a clump of hair missing. She told him that Binion
had beat her up.

"She took a lot of crap from him," Loveday said. "She
would show me the bruises. She would put makeup on to
cover it, but you could still see it. She got beaten a lot. Ted
had a temper."

In her sworn deposition, Murphy recalled one altercation
with Binion over his daughter early in their relationship.

"I was very angry with Bonnie, and I have a hot temper
at times," she said. "I shoved him back, and he almost fell
over the coffee table, and he grabbed onto me so he wouldn't
fall and then—I had an attitude at this point—I grabbed his
hair to like pull him down . . . you know, I was mad. Sometimes everybody loses their temper. I'm not perfect. I do
have a very aggressive temper."

Murphy had called 911 during that fight, alleging "my
boyfriend beat me up."

The beatings were softened by the many other benefits
Binion showered upon Murphy, mostly perks from the
Horseshoe Club. She had use of a Horseshoe limousine and
wielded complimentary privileges at the popular downtown
Las Vegas casino, where she and her family could dine at its
world-famous steak house. She once had the Horseshoe
send her a $2,000 case of white wine. Binion even sent her
to Taiwan to schmooze high rollers for the casino.

Murphy also was privy to Binion's secret world on the
streets, a world in which handshake deals were struck with
the likes of Herbie Blitzstein and his underworld associates.

"Sandy was just in over her head," Loveday said. "She
thought she knew what she was doing, but he just had her
there because she was pretty."

Behnen said she knew Murphy and her brother didn't love
each other.

"To love someone, you have to have some respect," she said. "But these two did not respect each other. They just filled a void. And finally, it got too brutal, too out of hand."

Binion's divorce lawyer, Thomas Standish, described Murphy toward the end of her relationship with Binion as a "psycho" with a wicked temper who worked overtime trying to manipulate Binion. She even secretly monitored his telephone conversations from a series of tape recorders in her bedroom.

Behnen said Murphy was always on drugs, mostly marijuana, and behaved erratically the last year of her relationship with Binion.

"She was always threatening my life and telling me how she was going to do it," Behnen said.

One time, Behnen said, Murphy telephoned her sixty times in a row with threats and even circled her house in her car.

"She used to say, 'Do you have your pencil bitch [Behnen's secretary] there?' " Behnen said. "Then she'd explain how she planned to harm me."

As Binion lost his battle with regulators and was forced out of the casino industry in March 1998, his life once more became clouded in alcohol and heroin. And it took its toll on his relationship with Murphy. The two rarely slept together. Often, Binion would remain holed up in his den drinking alcohol, or in his secret basement hideaway "chasing the dragon," his usual method of smoking heroin. On most of those evenings, Murphy was seen nightclubbing with her girlfriends and with a new man at her side, Rick Tabish, the thirty-three-year-old son of a wealthy Missoula, Montana, businessman.

Tabish, who had befriended Binion months earlier, was young, strong and dashing, the opposite of the strung-out fifty-five-year-old Binion. Always looking to make a score, Tabish had begun hanging around Binion with the hope of tapping into his wealth for his own business ventures.

Murphy and Tabish, it seemed, had a common goal.

CHAPTER 5

•••••••••••••••••

A New Friend

•••••••••••••••••

As RICK TABISH told it, about seven months before Ted Binion's death, the two met in the bathroom of Piero's restaurant, an upscale hangout for the rich and famous in the shadow of the famed Las Vegas Strip.

Most evenings would find Piero's owner, Freddie Glusman, playing host to mob figures, politicians and national sports heroes all at the same time. They would come to be seen—and, of course, to dine on Glusman's famous Florida stone crabs and slow-cooked veal shanks. Pictures of the restaurateur's best friend, Jerry Tarkanian, in his glory days as UNLV's basketball coach a decade ago, graced the wood-paneled walls of this dimly lit, intimate establishment. It was one of Binion's favorite restaurants. Tabish, as a newcomer to Las Vegas, learned quickly that Piero's was a great place to meet people who could further his ambitious business career. Charlie Skinner, Glusman's son, had introduced him to life at Piero's in February 1998, and Tabish, the good-looking smooth talker from Missoula, Montana, took over from there. Binion, vulnerable and on the brink of losing his coveted gaming license, turned out to be a prize catch.

"I'm in the bathroom. He comes in and says, 'Hey, Rick Tabish, where are you from, Montana?'" Tabish once told police. "He says, 'You know, I had a ranch in Montana. The best times in my life were in Montana.'"

As Binion talked about himself, Tabish took an interest in his words, and by the time the two left the bathroom, Binion had invited him to his 125-acre ranch in Pahrump.

"We just hit it off," he said. "After a couple of months, he consulted me about his problems, how he'd like to quit doing the drugs."

Tabish then described how Binion returned to using heroin after Nevada gaming regulators had taken away his license at the Horseshoe Club.

"I started helping the guy out," Tabish told police. "He basically got piss-poor write-ups in the newspaper. Everybody's against him . . . and I just took him for what he was."

Binion, it seemed, took Tabish for what he was, too.

Lawmen in Missoula knew Tabish long before he landed in trouble in Las Vegas. Tabish grew up amid affluence in the city of 50,000, the second of three sons of Frank Tabish, who had become wealthy building up a petroleum distribution business. His father had bought his first gas station at the age of eighteen, and later parlayed his profits into a booming convenience-store business.

After graduating from high school in 1983, the younger Tabish tried college, but dropped out after two terms. Soon he took up with the "Pretty Boys," a group of young well-to-do Missoula men known for their hell-raising. The group's members loved to pump iron, chase women and party, but rarely did they work. Tabish often landed in jail from drinking too much and brawling too often. Most of the time his well-respected father was there to bail him out of trouble.

"Basically, it was a case of a wild kid with more money than sense," a Missoula detective familiar with Tabish told the *Las Vegas Sun*. "With his name, he knew he could push it."

By 1985, at the age of twenty, Tabish was a regular on the Missoula police logs. He was arrested in May on a felony criminal mischief charge for damaging a borrowed car. Then, in July, he pleaded guilty to a misdemeanor assault charge and received a deferred six-month sentence. One month later, Missoula police considered him a suspect in a string of burglaries, but he was never charged. Lawmen said many of those cases had a way of disappearing because of the prominence of his father.

But in September 1985, Tabish was charged with stealing a seventeenth-century painting, valued at the time at $600,000, from Milt Datsopoulos, a family friend and well-known attorney who was representing Tabish in some of his legal troubles. The case moved slowly through the court system until Tabish was arrested two years later for cocaine trafficking. Tabish and two other men were charged with shipping a quarter pound of cocaine from Arizona to Missoula by Federal Express. While the case was pending, Tabish was taken into custody again for assault, this time for fracturing a man's eye socket at a local restaurant. That case was plea-bargained to a misdemeanor. Tabish also pleaded guilty to the theft of the painting, receiving his first felony conviction along with three years probation. A year later, he pleaded guilty to the cocaine charge.

"Tabish is a classic example of an arrogant rich kid who has been able to commit numerous crimes with almost complete impunity because his father has been able to buy his way out," then Missoula County District Attorney Dusty Deschamps wrote in arguing for a jail term for Tabish.

In December 1988, Tabish was sentenced to ten years behind bars, seven of which were suspended. He spent nine months in a Montana prison before entering a pre-release center and later earning parole.

While on parole, Tabish went to work for Marvin Rehbein Sr., who ran a rock-crushing business in Missoula. There, he married Rehbein's daughter, Mary Jo. By 1992, Tabish took a stab at business himself. He started a truck-washing company, then a telecommunications business and ultimately a trucking and hauling firm called MRT Transport. All of his business ventures, except for MRT Transport, struggled in Missoula while his family was beginning to grow.

"We ended up having a child, Amanda Jo, the love of my

life," Tabish later testified. "Man, I wanted to stay home. But I'm in too deep. I have to run this equipment year-round. There's no way it can sit in the snow months.

"You start putting the kids No. 1. You start putting your marriage No. 2, and that's what happened in my case. I started working hard, and the next thing you know, we have another child."

His son, Kyle, was born about three years after Amanda.

When his probation on the drug-trafficking charge ended in 1997, Tabish decided it was time to expand to Las Vegas. He started MRT Transportation of Nevada, MRT Contracting and MRT Leasing. Tabish would leave his wife and two small children behind in Missoula for days at a time to fly to Las Vegas to conduct business.

Described as a go-getter with much energy, Tabish made friends quickly in Las Vegas.

"He was able to meet contacts fast," Skinner told Las Vegas police. "Rick has a talent for getting an introduction and then being able to meet five to ten more people from that introduction. And he met a lot of people in the short time he was here."

Tabish even once attempted to get into a real estate venture with Las Vegas private detective Tom Dillard, who would later zero in on Tabish as a suspect while investigating Binion's death.

But dining at Piero's wasn't the only way that Tabish was able to insinuate himself into the Las Vegas business community. He networked at the Las Vegas Sporting House, an athletic club that caters to the city's movers and shakers. The Sporting House was a natural for Tabish, a former high school football player who prided himself on his physical shape. He stood six-two and weighed a solid 220 pounds. The Sporting House was also where Tabish's secret romantic relationship with Sandy Murphy took shape. And where schemes of gaining access to Binion's millions were hatched.

Soon after his arrival in Las Vegas, just as in Missoula,

Tabish began failing at business. His ambition seemed to get the better of him.

Skinner described Tabish as a "meat-and-potatoes guy" when he first came to the city. But after getting a taste of the fast lane there, a step above rural Montana, Tabish changed. He developed a desire to maintain a high lifestyle.

By the time Tabish met Binion at Piero's, MRT Transportation of Nevada was losing money, and losing it fast.

"I was an overachiever," Tabish later testified. "I should have listened to my father. He told me all of the time, 'Learn how to walk before you run, Rick.' I never listened."

One way out of his financial difficulties was to stay close to Binion.

After his gaming license was revoked in March, Binion knew he eventually would have to remove his $6 million silver fortune from a basement vault at the Horseshoe Club. His sister Becky Behnen was close to finalizing a deal to take over the family business.

Tabish and Murphy, looking for a finder's fee, had persuaded Binion to sell the silver bars and coins, most of which he had inherited from his mother, Teddy Jane, after her 1994 death.

In April, while on a visit to Disneyland with his wife, Mary Jo, and the two small children, Tabish set the wheels in motion. He arranged a dinner meeting with Billy Marin, a well-known Los Angeles street merchant, at a posh Beverly Hills restaurant. The fifty-one-year-old Marin liked the proposition and agreed to become involved, but the silver was too much for him to move alone. So he brought in Mark Goldberg, a veteran coin dealer with experience in large deals. Goldberg, who ran Superior Stamp & Coin in Beverly Hills, agreed to come to Las Vegas in May to examine the silver at the Horseshoe vault.

Tabish picked up Goldberg at the airport when he arrived in Las Vegas and took him to the Horseshoe, where they met Murphy. After a brief examination of the silver, Goldberg, who liked what he saw, returned to Beverly Hills to await further instructions. A couple of weeks later, an excited Murphy telephoned Goldberg and told him that Binion was ready to sell the silver. The coin dealer promptly sent dozens of silver-dollar tubes to Murphy and Tabish so that the most expensive coins could be repackaged in anticipation of an auction in Los Angeles.

Goldberg had hoped to transport the silver in several armored cars. But first he made plans to return to Las Vegas in June to conduct a tedious appraisal of the coins and bars. He spent three days there with a crew of three employees evaluating the silver inside the Horseshoe vault. He estimated it was worth $5 to $7 million.

When the appraisal was complete, Goldberg was summoned to meet Binion at his ranch in Pahrump. But the news was not good. Binion, who appeared "stoned drunk" to Goldberg, said he had decided not to sell the silver because its price had fallen too much on the market.

Goldberg was particularly dejected, since he had been looking forward to seeing a bag of 1889 Carson City-minted silver dollars that Binion said was part of the collection locked away in a separate place at the Horseshoe Club. The coins, worth millions by themselves, were rare because the Carson City mint had been in operation only for a couple of years. Binion told Goldberg he had 1,000 of the rare silver dollars.

Binion, in the meantime, had told Tabish that he wanted to bury the silver on vacant land he owned in the heart of downtown Pahrump, about an hour from Las Vegas.

Tabish suggested that he could help Binion build an underground vault, and Binion took him up on his offer. He agreed to pay Tabish $40,000.

The vault was almost completed by the time Becky Behnen took control of the Horseshoe Club on July 2, 1998. About twelve feet long, ten feet wide and ten feet deep, the vault was made of concrete with a large steel door. The only way to get inside was through a small manhole on the concrete cover, which was at ground level. All around was a chain-link fence with barbed wire.

Just after midnight on July 2, Binion armed himself to the hilt and corralled his trusted nephew, Key Fechser, into helping him move the silver out of the Horseshoe. The two men met Tabish and his crew at the casino. Even Sandy Murphy showed up. There, under the watchful eye of Horseshoe security officers, Binion and company spent several hours loading dozens of crates of silver bullion and hundreds of bags and tubes filled with silver coins, some uncirculated and dating back to the late 1800s, into a large truck that Tabish had brought. The truck was parked on the side of the neon-lit hotel, just off the famous Fremont Street Experience, a downtown pedestrian mall for tourists.

"We had kind of an assembly line going," Fechser said in court documents. "We would bring the stuff up from the vault, up the elevator, and drop it there and load it. We had three different crews."

As daylight broke, all of the silver had been loaded onto the truck. Tabish and his crew drove to Binion's home a couple of miles away. Binion, Murphy and Fechser followed in separate cars. The truck remained parked on Binion's front lawn inside his gates for two days until another early-morning run was made to Pahrump to put the silver in its new resting place underground. This time, on the Fourth of July, a heavily armed Binion rode shotgun with Tabish as his entourage made the sixty-mile trek through the Spring Mountain Pass to Pahrump. Hours later, the silver was safely buried.

Some of Binion's friends, meanwhile, were wary of the trust Binion had placed in Tabish.

"It's hard for me to believe that he would let somebody he didn't know that well build him a vault," his longtime pal Sid Lewis later told investigators. "I'd never heard of Tabish, and I'd been around Ted for thirty-something years."

CHAPTER 6

....

Love and Betrayal

....

MARK GOLDBERG WASN'T the only one who saw romantic sparks between Sandy Murphy and Rick Tabish while appraising Ted Binion's silver fortune at the Horseshoe Club in the spring of 1998.

Security officers Donald Kershaw and John Boylan couldn't help but notice the gleam in the eyes of Murphy and Tabish one day as the two Binion confidants gazed at each other inside the casino's basement vault while Goldberg was working.

By then, Murphy had been living with Binion, who was more than twice her age, for three years. Their relationship had been deteriorating within the past year, often marred by violent arguments, which usually resulted in threats against each other's lives.

Kershaw said he just "kept his mouth shut" about his observations and didn't tell his supervisors that Binion's girlfriend had taken a liking to Tabish. He said there was little doubt in his mind that Murphy and Tabish were more than just business partners.

"They were just too touchy-feely," he would later tell investigators.

Boylan said the two weren't making it obvious, but he also sensed that they were "very friendly."

When Goldberg later ran into Murphy and Tabish at Bin-

45

ion's ranch in Pahrump, the two lovers went out of their way to disguise their relationship in front of Binion, who was drunk on tequila at the time.

"Oh, they didn't show it," he said. "I mean, they were cautious about it. If anything . . . Sandy was all over Ted."

But Goldberg said he knew better.

After state regulators had forced Binion to give up his interests in the Horseshoe Club a couple of months earlier, Binion kept up his spirits, but he took the news hard. He returned to a life of alcohol and drugs, further straining his relationship with Murphy, who had grown accustomed to spending $5,000 a month, sometimes much more, of his money on clothes and dining at gourmet restaurants.

Anticipating a breakup, Murphy was looking to profit financially from the three years she had invested in the relationship so she could continue to lead a life of luxury. She knew that she had signed a cohabitation agreement and that Binion had not put her in his will.

Tabish, meanwhile, was deep in debt and saw Binion's wealth as a quick way to ease his financial troubles. There also was temptation to run afoul of his marriage. Tabish's business ventures in Las Vegas had forced him to spend long periods of time away from his wife, Mary Jo, and their two young children. And Murphy had the kind of charm and sexually expressive personality that played up to Tabish's virility. Even better, Murphy was close to Binion, his potential cash cow.

And so began the plot to kill the wealthy fifty-five-year-old gambling figure.

Tabish bragged to business partner Leo Casey, the operator of a sand pit outside Las Vegas, that he intended to bring about Binion's demise. Casey, a slender, sixty-four-year-old man who sported a toupee and wore thick glasses, later told homicide detectives that Tabish boasted of pumping Binion with drugs and making it look as though his death was an overdose. And as it became clear that Tabish would be unable to broker the silver deal, he told the soft-spoken Casey that he planned to steal the fortune instead. He also confided that he was "laying the pipe" to Murphy and that his relationship with her would make it easier for him to pull off the massive theft.

Private detectives working for Binion's estate found records that showed there were regular cellular phone calls between Murphy and Tabish beginning in April 1998. Gradually, the calls became more frequent and longer. They were made at all hours of the day. By late June, Murphy and Tabish were calling each other as many as two dozen times a day. Investigator Bob Leonard, who pored over hundreds of minutes' worth of cell phone records, concluded that Murphy was the predominate caller.

"Many of Tabish's calls appear to be in response to a series of calls from Murphy," he wrote in a secret report. "The pattern of Murphy's calls suggests she is either extremely impatient or agitated by not getting an immediate answer and would repeatedly call the same number. . . ."

With Binion intent on burying his silver, Tabish had persuaded the casino man to let him supervise the building of the vault in Pahrump. That way, Tabish would have the inside track on removing the fortune when the time was right. Binion, meanwhile, was becoming more and more withdrawn in his relationship with Murphy. He would stay up all night smoking heroin and watching The History and Discovery channels on cable in his den, while Murphy would hit the nightclubs on the Las Vegas Strip with her girlfriends and Tabish whenever he was in town.

Perhaps because of the slaying of his good friend Herbie Blitzstein and his bitter family infighting over the Horseshoe Club, Binion was gripped with paranoia during the remaining months of his life. He was in constant fear that someone might try to kill him. Around his sprawling estate, he had installed a series of eight television cameras that could be viewed on monitors in his bedroom and den. The cameras were hooked to a video recorder so that he could keep track of people coming and leaving his home when he wasn't there.

At the same time, Murphy had become obsessed with keeping track of Binion and manipulating his life. She would eavesdrop on his telephone conversations and secretly record his calls from her bedroom. Nick Behnen, Binion's brother-in-law, said Binion once told him Murphy would use a parabolic microphone inside his home to monitor conversations with friends and business associates who visited him. Binion was aware of Murphy's clandestine activities and often was guarded when speaking on the telephone. Still, Behnen said, Binion told him he believed she had tapes that could land Binion in trouble with the law. Murphy had led Binion to believe the tapes were her insurance that she would get a handsome financial windfall if the couple ever broke up. When later asked about the tapes by a reporter, Murphy did not deny that they existed.

Shortly after Tabish had helped Binion transport his silver to the underground vault in Pahrump on July 4, Murphy began pressing Binion to put her in his will. On July 9, Binion caved in and amended the will. He agreed to give Murphy his home, which had been appraised at $900,000, its contents and $300,000 in cash to cover inheritance taxes. At the same time, Murphy had confided in her good friend from Southern California, Linda Carroll, that she was having an affair with Tabish. Carroll would later tell one of Binion's lawyers, Richard Wright, that Tabish hated Binion with a passion and wanted him dead.

Tabish's darker side, it seemed, began to surface as his financial troubles worsened. He had come to Las Vegas in 1997 looking to parlay his trucking experience into a gold mine in the sand-and-gravel business, the core of the booming southern Nevada construction industry. Sand and gravel are used to make the concrete that provides the foundation for the megaresorts of the Las Vegas Strip and the hundreds of residential subdivisions around it. Tabish had the ability to get the valuable resource, where millions could be made, to the concrete companies.

By early 1997, Tabish had hooked up with Leo Casey,

who had obtained the mining rights to a lucrative sand pit in Jean, Nevada, a tiny town off Interstate 15, about forty miles west of Las Vegas. Casey later struck a deal to sell his rights to John Joseph, a balding sixty-year-old banker from Southern California. In return, Casey became a joint owner in Joseph's gravel and rock-crushing companies. Homicide detectives probing Ted Binion's death later learned that the deal appeared shady from the start. Joseph wasn't willing to pay Casey the full value of his mining rights out of fear that too much debt in the companies would drive away much-needed investors to produce the sand. So the two men agreed to allow Casey to buy expensive rock-crushing equipment at wholesale prices and sell it back to their companies at retail prices. Casey would be able to keep the difference, as much as $50,000 for each piece of equipment. The scheme worked well for Casey and Joseph as they mined the sand and gravel. But it had the potential to defraud investors, who would be shortchanged hundreds of thousands of dollars.

Tabish, meanwhile, had been hauling sand and gravel for the two men from Jean to the California border, where there was a casino boom. In February 1998, Tabish found another sand pit in Mesquite, Nevada, a small town about sixty-five miles northeast of Las Vegas. He made a deal with Casey and Joseph to run the pit and then share the proceeds of the sale of sand and gravel. Tabish hoped to earn $1.6 million over the next three years in the business venture. But it all began to unravel in July 1998. Casey and Joseph were months behind in their bills to Tabish. He was owed $500,000. Then Casey and Joseph became embroiled in a bitter business dispute, forcing them to pull out of the Mesquite operation and close the Jean sand pit. That left everybody, including Tabish, in a tough financial bind. And it led to some desperate measures.

On July 28, Tabish, Joseph and another business partner, Steven Wadkins, drove Casey to the sand pit in Jean under the guise of inspecting some equipment for a possible sale. As they arrived at the 1,900-acre pit, Wadkins, seated next to

Casey in the backseat, allegedly pulled out a revolver and pointed it at him. Tabish then ordered Casey out of the car. His arms were pulled behind his back and his hands were restrained with thumb cuffs. Tabish reached into the car and brought out a thick phone book and immediately began hitting Casey in the head with it.

"You stole from us, and you stole from John Joseph," Tabish said.

"No, I didn't," Casey responded.

"Yes, you did, and you're going to confess," Tabish yelled back as he continued to hit Casey with the phone book.

Casey was knocked to the hard desert ground several times, his toupee shoved to the side of his head, during what amounted to an hour-long torture session aimed at persuading Casey to turn over his interests in the sand pit operation to Tabish.

"I'd just gotten the hell beat out of me," Casey later testified. "They were going to cut my fingers off and cut my wrists."

At one point, Wadkins, a stocky, tough-looking man, allegedly stuck his gun in Casey's mouth and said: "You're going to sign this confession. You're going to sign over your interest in this equipment."

When Casey still refused to confess, a knife was stuck under all of his fingernails, causing unbelievable pain. But Casey again would not cave in.

Losing patience, Tabish told Wadkins: "Go get the front loader over there and dig a grave for this guy."

After a three-foot hole was dug, Casey was dragged over and told by Tabish, "This is going to be your grave."

Casey finally relented, saying, "OK, I'll sign the documents."

Still restrained with the thumb cuffs, Casey was driven back to Las Vegas with a gun pointed to his head. On the way to town, Tabish telephoned Joseph from the car and asked him to meet them at Tabish's MRT Transportation of Nevada offices on the far south end of the Las Vegas Strip.

Once there, Joseph got into the car, and they all drove to All Star Transit Mix, a cement-making company owned by Wadkins in the north end of the city. A shaken Casey was instructed to confess in writing that he had been stealing money from Joseph and had agreed to give up the rights to the sand pit equipment. After completing the confession, Casey was taken to a law office, where an attorney drafted a three-page formal "asset transfer agreement" for Casey to sign in the presence of a notary. The lawyer, surprised by the unusual event, noticed that Casey appeared very distressed in his presence.

When they left the lawyer's office, Tabish and Wadkins allegedly told the frightened businessman not to "meddle" in their business and to leave town or they would take Casey's daughters and "fuck them to death and blow their heads off." The next day Casey went to the bank, withdrew $200,000 and fled to California. Tabish, in the meantime, had instructed another lawyer, William Knudson, to draft an investors' summary looking for $500,000 to reopen the sand pit in Jean. The summary indicated Tabish was made a very favorable offer to run the operation for the next fifty years because he had caught someone embezzling from the company. On August 26, 1998, Joseph formally gave Tabish the mining rights to the pit.

Tabish needed to open the sand pit to recoup the $500,000 Casey owed him and the $1.6 million he had lost in the failed Mesquite mining project. But more important, he needed quick cash to pay off mounting IRS debts that had soared to more than $1.3 million. In January 1998, the IRS began slapping five- and six-figure liens on his Montana businesses for unpaid taxes dating back to 1996. The Montana Department of Transportation also hit Tabish with a $257,189 lien. And a bank in Missoula was moving ahead with efforts to foreclose on property Tabish owned there because of a delinquent $75,000 loan.

In Las Vegas, Tabish's debts began piling up as well. He was having trouble making his payroll at MRT Transportation of Nevada, and creditors started filing default notices for failed lease payments on his trucks. He had missed payments in March, April, May and June of 1998. Adding to his troubles was a $200,000 bank loan that was due on September 19, 1998.

Despite his mounting financial problems, Tabish still had Murphy to console him. On July 27, 1998, the day before Tabish kidnapped Casey in the desert, Murphy went on one of her usual shopping sprees with Binion's credit card at the upscale Fashion Show Mall on the Las Vegas Strip. This time, however, she was shopping for Tabish, her new lover. Brian Hall, a salesclerk at Neiman Marcus, said Murphy charged a $310 pair of stone-washed Gucci jeans to Binion's account and asked that they be gift wrapped. The thirty-six-inch-waist jeans, with a "G" etched in rhinestones on the back pocket, were given to Tabish. A week later, on August 3, Murphy returned to Neiman Marcus and bought a $240 pair of black Armani slacks, a $445 black velvet Armani shirt and an $85 Wilke Rodriguez top. Once more, the bill was charged on a credit card Binion had given Murphy. Hall said Murphy had asked that these items be gift wrapped, and he overheard Murphy tell a friend that she was going to surprise Tabish by placing the present "on the bed."

Five days later, on August 8, Murphy and Tabish checked into a $350-a-night suite with a deluxe king-sized bed at the posh Beverly Hills Hotel in the first of their secret weekend trysts in Southern California. Murphy signed in as "S. M. Tabish." The couple had drinks that night at the hotel's famed Polo Lounge, and the next day they rented a $125 poolside cabana.

Later that month, while back home in Missoula, Tabish solicited the help of high school friend Steven Kurt Gratzer, a thirty-six-year-old Army veteran who was working for a Tabish-run telemarketing firm, in killing Binion. Tabish told Gratzer, who had received training as an Army Ranger, that the wealthy casino man was a heavy drug user who owed him $13,000 for building the vault in Pahrump and was abusing Murphy constantly. Tabish described Murphy as "one of the pigs he fucks" and said she was "in his back pocket" and would do whatever he wanted her to do. He said he had plans to acquire an $875,000 life insurance premium that Murphy stood to gain upon Binion's death and that he also intended to steal Binion's silver in Pahrump and his valuables at his Las Vegas home. Tabish promised to buy Gratzer a new 1999 Pontiac Trans Am and give him part of the life insurance proceeds for his help.

In September, cellular phone records showed that calls between Murphy and Tabish were at an all-time high, as many as thirty-one times a day. And Murphy was making it clear in public that her relationship with Binion was on the rocks.

On September 7, Murphy walked into the Gianni Versace store at the Forum Shops at Caesars Palace, shopping for fall clothes. There, she was greeted by salesclerk Christopher Hendrick, who observed her to be "drunk or high on cocaine." She began rambling about her deteriorating relations with Binion, saying the two no longer were sleeping in the same bed, nor were they having sex. Murphy said she had seen a lawyer about obtaining a settlement from Binion and was told she could get as much as $2 million. She also reported that she had a new boyfriend. A couple of days later, Hendrick telephoned Binion and told him the clothes Murphy had purchased were ready, but Binion ordered Hendrick not to ship them, saying Murphy soon wouldn't be able to afford them.

About 10:30 A.M. on September 10, Murphy and her friend Linda Carroll showed up at the Neiman Marcus beauty salon for a day of pampering. Right off the bat, manicurist Deana Perry noticed that Murphy appeared to have been drinking or taking drugs. While doing Murphy's nails, Perry mentioned that she was getting a divorce from her husband. Murphy responded that she, too, was having trouble with "her husband." Perry asked Murphy why she didn't get a divorce from Binion, and Murphy responded she wouldn't get any money if she left him. She told Perry, however, that she stood to receive $3 million and Binion's $900,000 Las Vegas house if he died and that she would just have to "hang in there."

Then Murphy made a startling prediction. She said Binion was going to die of a heroin overdose within the next three weeks, and that would allow her to obtain her inheritance and proceed further with her new boyfriend, whom she identified as Richard.

Even more ominous, Murphy was laughing about Binion's demise and planning to go to upcoming social events in his absence. Murphy suggested it would be too soon in the wake of Binion's death to attend the annual Andre Agassi children's benefit with Tabish at the end of the month. But she thought that Tabish could accompany her to the grand opening of Steve Wynn's new Bellagio megaresort on the Strip the following month. Perry also heard Murphy say that Tabish and his friends planned to recover Binion's assets after his death.

Perry, it turned out, wasn't the only one who had heard Murphy boast of Binion's upcoming death. Hair stylist Michelle Gilliam reported that she was within earshot when Murphy made the prediction to Perry. She also heard Murphy talking about her "secret love affair." And Georgia Gastone, a hair stylist who worked next to Gilliam, said she heard Murphy say she would be able to get more money if Binion passed away. Murphy even boasted in front of the beauty salon employees that Tabish had the combinations to all of Binion's safes.

Later that evening, Murphy met Tabish and another man, Larry Stockett, who was thinking about buying one of Tabish's businesses. During a conversation at the Voodoo Lounge, a trendy nightclub atop the Rio hotel-casino, Murphy told Stockett that Binion was likely to overdose on heroin soon. And she confided in Stockett that she was in love with Tabish and wanted to marry him.

The next morning, as her relationship with Binion was

fast disintegrating, Murphy checked into the Peninsula Hotel in Beverly Hills. She identified herself as "Mrs. Tabish" and requested a room with a Jacuzzi, an expensive bottle of red wine and two dozen long-stemmed roses, all as a "surprise for her husband." The following morning, a Saturday, Murphy and Tabish spent the entire day at a cabana at the pool. On Sunday, they went back to the cabana and that evening ordered his-and-her massages in their room. They checked out on Monday, September 14, and returned to Las Vegas.

Three days later, Binion was dead.

CHAPTER 7

. . . .

Paranoia and the Last Day

. . . .

IT WAS NO secret to those close to Ted Binion that during the last month of his life, his relationship with Sandy Murphy was deteriorating rapidly.

His housekeeper, Mary Montoya-Gascoigne, said the two were constantly arguing, generally about her spending habits. Records showed Murphy charged $52,000 from January through September of 1998, over $5,700 a month, on a credit card Binion had given her long ago. About a week before his death, Binion instructed his bookkeeper, Cathy Rose, to cancel the credit card. He had made this request before in the heat of a fight with Murphy, so Rose always waited several days before actually calling up the credit card company. Usually Binion would call her back within that time and tell her not to go through with it. But this time there was no callback, and Rose went ahead and canceled the card.

During that stormy month, Binion twice asked Montoya-Gascoigne to accompany him around the house to remove the bullets from the weapons scattered about. He was afraid Murphy might use one of the guns during an argument. Binion also began to talk openly to the housekeeper about his suspicions that Murphy was cheating on him. He even asked her whether he should hire a private detective to follow Murphy around town.

56

"He said, 'I don't know, she goes out a lot and dresses too nicely to go to the store. I think something's wrong there,' " Montoya-Gascoigne later told investigators.

She said Binion also suspected that Murphy stole 1,000 silver dollars from his safe the week before he died and took them to her stepmother in Bellflower, California, during a visit over the weekend. Murphy, the housekeeper said, had the combination to Binion's safe. What Binion didn't know was that Murphy secretly had hooked up with Tabish at the Peninsula Hotel that weekend. Binion was led to believe that Murphy had traveled to California to attend her nephew's birthday party at her stepmother's house.

That weekend, on Saturday, September 12, Binion found himself lonely, and he reached out to Murphy in California, begging her to come home. He tried to entice her back by lying to her, saying their dog, Pig, had run away.

Brad Parry, who had installed the television cameras around Binion's home, was present when the distressed casino man pleaded with Murphy to return to Las Vegas.

"He was in bad shape," Parry later said.

Binion told Parry he believed Murphy was "chipping around on him," and he asked him to play a recent surveillance tape of Murphy talking to a man in a truck outside his house. While reviewing the tape, Parry noticed that someone had tampered with the video recorder hooked to the eight cameras around the house, and he promised to come back and have it fixed. Binion asked the electronics expert to plant a bug in Murphy's bedroom phone so that he could secretly monitor her conversations. It was only fair, after all, because Binion knew Murphy was keeping tabs on his phone calls with recorders in her bedroom. So Binion gave Parry money to buy an eavesdropping device, and Parry promised to return in a couple of days.

On Sunday, Binion, growing more apprehensive, telephoned his brother-in-law, Nick Behnen, and asked him to send over a Horseshoe Club locksmith to get into Murphy's bedroom, which she had bolted shut before leaving for California. But no locksmiths could be reached. And when Parry came back to the home the following Tuesday, Murphy had returned from California, and it was impossible to install the bug. Parry, however, did unhook the video recorder and take it to a repair shop. That left Binion with no way of recording people coming in and out of his home the rest of that fateful week.

On Monday evening, Binion's friend and lawyer Richard Wright paid a visit to drop off $40,000 in cash for Binion to give to Las Vegas Mayor Jan Laverty Jones, a Democrat who was leaving City Hall to run for governor. Wright had always kept cash for Binion in his safe at his law office.

Binion, though down about his relationship with Murphy, was optimistic about one day seeing a governor in office who would consider giving him a chance to get his gaming license back. He thought that Jones, a wealthy businesswoman who traveled in his same social circles, was the perfect candidate for him.

Wright had a pleasant talk with Binion in his den. Binion sat in his usual spot on the left side of his worn-out couch, within arm's reach of an ashtray on the end table. He talked about buying a new ranch in Oregon and the proper way of giving Jones her campaign contribution. Wright had suggested a check, but Binion wanted to give her cash. That was the way his legendary father had always done it. As the two chatted, Binion showed Wright his $300,000 collection of antique coins and currency. He was proud of the collection, which contained dollar bills dating back to the Civil War era. Wright left Binion in good spirits.

The next morning, Tuesday, Binion was happy again, and he decided to make some more investments with his money. He summoned Kevin Page, a senior vice president at First Security Bank of Nevada, to his home and told him to put together a $1 million portfolio. Binion had also decided that he wanted new $100 bills to give to Jones, who was to visit him on Wednesday, so he gave Page an extra $40,000 check and told him to return with the cash.

Wednesday was indeed a big day for Binion. Mayor Jones was expected in the morning, and Binion was excited. He instructed Montoya-Gascoigne, who had arrived for work early that day, to make sure the house was in special shape for the mayor. Then he ran into his next-door neighbor, Enrique Lacayo, a local physician, who was getting ready to play tennis in his backyard. Whenever Binion needed to get off heroin, he went to Lacayo to get a prescription for the sedative Xanax. On this morning, Binion told his neighbor that he wasn't doing heroin, but was "anxious" because of the mayor's visit and needed something to calm him down. Lacayo promptly wrote him a prescription for a month's supply of Xanax. Within a short time, Tanya Cropp, Murphy's twenty-four-year-old close friend, arrived at the house. Cropp, blond and slender with a pretty face, was learning how to become Binion's new bookkeeper because Rose was leaving the state for a new job.

"We've got a lot of work to do, Tanya," Binion told his new bookkeeper. "But the mayor's coming over. Can you come back in a couple of hours?"

Cropp obliged her new boss and left the house.

About 10 A.M., shortly before Jones arrived, Binion received a long-distance call from his longtime friend Jay Kerr, whose car had broken down on a Texas highway. Kerr asked Binion to wire him $300 in cash to get the car fixed. During the conversation, Binion told Kerr that he was mad at himself for going back on heroin. He said he had tried to stop.

"But sure enough, as soon as I do," Binion said, "I run into a guy that can get me some good dope, and he's on his way over here."

Binion described the new drug supplier as a "young, sharp guy." It was the same way he had talked about Tabish in an earlier conversation with his lawyer and good friend James J. Brown. Later that day, when Tabish was chatting at his home with Murphy in the living room, Binion pointed toward the two and told Roy Price, one of his Pahrump ranch hands, "They got me the best shit that I have had in a long time."

Mayor Jones arrived with her driver a few minutes after 10 A.M. She was greeted by Binion, who was barefoot and dressed in jeans with a plaid button-down shirt. The first thing Binion did was take the mayor on a tour of his remodeled house.

They walked through the spacious living room with its white marble floor, white baby grand piano and French doors that opened onto a view of his large backyard. For a moment, Jones peered into the backyard, which was graced by large plum and olive trees and plenty of grass. To the left of the modest rectangular pool was a small gazebo surrounded by flowers. To the right and farther back was the small playhouse Binion had built years ago for his daughter, Bonnie, when she was a child. The entire estate stood on a little more than two acres.

"He loved his backyard," Jones later said. "He talked about why he would never want to leave that house, because the backyard was, you know, such a great, great place for parties and for his dogs and how it didn't feel like you were in Las Vegas."

The tour took Jones to Bonnie's wood-floored bedroom and Murphy's huge, elegant sleeping quarters, which had been designed by Binion's ex-wife, Doris. When they got to the kitchen, on the other side of the house, Binion handed Jones $40,000 in cash as promised.

"He wasn't in any way depressed at all," Jones told homicide detectives. "I mean, Ted was in a really good mood. He was quite nostalgic."

Binion took out photo albums and showed the mayor pictures of his father and of himself as a youth riding a horse. Then he showed her his prized coin and currency collection in the living room. Jones described Binion as "real talkative" that morning.

"He was talking about the future," Jones said. "And he talked about losing his license and how he felt and what he was going to do to try and get it back."

Binion even discussed his heroin problem: "He said, 'Look I had problems in the past, but I've really got this under control . . . I'm doing the things I need to do . . . And I'm going to go in front of the [Gaming Control] Board and show them that, you know, I deserve to be licensed.'"

The infighting within his family was also on his mind that day. Binion believed the split between the brothers and sisters had begun in 1994, after the death of his mother, Teddy Jane. The inheritance wasn't as large as everyone had thought, maybe $3 million after taxes for each of her children, Binion told Jones. His sisters had become jealous of his brother, Jack, who had made millions expanding the Horseshoe Club operations outside Nevada into Louisiana and Mississippi. Early on, Jack had offered his sisters a chance to invest in his properties, but they had declined. Binion said he had made out fine financially. He had received about $10 million in cash toward his 20 percent interest in the hotel and was doing well because of real estate investments he had made in Pahrump.

Binion didn't hold out much hope that his sister Becky would be successful at running the Horseshoe. He felt that his brother was the only person who really could handle the downtown casino, which he called an old-time "joint."

That was why he was looking forward to getting back his license, Jones said. Binion felt that his brother would end up with the Horseshoe in the long run, and he wanted to be there to help him run it.

As Binion walked Jones out to her car at the end of her hour-long visit, he told the mayor that Murphy, "his old lady," was out shopping and would be sorry that she had missed her.

Homicide detective Tom Thowsen later pressed Jones about her impressions of Murphy.

"In the brief time that you did spend around Sandy, either alone or when she was with Ted, and seeing her interactions, did you form any opinions as to whether she seemed like somebody that was genuinely in love with Ted or somebody

that was along for the ride with Ted for the money?"
Thowsen asked.

"She was along for the ride," Jones responded.

"No doubt about it?"

"You know, the only time I ever felt differently was the
day Ted was talking to me on the tour of the house, and it
was more the way he talked . . . how proud he was, how neat
the house was . . . The pictures that were out were nice pictures of Ted and Sandy. They looked happy, they looked loving. And I thought, you know, maybe everybody's really
wrong."

But everybody wasn't wrong.

After Jones left shortly after 11 A.M., Cropp returned to
begin her new duties. Her first task was to set up a Rolodex
for Binion, who still seemed to be in good spirits, even
promising to help Cropp make some financial investments.

But Binion's suspicions about Murphy were weighing
heavily on his mind. He knew Cropp was close to her, so he
pulled the young woman aside and asked: "I want you to be
square with me. Is Sandy having an affair?"

"No," Cropp replied. "But I think she intends to have an
affair on you."

Cropp knew she wasn't being totally truthful with her new
boss. A month earlier, Murphy had confided in her that she
was carrying on a romantic relationship with Tabish, but
Cropp didn't want to break that confidence. She did, however, say enough to cause Binion great concern.

Minutes later, Binion telephoned private detective Don
Dibble and asked him to put a tail on Murphy, who he now
firmly believed was cheating on him. Binion told Dibble he
suspected Tabish was Murphy's new lover, and he suggested
Dibble start the surveillance at the Las Vegas Sporting
House, where he knew they both exercised. Then he called
his friend James Brown, but was told by his wife, Laura, that
Brown was playing golf.

"Just tell Jimmy to take Sandy out of the will and put
Bonnie in," he said. "Bonnie gets it all."

"Is Sandy gone?" Laura Brown asked.

"No, but she might as well be," Binion replied.

About an hour later, Brown came home from his golf game and returned Binion's call.

"Take Sandy out of the will, if she doesn't kill me tonight," Binion told his lawyer. "If I'm dead, you'll know what happened."

"OK, I'll get it done," a startled Brown replied.

While Murphy was still away, Binion asked Montoya-Gascoigne to go around the house one more time with him while he unloaded his guns. Binion, anticipating a confrontation with Murphy, told his housekeeper he was afraid Murphy might try to shoot him. He told Montoya-Gascoigne that if Murphy did try to grab one of his weapons, "I'll be already on top of it."

That afternoon, Binion's trusted nephew, Key Fechser, telephoned to ask his uncle whether he wanted to attend the premiere of the documentary *Mob Law,* about the career of attorney Oscar Goodman. Binion declined the invitation, but informed Fechser that he was writing Murphy out of his will and "getting rid of her."

Murphy was in the living room at the time, talking with Tabish. Binion then turned his attention to ranch hand Price. He pointed to Murphy and Tabish and told the ranch hand: "She's closer to him than a cheap suit."

Price gave Binion even more reason to be suspicious of Tabish. He told his boss about a strange incident a day earlier, when he had observed people taking photos of the Pahrump ranch from a van outside the property. Price followed the van to the nearby site of the underground vault, where only a few people, including Tabish, knew the silver was buried. Binion began to suspect that Tabish was trying to double-cross him.

Before this, Binion had demonstrated to Murphy that things were going to change at his house. In a chore usually reserved for Murphy, he had asked Montoya-Gascoigne to go to the bank and deposit half of the $40,000 that Wright had brought over earlier in the week. That left at least $20,000 in the house.

By 2:30 P.M., Price went back to Pahrump, leaving Binion in the home with his housekeeper, Murphy and Tabish.

As Montoya-Gascoigne was cleaning Murphy's bathroom, an angry Murphy, who had noticed Binion's changed demeanor, confronted Montoya-Gascoigne.

"I don't trust you anymore," said Murphy, who was concerned that the housekeeper might have informed Binion about her affair with Tabish. "I want you to leave now."

Baffled by Murphy's words, Montoya-Gascoigne promptly put down her mop and bucket, said good-bye to Binion and left the house.

About six minutes later, Binion telephoned David Mattsen, who managed his Pahrump ranch, to ask whether he knew anything about the mysterious van Price had followed outside the ranch the previous day. Binion also had learned from Price that Mattsen was seen driving around in a new pickup truck registered to Tabish. Shortly after that phone call, Mattsen telephoned Tabish, who was still at Binion's house, to report his conversation. Binion now was suspicious of Mattsen.

Meanwhile, Binion had misplaced his prescription for Xanax and gone back to Lacayo next door to get another one. He then took it to a nearby pharmacy to get it filled.

Later that evening, Binion received a phone call from Barbara Brown, his real estate agent. Brown was working on a deal for Binion to buy four acres of land next to the Texas Station Gambling Hall & Hotel on the north side of town. Binion was planning to open an adult nightclub on the site, and Brown had arranged a 1 P.M. meeting with Binion in two days to discuss the deal. Binion confirmed his Friday appointment with Brown.

A half hour after Brown's call, Peter Sheridan, one of Binion's longtime drug suppliers, showed up on his doorstep with twelve balloons of black tar heroin, just as Binion had ordered. Murphy gave Sheridan a cold stare when she let him inside. Binion usually went through one balloon a day and would buy three or four at a time from Sheridan. But this time he wanted an extra supply because he was planning to spend a week at his ranch riding horses. The forty-four-year-old Sheridan, a heroin addict himself for more than twenty years, had been supplying Binion with the raw street drug since 1980. Sheridan had always gotten Binion black tar because he knew that was the best kind to smoke. Binion preferred the method of "chasing the dragon," which is lighting up the heroin on tinfoil and inhaling it. He never injected the drug into his veins.

After a friendly chat in his den, Binion paid Sheridan for the heroin and gave him a bonus of thirty Xanax tablets for getting him the balloons on quick notice. That left Binion with ninety tablets. Sheridan later told homicide detectives that Binion had a lot on his mind, but did not appear suicidal. Binion, however, seemed "stoned" to Sheridan, as if he had taken some Xanax.

Sheridan knew that Binion found it easier to cut back on his heroin use if he took a couple of Xanax and went to sleep.

This night, however, Binion wasn't planning to sleep.

CHAPTER 8

•••••••••••••••••••

Death of a Casino Boss

•••••••••••••••••••

BY 4 A.M. ON September 17, Ted Binion, the night owl, was still awake. He left his house then to meet his good friend Willis Rieker, a Vietnam veteran who shared Binion's love of guns.

Rieker, a graveyard-shift engineer at a clinic several blocks from Binion's house, would regularly run into Binion in the early-morning hours buying cigarettes at a nearby 7-Eleven convenience store.

This time Binion had a specific reason to meet Rieker at the clinic. Rieker had learned that a relative of Sandy Murphy's who was a steady visitor to Binion's home, had been seen exchanging sacks of coins for cash at the Smith's Food King in Binion's neighborhood. Binion was intrigued by that news because he suspected Murphy had stolen a bag of 1,000 silver dollars from his safe.

"He was there to thank me for having given him a tip and told me that he was going to generate appropriate action to resolve the issue—'get rid of the broad and her family,' " Rieker later told investigators.

Binion also told Rieker that he believed Murphy had been cheating on him, and Rieker offered to help get her out of the house.

"I said I'd go over and rent a place for her for six months, and we'd just move her out and tell the bitch she was gone,"

Rieker explained. "Ted said that was a good idea and if he wanted me, he'd call me. And he thanked me for being available."

Rieker said it was obvious to him that Binion had been on a drug binge, but that he appeared alert and in control of his faculties. He was not suicidal.

"We shook hands and I told him I wanted him to press on, and I suggested that he get himself straightened up and get his gaming license back and . . . eliminate these women problems by running with a different caliber of female," Rieker said.

After leaving Rieker at 5 A.M., Binion went to the 7-Eleven to buy a couple of packs of Vantage cigarettes. There, he ran into store clerk Marvin Reed, who usually waited on him.

Reed said Binion came in two to three times a week, always just to buy two packs of cigarettes. Binion was often talkative, but this time he appeared "high" and agitated and left without carrying on a conversation.

"He was pissed off about something," Reed told investigators.

Reed then recalled that Binion often voiced concerns about Murphy carrying on sexual affairs behind his back, even with women.

"He said something about her fooling around with the dikes again," the store clerk reported Binion once told him.

Reed said he saw a couple of gay women, including one who worked with him, strike up a relationship with Murphy. The girls, he said, used to go to Binion's house to see Murphy when Binion wasn't home. But Binion didn't talk about Murphy that morning.

From the 7-Eleven, Binion returned to his home. About 5:30 A.M., his neighbor's maid, Eunice Rios, who was leaving for another housecleaning job, saw Binion in front of his house. His demeanor appeared normal. Rios said good morning and handed him his newspaper. She would be the last person outside his house to see him alive.

Cell phone records later showed a buzz of activity between Binion's ranch manager, David Mattsen, and Rick Tabish on September 16 and 17. It turned out that Tabish indeed had given the ranch hand a new pickup truck. He also had put him on his payroll. Between September 16 and September 18, Mattsen was calling Tabish more than a dozen times a day. On the evening of September 16, Mattsen's whereabouts were unknown from 6 P.M., when his wife reported him leaving Pahrump for Las Vegas, until he returned to telephone Tabish at 10:47 P.M. and then Binion's home at 10:48 P.M. and 10:56 P.M. Mattsen later called Tabish at 12:16 A.M. and 1:02 A.M. on September 17 from his home in Pahrump and again at 6:28 A.M. from the Binion ranch before heading back to Las Vegas.

At 9 A.M. on September 17, Montoya-Gascoigne received a call from Murphy.

"Ted isn't feeling very well," Murphy said. "Don't come to work today."

Murphy told the housekeeper to do her cleaning chores at another home Binion owned several blocks away.

About the same time, Binion's longtime gardener, Thomas Loveday, showed up to cut the grass. Loveday had been coming over to the house every Thursday for the past twelve years. This time he noticed some unusual occurrences. Murphy's black Mercedes sports coupe was parked under a large green-and-white canopy by the kitchen, on the east side of the house, instead of in its usual spot inside the garage, on the west end of the home. Binion's white Dodge pickup truck was in its usual place in the circular driveway out front, and there were no other cars on the lot. But as Loveday began working on the backyard, he noticed that the large drapes in the living room were drawn shut, restricting the normal view into the den, where Binion spent most of his time, and where his body would eventually be discovered. Loveday, a handsome, dark-haired man who often was invited inside to chat with Binion and Murphy, later said he had never seen those drapes closed. Loveday began to wonder what had happened to Montoya-

Gascoigne. She usually got to the house by 10 A.M. and always spoke to him.

Binion's dogs, Princess and Pig, also appeared to be acting strange to Loveday. Generally, the dogs would run up to him once he went through the back gate. Then Pig, a year-old puppy, would follow him around the yard while he did his trimming. Princess would return to the back porch and lie down. This time the dogs greeted him at the gate, but they quickly returned to the back door. After trimming the grass around Binion's pool, Loveday noticed the dogs still seemed to be acting odd.

"So I put my trimmer down, and I walked to the back door and petted the pup. They kind of wanted to get in," Loveday said. "I looked through the kitchen window, the door to the kitchen, and it was almost totally dark, except there was a light above it to the bar area that was on. But it was dim like you leave it on for the night. I couldn't see anybody. . . ."

Loveday said he went back to finish his trimming while the dogs stayed glued to the back door. As he began to mow the backyard, Princess went over and lay down in the bushes near Binion's bedroom. Loveday, becoming more suspicious, looked inside the bedroom window and saw that Binion's twenty-inch television monitor with its split screens was working. The screens captured the view of the front portion of his home from strategically positioned cameras. Binion's room was immaculate, another site Loveday had never seen before. His bed was made, and there were no clothes strewn around the floor. As Loveday peered around the corner into Murphy's bedroom, he found it equally clean. He remembered that Binion had told him a couple of weeks earlier that he was thinking about buying a ranch in Oregon.

"So I figured, well, maybe this is the time they decided to go to Oregon," the gardener said. "So maybe the dogs were just waiting for the maid to come . . . Well, there was no maid that day."

Loveday completed his yard work about 1:30 P.M. and left

the Binion home without seeing anyone inside. He learned of Binion's demise several hours afterward from a friend.

Investigators later theorized that Binion was killed while Loveday was working on his lawn, most likely between 9 A.M. and 10 A.M. Murphy's car never left Binion's house the entire time Loveday was working.

Mattsen entered the picture again at 12:03 P.M., when he telephoned Binion's home from Pahrump while his killers were believed to be looting the house and cleaning up the death scene. A minute later, Binion's real estate agent, Barbara Brown, called and Murphy answered the phone. Brown, a middle-aged businesswoman who had known Binion for years, asked to speak with him. She once more wanted to confirm their 1 P.M. luncheon appointment the next day to discuss the land deal near the Texas Station. They had planned to meet with the owner of the four acres at a Starbuck's coffee shop near the property.

Brown later recalled her conversation for investigators.

"Hi, Sandy," Brown said. "It's Barbara. Is Ted there?"

"No, Barbara, he's out," she responded.

"Out?" Brown asked.

"He's out," Murphy said again, this time in a crying voice.

"What's wrong? Are you OK?"

"No. Nobody understands what it has been like living with a drug addict. I've got this mess to clean up in the bathroom."

Sensing the distress in Murphy's voice, Brown asked if she wanted her to come over to the house.

"No," Murphy said. "He doesn't want anybody to see him, and be careful if you bring anybody. He'll be very upset."

"That's strange," Brown replied. "We have an appointment tomorrow at one P.M. You know we've been at this all week."

"Well, you better call tonight to see if he can make that appointment."

"Why don't you let me come over, and we'll go out to lunch and talk."

"No. Every time I go out, he interrogates me."

Murphy then promised to try to get Binion together to talk to her later in the afternoon.

"She just kept referring to this mess she had to clean up," Brown later recalled.

The real estate agent knew something was tragically wrong. She had talked to Binion the day before, and he had appeared fine to her.

"It was really a disturbing phone call," she said.

Cellular phone records analyzed by investigators working for Binion's estate later showed that from 12:15 P.M. to 1:32 P.M., there were several more phone calls between Tabish and Mattsen in Pahrump. During this time, Tabish also telephoned his young civil lawyer, William Knudson, who Tabish later said had met him and Murphy for a midafternoon lunch at Z'Tejas Grill, a local Southwestern restaurant.

By 1:32 P.M., Murphy had left Binion's home. She called her father, Kenneth Murphy, in Downey, California, from the cell phone in her car and had a four-minute conversation. Later, Murphy telephoned Cathy Rose, Binion's departing bookkeeper, at her office and then Murphy's sister in Compton, California. Tabish, meanwhile, had additional conversations with Mattsen and Knudson later that day.

At 2:45 P.M., Murphy showed up at Rose's office. She got Rose out of an important meeting to give her a $150 check from a Las Vegas couple who had opened a small restaurant with a loan from Binion. Rose was dumbfounded. Murphy had never brought her such a small check before. Rose didn't even know the couple, Richard and Debra Craig, who she later learned had been repaying Binion directly for months. Investigators would surmise Murphy's visit was an effort to help set up an alibi.

While there, Murphy told Rose that Binion had obtained some Xanax to help him "detox" from heroin.

"She said that Ted had gotten a prescription and that he'd been up all night," Rose told investigators. "She said he had asked her to stay up all night with him, and she did. And he had now gone to sleep, and she was running out to get a bite to eat and then go back and check on him."

Rose recalled that Murphy also suggested Binion might be out of control on drugs.

"She said if something happens, I'm just going to lock myself in my bedroom and hope that he doesn't shoot off the door like he did before," Rose explained.

At 3:16 P.M., shortly after leaving Rose, Murphy telephoned the bookkeeper from Tabish's cell phone asking for a number for Mike McDowell, a Binion fishing buddy in Alaska. Rose found that odd as well. She didn't believe Murphy knew McDowell.

Murphy telephoned her sister again in Compton at 3:40 P.M., and then received a call from Tabish at 3:47 P.M.

At 3:55 P.M., Murphy was in Binion's house when, in an apparent hysterical state, she called 911 to report that her "husband stopped breathing." Paramedics arrived a couple of minutes later and saw immediately that Binion had been dead for hours.

PART

II

The Investigation

CHAPTER 9

••••••••••••••••••

Suspicions Mount

••••••••••••••••••

POLICE ARRIVING AT the chaotic scene of Ted Binion's death on September 17, 1998, had no reason to suspect foul play.

The fifty-five-year-old Binion was a known drug and alcohol abuser who had lost his gaming license only months earlier because of mob ties. There were no signs of trauma to his body, which was laid out neatly on a blue sleeping mat on the floor of his den in front of his television set.

The empty bottle of Xanax next to his body and the discovery of a small amount of black tar heroin on a knife in a nearby bathroom prompted officers to surmise that Binion was the victim of a suicide or an accidental overdose.

The antics of his then twenty-six-year-old girlfriend, Sandy Murphy, gave police more reason to speculate about an overdose. In her frantic 911 call, Murphy led paramedics to believe Binion had suddenly stopped breathing. At the home, while Binion's body was being examined, Murphy appeared so distraught and hysterical over the loss of Binion that paramedics felt the need to transport her to the hospital. There, in the only interview she ever gave police, she told a detective that she believed Binion had killed himself on drugs.

Police later would learn that it was all an act on Murphy's part. In his last hours, it turned out, Binion had been taking steps to sever ties with his beautiful live-in lover. But for the moment, officers were persuaded by Murphy's theatrics.

"At first glance, the scene indicated that this was not intentional," Sergeant Jim Young told reporters outside Binion's house. "We're not 100 percent sure that it was accidental or intentional, but there is no evidence to make us believe it was intentional."

The next morning, homicide Lieutenant Wayne Petersen, who was briefed from the scene by Young, issued an even stronger statement.

"There was absolutely no evidence at the scene to suggest foul play," he said.

Those close to Binion, however, knew otherwise.

His longtime friend and estate lawyer, James J. Brown, recalled in horror that just a day earlier, Binion had instructed him to take Murphy out of his will before she killed him. Brown received word of Binion's death in a 4:30 P.M. cellular phone conversation with Richard Wright, another one of Binion's trusted lawyers. Brown, who had gone to high school with Binion, took the news hard. He asked Wright whether he should come to the house, but Wright told him he had things under control. The police had arrived and Wright had hired a security firm to keep watch over the house and Binion's ranch in Pahrump.

A shaken Brown stayed in his law office until 6 P.M. to collect himself and then drove home to his wife, Laura. Once there, he reconstructed Binion's chilling words to him the previous day on a legal notepad.

"I knew that something . . . that some kind of foul play had happened to him," Brown later told investigators.

The next morning, Brown confided in Wright about his last conversation with Binion, and was advised not to tell police until an autopsy on Binion's body had been completed. Wright, an experienced criminal defense attorney, wanted some sound medical evidence before airing Binion's troubles with Murphy in public. But the night before, Wright had told reporters he was stunned over Binion's untimely death.

"I'm just totally shocked," he said outside Binion's home. "I saw him last night, and he was in fine spirits. We talked about the future and what he always talked about, looking for a new ranch."

Wright described Binion as the "most unlikely Renaissance Man" he had ever known, and he said the ousted gaming executive had told him he was anxious to appeal the decision that had revoked his gaming license.

Then Wright urged a "total and complete autopsy" be conducted, as well as toxicology, or drug tests, on his body.

"We just don't know what really happened until we see the test results," he said.

Binion's sister Becky Behnen was less shy with a reporter about discussing her suspicions. That evening, she told the *Las Vegas Sun* that she believed her brother might have been murdered.

"I just feel it should be treated as a homicide until proven otherwise," she said. "I talked to him all week and he was not despondent. Ted would never take his own life."

At the same time, Behnen said her brother was not one to mix his drugs and allow himself to accidentally overdose.

Behnen then revealed that Binion told her he had been fighting all week with Murphy.

His brother, Jack, to whom Binion was closest, was in Mississippi on gaming business and immediately hopped on a plane for Las Vegas upon hearing of his death. So did his eighteen-year-old daughter and chief heir, Bonnie, who was away at college.

The next morning, Behnen kept the pressure on the police, expressing her affection for her brother, whom she described as "honest to the point of being too honest."

"I loved my brother very much," she told the *Las Vegas Sun*. "Even though we had disputes, we spoke on a daily basis. The funny thing was that Ted was so outspoken, you'd never know what he would say. Right in the middle of cussing me and my husband out, he would say, 'You know, I miss you guys.' "

Behnen did not go to her brother's home that evening, but among the onlookers outside was Rick Tabish, who told reporters he'd been on his way to the airport when he heard the news about Binion's death and decided to pay his respects. Investigators later would conclude, however, that Tabish returned to the death scene to look after Murphy. It was Tabish who persuaded Wright to go to nearby Valley Hospital with him to stop police from "interrogating" Murphy.

"I told him no . . . you're mistaken. They're not interrogating her, and she is not in custody," Wright later testified. "And he persisted and wanted me to go with him there. So my preference was not to leave the house, but he was adamant, and I agreed to go with him."

When they arrived at the hospital, Wright ran into Janis Tanno, a Binion neighbor who had gone on her own to comfort Murphy. Wright made arrangements with nurses to discharge Murphy in Tanno's custody, and then he and Tanno went to see Murphy, who was sobbing uncontrollably.

"She was saying over and over, 'I'm so sorry. I'm so sorry. Tell Harry I'm so sorry. I should have never left him. He begged me to stay. I shouldn't have left. I shouldn't have left.' "

Harry was Harry Claiborne, an eighty-one-year-old lawyer and confidant of the Binion family. Claiborne would later deliver a moving eulogy at Binion's funeral.

Nurses trained in observing psychological trauma told investigators that Murphy's hysteria appeared to be "almost theatrical" in nature. One nurse heard her yelling, "Boo-hoo, Boo-hoo," in the hallway as she was wheeled in on a stretcher. Before releasing her, doctors wanted to give her some Valium to keep her calm, but she refused to take it.

Murphy was discharged about 8 P.M. on the condition she spend the night at Tanno's home. Tanno took her car and Wright accompanied Murphy in Tabish's black four-door

Mercedes. On the way over, however, Murphy said she wanted to return to Binion's house, which she called "home."

"I told her she could not go home, that it was not possible," Wright testified. "She said, 'The house is being looted.' And I said, 'It isn't being looted. The public administrator has taken control of the house, and I have security at the house, and the property isn't being stolen.' "

Tabish joined in the conversation, saying he wanted to take Murphy to the Desert Inn to keep her away from the media that had gathered in the neighborhood.

"I said, 'You're not,' " Wright explained. " 'We're going to Janis Tanno's house because those are the conditions of her discharge. And so turn the car around.' "

Tabish at one point suggested getting Murphy some Rocky Road ice cream, which always made her feel better. A startled Wright, who wasn't aware that Tabish was close to Murphy, responded, "No ice cream. We're going to Tanno's."

Eventually, the Mercedes arrived at the neighbor's home, where Murphy was given a guest room to go to sleep. Tabish then left. Shortly after Murphy had gone to bed, Linda Carroll showed up on Tanno's doorstep and begged to see her friend for a few minutes.

Wright, meanwhile, returned to Binion's home, where police were wrapping up their death-scene investigation. By 9:30 P.M., police had turned over the house to Public Administrator Jared Shafer. Wright and Shafer walked through the 8,000-square-foot house looking for anything of value that could be kept in the administrator's vault overnight.

"I was looking for cash, the coin collections, things like that," Wright testified. "So we went through every single room looking for valuable property."

But the two men found nothing of value, including the $300,000 collection of antique coins and currency Binion had showed Wright in his den a couple of days earlier.

"We didn't find anything but a couple of dollars and coins spread about the floor of the garage," Wright said.

To Wright, who knew Binion liked to keep a lot of cash and coins around the house, that seemed odd. Wright and Shafer left the house in the care of security officers, who stood guard for the rest of the night.

CHAPTER 10

....

From Grief to Greed

....

WHEN SANDY MURPHY woke up on September 18, the morning after Ted Binion's death, Janis Tanno saw a changed person.

"She was fine. She was calm," Tanno told investigators. "She was completely different from her hysterics the night before."

Tanno, a longtime Binion neighbor, had let Murphy stay overnight at her home until her father, Kenneth, and stepmother, Sandra, arrived from Southern California to take care of her.

It was a sunny Friday morning, and Murphy was still sleeping when Tanno went to 8 A.M. mass. She had instructed her teenage children not to let anyone inside the house. On her way home from the half-hour service, Tanno stopped by McDonald's to bring back some breakfast for Murphy and her kids. When she returned home, she was startled to see Murphy and Tabish sitting together in her poolside cabana.

Tabish walked up to Tanno and said he was "taking her for a little ride." They returned fifteen minutes later, and Tabish then left.

Like many others, Tanno noticed that the relationship between Murphy and Tabish seemed more than platonic. She also noticed that Murphy was determined to get back into the $900,000 home she had shared with Binion the past three years—the home Murphy said had been willed to her.

While waiting for her parents to arrive, Murphy began making phone calls to those close to Binion. Her first call went to James J. Brown, who still remembered Binion's chilling words two days earlier, instructing him to take Murphy out of his will.

"She said they wouldn't let her into her house, and she needed to get into her house," Brown told investigators. "She said, 'I don't have anyplace to go. I've only got $5 to my name and Ted took $20,000 from me.'

"I said, 'Well, you know . . . everything's up in the air now . . . It's going to take a couple of days to figure things out.' "

Murphy also telephoned Binion's departing bookkeeper, Cathy Rose, complaining about not being allowed in the home. And she inquired about Binion's upcoming funeral.

"I said, 'Sandy, you don't have to worry about that . . . Jack [Binion] will worry about that.' And she said, 'Fine.' And then she called back a couple of more times, and each time she got a little more upset."

Tanno and the others saw the change in Murphy's demeanor that morning. They saw that her greed regarding Binion's wealthy estate was overcoming her grief of the night before.

Later that morning, Murphy's stepmother showed up at Tanno's house with Tabish to take Murphy to get a room at the Desert Inn. About the same time, maybe a mile a way, Brown and Richard Wright headed to the office of Public Administrator Jared Shafer to formally obtain control of Binion's house. Shafer then walked the two lawyers to the office of Clark County Coroner Ron Flud, who was overseeing the medical investigation into Binion's death. Brown and Wright were informed that Flud's chief medical examiner, Lary Simms, was conducting the autopsy on Binion's body that morning. Both attorneys told the coroner that they believed Binion had met with foul play, and they insisted that as many tests as possible be done to make sure of the cause of death.

"I told him I wanted every test in the world done," Brown later said.

Added Wright: "We wanted double samples of everything. That was our way of letting him know we were looking over his shoulder."

Wright said Flud was very accommodating, even sending messages to Simms in their presence while the medical examiner was performing the autopsy.

"When we left I got the impression he was thinking they were doing the autopsy of a lifetime," Wright said.

Flud, a serious public official who had grown up in Las Vegas, was well aware of the prominence of the Binion family, as well as of Ted Binion's drug addiction and notorious past. Flud expected his death would attract much media attention. As a result, he had instructed Simms—who was just settling into his job following his move to Las Vegas from Chicago two weeks earlier—to treat the autopsy as if it were a homicide.

"When you have a high-profile case, you have a lot of conspiracy theories and a lot of questions about what you do," Flud said. "I didn't have a crystal ball or know that this was going to be a homicide. We just handled it that way so there would be no questions."

He said he tried to calm the concerns of the lawyers.

"I assured them at that point," he said, "that we were doing everything we could."

Tabish, meanwhile, was seen over the lunch hour at All Star Transit Mix, a North Las Vegas concrete company owned by Steven Wadkins, whose brother had helped Tabish build Binion's underground vault in Pahrump. Jared Pace, a truck driver for Tabish, had gone into the All Star yard to ask Michael Milot, a Tabish supervisor, why his paycheck had bounced. As he approached, he saw Milot and Tabish loading plastic tubes into a toolbox in the back of Milot's pickup truck. Pace recalled that the tubes looked the same as those he had helped Tabish and Binion remove from the Horse-shoe Club several months earlier. Investigators later would allege the coins were stolen from Binion's safe.

After lunch, about 2 P.M., Brown picked up Binion's daughter, Bonnie, who had flown in from college back East to tend to her father's funeral. He drove Bonnie, a pretty but frail-looking young woman who stood to inherit Binion's entire $55 million fortune, to the casino man's home, where she gathered some photographs and small personal items of her father's for his funeral and put them in a knapsack. While there, Brown heard a knock on the door. He opened it and in walked Murphy.

"I said, 'Sandy, you can't be in here,' " Brown later reported. "And she asked 'Why?' And I said, 'Well, you know, Bonnie's in here, and I'm not going to have you in the house.' And then she made something up about, 'Well, she's going to take everything.' And I said, 'You've got to get out of the house.' "

As he backed Murphy out of the doorway, Brown noticed that her mother and two of her friends, Tanya Cropp and Linda Carroll, were outside. All four had been able to get past the locked steel gates and a security officer. Upset at the officer for disobeying his order not to let anyone inside the gates, Brown instructed him to call the police immediately. By that time, Murphy and her entourage voluntarily agreed to leave. Brown went back inside to check on Bonnie, who had found her father's empty wallet.

Bonnie later testified that as she was going through the house, she checked several of her father's favorite hiding places for cash and valuables and found nothing. In the kitchen, she came across the rest of a set of crystal glasses that were supposed to have been given to her mother in the divorce settlement, and she wanted to take them. But Brown instructed her to leave them behind.

"I told her, 'No,' " Brown said. " 'We're not going to be taking these things out . . . because I could see the hand-writing on the wall, that if we walked out of there with anything, we were going to be accused of taking things. So I said, 'No, just don't take these. This will all get resolved.' "

Brown, however, allowed Bonnie to take a small, stuffed teddy bear her father had given her as a child.

In the meantime, Murphy placed a call to Wright complaining about Brown.

"She said she needed my help—that Jimmy and Jack, meaning Jimmy Brown and Jack Binion, were evicting her from the house and that they couldn't do that," Wright said in court. "She told me that I knew the house was hers and that she was to get the house and $300,000 and a $1 million life insurance policy. And she's saying, you know, will you please help me because Jimmy Brown is looting the house and they're going to evict me.

"And so I responded by trying to tell her that it wasn't an eviction, that Jack Binion was the executor, that they were marshaling and preserving the assets . . . And I said, 'I'm telling you no one can loot anything. No one can take any property at all. It has to be preserved and go through probate.'

"And it ended with her saying, 'Well, it's clear they're looting it. There are gold plates on the table that they are taking.' And she said, 'I am going to film everything that's there—videotape everything that's there.' And I told her that I thought that was a good idea, that she should do that."

By 3:30 P.M., on September 18, Brown returned to Binion's house, where he ran into a uniformed police officer who told him he had received a complaint from someone having trouble getting inside the home. Within minutes, Murphy and her entourage arrived at the gates, this time with William Knudson. Brown surmised that Murphy had called the police from the home of Knudson's mother, Jean, who lived down the street.

Knowing there still were valuables in the house and desperate to keep Murphy from going inside, Brown told the officer he didn't believe Murphy was a legal resident of the house. He said he thought she lived in California. But after

Murphy showed the officer her driver's license that listed Binion's 2408 Palomino Lane address as her residence, the officer informed Brown that he was going to allow her inside. Brown then was ordered to stay out of the house. He promptly telephoned Wright in front of Murphy and the officer, and a shocked Wright told him to get an emergency court order granting the estate custody of the home. Brown left Murphy and her friends inside the home and headed downtown to court. He returned about ninety minutes later with an order from District Judge Jack Lehman appointing him special administrator of Binion's estate and giving him control of the house. It took Brown another thirty minutes to negotiate with Knudson and one of Murphy's other lawyers, David Chesnoff, who was in contact with her by cellular phone, to get back inside the home. Knudson and Murphy came outside the house after Brown assured the lawyers that the assets inside would be protected until Binion's estate was resolved in probate court. Murphy, however, was very upset.

"She said, 'Why are you doing this to me? You're my friend. Why are you doing this to me?' " Brown told investigators. "And I said, 'I'll tell you exactly why I'm doing this to you. Because the day before Ted died, he told me to take you out of the will if you didn't kill him that night.' And she said, 'You're lying. You're a liar.' "

Knudson and Murphy went back inside, and five minutes later, by 6 P.M., Knudson came out and told Brown that Murphy had agreed to leave, but she wanted to videotape the contents of the home first.

"I said, 'That's fine, we'll videotape it,' " Brown said.

Tabish and Milot later showed up with a brand-new video camera. Tabish left after a few minutes, but not before letting it be known he was going to take care of something before Brown got "his hands on it, too." Investigators would learn Tabish was referring to Binion's $6 million silver fortune buried in an underground vault in Pahrump.

The twenty-minute tour, with Knudson doing the taping,

began at the far west end of the house, in Bonnie Binion's hardwood-floored bedroom. An agitated Murphy, wearing black slacks and boots and a white jacket, led the way, pointing out items of value with her stepmother, Carroll, Cropp and Brown in tow. Murphy carried a large black shoulder bag over her right shoulder.

Her demeanor had radically changed from the grief-stricken girlfriend of the previous evening. Murphy, often shouting obscenities, became obsessed with ensuring that she would receive her share of Binion's $55 million estate.

"I want to take my perfume bottles because that's what I'm afraid they might steal, since they tried to steal the china," Murphy yelled in a deliberate voice as the group made its way to her posh bedroom, which was twice the size of Binion's. "They already loaded up some stuff in the car. The security guard said so. They already stole some stuff. Make sure you get a complete inventory of everything, because if anything's missing, I just want to make sure . . ."

Moving to Binion's bedroom, Brown noticed a purse on the floor next to the wood-framed, king-sized bed.

"That's my purse, Jimmy," Murphy said tersely. "Please stay out of it."

"All right," Brown responded. "Did you just bring it in here?"

"Yes, I did. Please stay out of it . . . I'm sorry, Jimmy. I thought you were my friend. Now, I don't know if this was entrapment. You lied to the cops and told them I'm a resident of California. You come in here and tell them that you guys are in here on good terms and you're here loading up my fucking shit to give to the court."

Knudson then interjected: "Can we try to get along just for the videotape, please?"

Murphy, still talking, walked over to Binion's writing desk, opened a drawer and took what appeared to be cigarette papers used for smoking marijuana. She then moved to his walk-in closet, where she pointed to a dresser against the wall in the entranceway.

"There's nothing in any of these drawers, just shoe horns," she said.

Then, pointing to the back of the dresser, she added: "I found his heroin deal behind here."

Outside Binion's bedroom, Murphy brought up the subject of a couple of pieces of valuable art she and Binion had bought. She told Brown she wanted to take the artwork, because "if it's gone, I'm screwed." Then she agreed to let it stay in the house after Brown said she ultimately could have it.

"I'll let you take it," she told Brown. "But you have to give me your word. And you have to understand that I know you don't trust me for whatever reason it is, but I don't trust you either."

Back in Murphy's bedroom, as the camera kept recording, Murphy brought up the subject of her personal belongings.

"OK, you don't care about my shoes or my jewelry?" she asked Brown as the camera panned her bedroom-sized, walk-in closet.

"No. No. No," Brown replied.

"My clothes. I need my clothes," she said.

One by one, Murphy then opened all of her dresser drawers, showing a large collection of belts, necklaces, bracelets and earrings.

"Everything in here is mine," she said. "I'm going to take it."

Knudson started complaining that he was losing battery power and asked Murphy to move on to another part of the house.

"Let's just go . . . because I only have so much battery life," he said.

As they moved to the sunken living room, Murphy pointed to the white baby grand piano on the far west end of the room and said: "Get my piano drawer . . . I got music in there. I got another pistol in there. I bet they forgot about that one because they weren't smart enough to fucking look." She walked to the piano, opened the bench and said: "Here you go," as she lifted up a gun.

From the living room, the taping moved to the dining room, on the east side of the house, where Murphy said: "Get the china. This is very important. And don't worry. They'll steal anything they can get their hands on."

In the kitchen, she showed off some antique plates and told Knudson: "Make sure you get a good view of this, because, don't worry, this is what they came to steal. Oh, we're taking this for certain, because this is too valuable to leave in the house."

Then Murphy did something startling, though no one picked up on it at the time. With her back to the camera, Murphy walked past an island countertop sporting a half-dozen wineglasses on the far end. While still talking, she coolly walked backward toward the camera, picked up one of the glasses with her left hand and appeared to transfer it to her right hand and put it in her shoulder bag. She also picked up a coaster from the countertop a couple of feet away. It wasn't until months later, after the videotape was watched by investigators, that the theft was noticed. Even Brown didn't see it until he viewed the videotape. Prosecutors later theorized that the glass was used to give Binion a deadly cocktail of heroin and Xanax.

At one point, Murphy ran across another weapon.

"Here's my pistol," she said. "This is my personal property. It was a gift. But I'll leave it so that Jimmy doesn't throw a fucking tantrum."

Murphy then walked into the den, past the site where Binion's body was found on the floor a day earlier. Without showing any emotion, she went into Binion's garage, where he kept his three-foot-tall safe. Keys, loose change and poker chips were scattered on the floor around the unopened safe.

"The safe's empty," Murphy said. "There's nothing in it. Get a picture of the keys there and the box being opened and the money missing."

"So there's money in there?" Knudson asked.

"Well, there's $20,000 in the house, and it's not here now," she responded.

Then she added: "I don't trust anybody anymore. I can only trust one person, my old man, and he's not around to protect me anymore so I've got to be tough."

From the den and garage, Murphy took the group back to the bathroom in her bedroom, where she was observed removing what appeared to be a computer disk from a drawer.

As they completed the videotape, Murphy asked, "Can I take my teddy bear that says Ted on it?"

CHAPTER 11

• • • • • • • • • • • • • • • • • •

Stealing the Silver

• • • • • • • • • • • • • • • • • •

AFTER RICK TABISH and Michael Milot left Ted Binion's home the afternoon of September 18, they headed to Pahrump to grab the wealthy gambling figure's silver fortune.

This was the $6 million in silver bars and coins, 48,000 pounds in all, that Tabish had buried for Binion in an underground vault on land Binion owned in the small town in neighboring Nye County, just southwest of Las Vegas.

With an excavator and a large belly dump, Tabish and Milot arrived in Pahrump as the sun was setting and worked into the early morning, digging up the silver with their heavy machinery. David Mattsen had joined them for the dig.

Weeks earlier, Binion privately had told his friends in Nye County law enforcement, Sheriff Wade Lieseke and Sergeant Steve Huggins, to keep watch over the silver, which was buried alongside the main thoroughfare in Pahrump.

Huggins had known Binion for more than twenty years. He even had once worked for him at the Horseshoe Club in Las Vegas. Through Huggins and Lieseke, Binion maintained good relations with the Nye County Sheriff's Department, often lending the department thousands of dollars at a time to make drug buys during undercover investigations. Huggins would pick up the cash himself at the Horseshoe Club's casino cage.

In August 1998, Binion told Huggins that he was concerned that someone might try to dig up his silver. Without mentioning Tabish's name, Binion expressed doubts about the guy who had built the vault, saying he had taken advantage of him by charging too much money ($40,000).

That conversation was on Huggins' mind the day after Binion's September 17 death. He called Sergeant Ed Howard, a colleague who was in charge of patrolling the streets of Pahrump that night, and informed him about the vault.

"I told him it wouldn't surprise me if somebody comes out now that Ted had died and tries to dig that up and take it," Huggins later testified.

Huggins also telephoned Richard Wright and suggested he station security officers at the site of the vault. Wright told Huggins he had already done that. But Wright mistakenly thought that the vault was at Binion's ranch a couple of miles away, and had placed the guards there. As a result, Tabish had free rein to do his digging.

By 2 A.M., after Tabish and his associates had loaded the silver into the belly dump and were cleaning up the site, Howard stopped by in his patrol car. He saw all three men loading the excavator onto a black flatbed trailer. Before doing anything, Howard called for backup. Then he talked to Mattsen, who told him that the three of them had been digging up ammunition with the excavator.

Deputy Dean Pennock was having dinner at Terrible's Hotel & Casino a few hundred yards away when Howard used his police radio to summon him to the vault. When he arrived, Tabish was telling Howard a different story. He said they had been cleaning up concrete in preparation for a sale of the property to the Herbst family, who owned Terrible's casino. The deputies, however, wanted to know what was inside the covered belly dump, which Tabish had insisted was empty. Tabish hit the upper portion of the truck with a flashlight to create a hollow sound.

"See, there's nothing in there," he told the deputies.

Howard hit the side of the truck a little lower and heard a thud, which indicated to him that indeed there was something inside. He then instructed Pennock to climb up the back of the belly dump and look under the canvas cover.

As he pulled back the cover, a startled Pennock saw stacks of silver bullion and dozens of bags of silver coins. Excited, he yelled down to Howard: "There's a shitload of silver in there, Ed."

Realizing he had been caught red-handed, Tabish told the deputies: "OK, I'm lying. I'm doing this for Teddy Binion. I'm taking the money to Vegas, where Wells Fargo will take it to California and put in a trust fund for Teddy's daughter when she turns thirty-five."

That was when Howard and Pennock decided they might have to make some arrests. At this point, Milot wasn't causing a problem. He had requested permission to go to sleep in the back of a pickup truck. Howard, nevertheless, called for more help. He informed Huggins what they had encountered and asked him to come to the scene. Huggins arrived within minutes.

About the same time, Tabish stunned the deputies when he began insisting that Lieseke knew about his efforts to dig up the silver. He said he had telephoned Lieseke three times earlier in the day to inform him that he was coming to Pahrump to pick up the silver. Mattsen indicated that he also had talked to the sheriff at Pahrump's annual Harvest Festival. All three deputies knew this incident had the potential to become a political firestorm in Nye County. Lieseke was up for reelection, and each deputy was supporting his opponent, Doug Richards.

While waiting for Huggins, Howard and Pennock woke up Milot and decided to search the three theft suspects for weapons. They found none, but they did see that Tabish and Milot each had $1,600 in fresh $100 bills on them. Prosecutors later would allege those bills, most of which had serial numbers in sequential order, were stolen from Binion after his death.

Once Huggins made it to the scene, he decided to call Lieseke and ask him to come over. In the meantime, Tabish told Huggins and Howard that Binion had authorized him to pay the sheriff $100,000 for his assistance in removing the silver.

The conversation made the two sergeants even more suspicious about their boss. Lieseke, who wore a hearing aid in each ear, was in an agitated state when he arrived. He immediately confronted Tabish and, while acknowledging that he had received phone calls from him, insisted in front of the two sergeants that he had no idea Tabish had come for the silver. He also said he gave no one permission to take Binion's buried treasure.

But one of the first things Tabish said in Lieseke's presence was: "Wade, I told you we were gonna take care of you as soon as we were done with this."

Huggins and Howard, meanwhile, became anxious to arrest Tabish, Milot and Mattsen on theft charges. But Lieseke, according to the two sergeants, started to question whether they had a strong enough case against the three suspects. When the sergeants insisted on going through with the arrests, an angry Lieseke told them to do whatever they wanted and stormed off.

By 5 A.M., the three suspects were handcuffed and driven to the county jail, while the deputies impounded the three vehicles at the scene and took the belly dump filled with silver to the sheriff's department. Off-duty deputies were called in on overtime to begin the tedious task of making an inventory of the silver. The inventory was made more difficult because many of the tattered canvas bags of silver had fallen apart.

While at the station, Tabish gave Huggins and Lieseke a taped interview, but when Tabish asked to speak to an attorney, the Nye County lawmen decided to terminate the interview. Tabish, however, kept talking, and the interview continued for a half hour.

Lieseke was anxious to allay the concerns of his deputies about his possible complicity in the theft.

"My only problem here is I want no one thinking or believing that I had a conspiracy going on with you or Dave [Mattsen]," Lieseke told Tabish.

"Absolutely not," Tabish responded.

A few minutes later, Tabish again said he wanted to talk to an attorney. But then he added: "I've got nothing to hide here. I mean, I'd have to be a complete fool to come out and load a steel trailer full of silver and think I'm going to steal it in broad daylight. I mean, I came out here at seven P.M. last night. I called you on three occasions, telling you I was coming. I said I would call you when I came to town. I wanted to meet you. I wanted to make sure everything was on the QT."

Lieseke responded: "The only thing that I understood you to say was that you were coming over here. I knew nothing about this vault."

Tabish insisted throughout the interview that he was carrying out Binion's wishes to remove the silver in the event of his death.

"I did everything that I was supposed to with you guys," he said. "The next step was to take it to the ranch. But it was all locked up out there, and we needed an attorney to get into the ranch."

Later he added: "I thought I was being prudent in coming out here . . . but evidently I was not. I mean, we never left the property with any silver . . . I thought we were open about it."

Tabish told Lieseke and Huggins that Wright was supposed to arrange for Wells Fargo to transport the silver to Los Angeles.

"[Binion] wanted it locked in a vault in L.A., where they could turn it into cash because it's been willed to Bonnie," he said.

"You probably should have brought Wells Fargo with you," one of the interviewers said.

"Probably," Tabish responded. "But you know, I've been doing things the Teddy way here and that's the way we've

done it for the last three months, and here I come out here
. . . I mean, my God, you guys. It's not like it was a secret
what I was doing out there. We had a patrolman come by
earlier in the night and flash his light out, and I figured after
talking to you, you'd tell somebody. That's why we asked
for you, Wade. We weren't trying to implicate you."

Wright later told sheriff's deputies that Tabish had not informed him or anyone else with Binion's estate about his
plans to dig up the silver.

Toward the end of the interview, Tabish became more
forceful in his denials.

"I didn't come out here to rip this man off," he said. "I
mean, I've got a year-and-a-half-old kid and a three-year-old
kid. I've got a hell of a business that's going public right now.
I mean, to walk out there with trucks painted MRT Transport
all over them and sit out there digging with an excavator and
thinking I'm going to go hike his silver? It wasn't the agenda.
And I know that's hard for you guys to believe . . ."

Tabish later would contend that Binion discussed having
him dig up the silver in the presence of another one of his
lawyers, Thomas Standish. But Standish told investigators
he had advised Binion against doing that, saying it was the
"dumbest thing" he had ever heard.

"I said to them, 'Hold on,' " Standish explained. " 'Nobody's going to go immediately and remove the silver if you
die, Ted. That's stupid. All you have to do is call the sheriff,
and they will post somebody there. Or you arrange to have
security guards go out there.' "

Standish said he told both Binion and Tabish that it would
be unlawful for anyone other than the executor of Binion's
estate to dig up the silver after his death. Binion ultimately
agreed with him.

When the interview with Tabish ended, Lieseke, who was
afraid of political fallout in an election year, commandeered
the tape. But a transcript was made for the criminal case.

Later that day, Wright became suspicious of Lieseke during a meeting with the sheriff in Pahrump. Wright found it

odd that Lieseke had asked him if Binion had included him in his will. The sheriff was not named.

Lieseke later testified that he brought up the subject only because Tabish had indicated at the scene of the theft that Binion wanted to "take care" of him financially. Lieseke also described Tabish to reporters as a "liar" and a "con man" who was trying to use him to set up an alibi in the theft.

"I had no involvement in this other than to answer my phone," he said.

At the scene, Tabish had given Huggins and Howard what would turn out to be a valuable piece of evidence in the Las Vegas murder investigation.

He disclosed that he was at Binion's house the day he died.

"Ted Binion told me that he was going to take a whole bottle of Xanax tablets and lie down and go to sleep, and when he woke up his body would be cleansed of all of the drugs," Huggins quoted Tabish as saying in a crime report.

Prosecutors later would use those words against Tabish during the murder trial to place him at the scene of Binion's slaying.

Nye County sheriff's deputies also found additional incriminating evidence during a search of one of the trucks. Inside a briefcase belonging to Tabish, Huggins discovered a newsletter for coin collectors, the combination to the vault and, most intriguing of all, a handwritten note from Murphy that said, "Love you! Sandy. P.S. I love my lover." That tied Murphy to the theft conspiracy and for the first time raised questions in the minds of investigators about the romantic relationship between Murphy and Tabish. Sheriff's deputies shared their information with Las Vegas police, who were receiving pressure from Binion's family to look closely at his untimely death.

Word of the Pahrump arrests began to reach the news media the evening of Sunday, September 20. KVBC Channel 3, the local NBC affiliate, aired a story on the arrests and showed footage of the silver, which it had obtained from its associate station in Pahrump.

On Monday, September 21, the *Las Vegas Sun* was the first to get the story in print. By that time, two of the suspects, Tabish and Milot, already had been bailed out by William Knudson. Murphy had put up her Mercedes sports coupe and some jewelry Binion had bought her as collateral for the $100,000 bonds for both men.

The *Sun* reported that Nye County Undersheriff Bill Weldon had estimated the silver was worth $13 million to $15 million. But Wright, who was more familiar with the fortune, said its value was closer to $3 to $4 million. An actual appraisal of the silver, commissioned by Binion's estate months later, found it to be worth $6 million.

Later, Huggins and several of his fellow deputies went back to the Binion property with a backhoe and reopened the vault, where they found nothing but a lone silver dollar in the middle of the floor. Tabish had told deputies that Binion wanted him to leave the silver dollar to send a message to his greedy family members. But the deputies thought otherwise. They suspected they had a signature crime on their hands.

The theft left little doubt in the minds of Wright and Brown that Murphy and Tabish had been conspiring to harm their client. Brown recalled the chilling conversation he had with Binion the afternoon before his death, and Wright remembered how Tabish was trying to keep Murphy from talking to police the evening of his death.

Wright issued his strongest words yet about his suspicions.

"This definitely raises concerns that require a more thorough investigation into the precise timing and cause of death," he told the *Sun*. "I'm positive Ted didn't intentionally cause his own death."

Harry Claiborne, another longtime attorney and friend of Binion's, added his concerns.

"These circumstances shocked the living hell out of me," he said. "I know he didn't purposely overdose."

At this point, homicide detectives in Las Vegas still weren't involved in the investigation, but homicide Lieutenant Wayne Petersen was fielding questions from reporters. On the morning of September 21, Petersen told the *Las Vegas Sun* that the death scene was "consistent" with what Murphy had told police when she reported his death.

But within hours, Petersen would receive a visit from Wright and Brown that would change his mind.

CHAPTER 12

••••••••••••••••••

A Slow Start

••••••••••••••••••

WHEN WAYNE PETERSEN arrived at the homicide bureau about 7:30 A.M. on Monday, September 21, he was having second thoughts about not assigning members of his unit to the scene of Ted Binion's death.

At forty-five, with twenty-one years of service under his belt, Petersen was one of the stars of the Las Vegas Metropolitan Police Department. Fit and trim as a result of running marathons most of his life, Petersen was a dedicated cop fiercely loyal to Sheriff Jerry Keller. His allegiance was rewarded in 1996, when Keller gave him the trusted assignment of heading the high-profile homicide unit, where he quickly became a regular on the evening newscasts. His good looks, pearly white teeth and wavy blond hair made him a natural in front of the camera. Reporters in the field were conditioned to seek him out at murder scenes. He liked to keep a tight rein over the flow of information coming from his unit and generally served as its chief spokesman.

As he began his day that morning, Petersen got the feeling he soon would be embarking on one of his more challenging cases.

Becky Behnen, who knew about the stormy relationship between Binion and Sandy Murphy, publicly was putting pressure on the police to treat her brother's death as a homicide. And over the weekend, Rick Tabish and his cohorts were busted in Pahrump for digging up and trying to steal the gambling figure's $6 million silver fortune.

"In twenty-twenty hindsight, I would have liked to be at the death scene," Petersen said. "It would have made our job much easier."

But Petersen didn't send any of his people to Binion's home the afternoon of September 17. He had received reports at the scene from Sergeant Jim Young, a general-assignment detective who had told him there were no obvious signs of trauma to Binion's body. When Young saw the empty bottle of Xanax nearby, he had even more reason to suspect that Binion, a man with a long history of drug abuse, was the victim of an overdose. Young also told Petersen that the death scene appeared to have been cleaned up—something that family members frequently do in drug overdoses before police arrive.

By Monday morning, having spent considerable time in Pahrump over the weekend taking care of Binion's affairs, Richard Wright and James Brown were ready to push for a homicide investigation. What they learned in Pahrump left little doubt in their minds that their longtime friend had met with foul play.

Furthermore, preliminary autopsy results on Binion's body had made it clear that the troubled casino executive did not die a natural death. Officially, however, Clark County Coroner Ron Flud still was listing the manner in which Binion had died as "undetermined" pending further investigation.

Wright and Brown showed up at Petersen's office about 9:30 A.M. to make their pitch. Petersen had brought in one of his sergeants, Ken Hefner, to listen with him.

One of the first things Brown did during the half-hour meeting was disclose the chilling details of his telephone conversation with Binion the afternoon before his death. That was the conversation in which Binion had instructed Brown to take Murphy out of his will if she didn't kill him that evening. Then Brown talked about the problems he had with Murphy and her entourage at Binion's home the day after his death.

Wright told Petersen and Hefner that the day before he died, Binion had asked him for the name of a private detective he could hire to follow Murphy. Veteran investigator Don Dibble, another ex-cop, later reported that Binion had asked him to put a tail on his girlfriend, saying he believed she was cheating on him.

The two lawyers also informed Petersen and Hefner that many of Binion's valuables were missing from his home. Though he was known to keep a lot of cash on hand, they said, none was found at the house. And Binion's collection of rare coins and currency dating back to the Civil War was gone.

Most intriguing, Wright and Brown reported that Nye County sheriff's deputies had told them about the love letter they had found from Murphy to Tabish in Tabish's briefcase after his arrest on the theft charges.

Deputies also had informed the attorneys that they had seized $3,200 in sequentially numbered $100 bills from Tabish and Milot. Wright said the serial numbers on the crisp bills were similar to the numbers on the $40,000 in $100 bills he had brought to Binion a week earlier.

To Wright and Brown, questions about Binion's death were rapidly mounting.

"It became clear to us that police needed to take some affirmative steps toward an investigation," Brown said.

But after the attorneys had finished making their case, they got the impression Petersen and Hefner weren't all that interested.

"I thought they were courteous, but weren't going to do anything," Wright said. "I felt like they were giving us lip service and that this wasn't a high priority for them."

Added Brown: "We walked away feeling that they were not going to pursue any kind of investigation until they were forced to by an autopsy showing a clear homicide."

Petersen told the lawyers he wanted to wait until the results of the toxicology tests on fluids taken from Binion's body were known before moving ahead with a full-blown homicide investigation.

"That Monday morning, I wasn't convinced," Petersen said. "We didn't have the evidence from the autopsy or anything else. It just wasn't clear at that point exactly how he died."

Despite the lack of evidence, Petersen assigned the case to Hefner and two of his top detectives, James Buczek and Tom Thowsen, after the lawyers had left the homicide bureau. Buczek didn't even hear about Binion's death until Saturday, September 19, when he returned from Hawaii, where he had been pursuing leads in a high-profile quadruple-homicide case. Buczek, who would become the lead detective on the Binion case, learned about Binion's demise from his wife, Denise Rosch, a television reporter with local NBC affiliate KVBC-TV. Rosch was one of the reporters covering Binion's death from the start.

Though he played it cool to Wright and Brown, Petersen indeed had concerns about the way Binion had died.

But before taking the plunge, he wanted to be sure in his own mind that Murphy and Tabish had killed Binion and weren't just opportunists taking advantage of a drug addict after his death. Petersen later would refer to Tabish and his fellow silver-theft suspects as the "Pahrump Pirates."

"There certainly were lots of suspicious circumstances that needed further investigation," he said.

Petersen said Chief Medical Examiner Lary Simms didn't discover anything at the autopsy that led to the undisputed conclusion that Binion had been the victim of a homicide. But Simms did find forty milliliters of a mysterious gray-brown fluid in his stomach that he had sent out for tests. He also found unusual marks on Binion's body that he thought could have occurred immediately before or after Binion's death.

There were abrasions on both of his wrists, which investigators later found odd because Binion wasn't wearing a watch. There were also two fresh bruises on his right lower back and another one on the left side of his chest near his rib cage. And two red marks were found near his breastbone that were circular in nature, one about the size of a dime and the other about as big as a shirt button. Simms wasn't sure what had caused those marks, but he suggested that they might have been the result of bug bites while Binion's body was on the floor of his den.

The medical examiner also saw redness and discoloration around Binion's nose and mouth, which could have been caused by vomiting. And Simms observed small red dots under Binion's lower eyelids, which he called vascular congestion and attributed to his body being facedown for a period of time after his death. Simms found it odd that there were two different patterns of fixed lividity on the body. Blood had settled on the right side of Binion's body and face, as well as on both sides of his back, which confirmed to Simms that the body had been in two different positions after death and had been moved. The depth of the lividity also indicated that Binion had been dead for a much longer time than Murphy had let on when she called 911 to report that he had stopped breathing.

After Wright and Brown had left his office, Petersen received a call from Binion's real estate agent, Barbara Brown, one of the more vocal of Binion's friends raising questions about his death. Brown talked about Binion's drug habits and gave Petersen details of her bizarre telephone conversation with Murphy at Binion's home on September 17. Later, Becky Behnen stopped by Petersen's office to make her own pitch for an investigation.

Wright and Brown, meanwhile, had hired a locksmith to drill open Binion's safe in his garage.

By 3 P.M., after two hours of work, the safe was opened. To their amazement, it was empty except for one dime in the center of the floor.

"I was expecting to find everything inside the safe," Wright said. "That was a real shock."

What Wright didn't know was that Murphy had taken a half-dozen bags of coins out of Binion's safe after his death. Investigators believed she and Tabish had removed the bags on September 17, but Tabish later would claim the coins were taken by Murphy and her friends late in the afternoon of September 18. Murphy first brought the coins to Knudson's home, where she had taken up a temporary residence. Within a day or two, she took the coins to the law firm of Oscar Goodman, which was planning to represent her during the police investigation and an expected civil court battle with Binion's wealthy estate. Murphy informed Goodman and his partner, David Chesnoff, that Binion had willed her his $900,000 home and contents, which meant she considered the coins her property now. She also told Goodman that Binion had given her the coins prior to his death. She wanted to use the silver as a down payment for her legal fees to the two lawyers. Goodman and Chesnoff reluctantly accepted the coins on the condition they be allowed to inventory them. But Murphy took back the coins before the inventory was completed.

At Binion's house on September 21, Wright and Brown saw the empty safe as further evidence that they needed to conduct their own investigation into Binion's death.

"The police weren't treating it as diligently as we would have liked them to treat it," Wright said. "It was clear to us that time was being wasted, and if we wanted something done, we'd have to do it ourselves."

After conferring with Jack Binion, who was preparing for his brother's funeral the next day, the decision was made to hire a private detective to conduct the investigation.

CHAPTER 13

·····················

A Cowboy's Funeral

·····················

ON SEPTEMBER 22, the day of Ted Binion's funeral, the homicide investigation into his death was hardly revved up. But detectives made it clear they were determined to solve the mystery.

Lieutenent Wayne Petersen told reporters that detectives were looking to talk to Sandy Murphy, and for the first time, he disclosed publicly that they were probing a possible love interest between the former topless dancer and Rick Tabish, the handsome, married contractor she had bailed out on charges of stealing Binion's silver fortune days earlier.

But Petersen remained cautious.

"Even if there's a romantic relationship between the two, it doesn't elevate this to a homicide," he insisted in an interview with the *Las Vegas Sun*.

Petersen continued to stress that police had developed no evidence that suggested Binion was the victim of foul play.

As for Murphy, Petersen said: "We would like to talk to her to clear up some things, but we haven't found her yet."

As he spoke, Murphy was on her way to meet with Nevada gaming agents to begin laying the foundation for her defense in her boyfriend's slaying.

Months earlier, while Binion was alive, Murphy had asserted her Fifth Amendment right against self-incrimination and refused to answer questions from the gaming agents about Binion's drug use and his business dealings with the mob. But on the morning of September 22, just hours before Binion was to be laid to rest, she had no trouble talking to agents. In fact, when she showed up at the offices of the Nevada Gaming Control Board with William Knudson, she demanded to see the agents.

Jerry Markling, the Control Board's deputy chief of enforcement, agreed to sit down with her. He described what he encountered in a confidential five-page report later obtained by the *Las Vegas Sun*.

Markling said Murphy, who cried throughout the interview, told him that Binion had killed himself. It was the same thing she had told police detective Jim Mitchell at the hospital on the night of Binion's death.

"Murphy stated that Teddy started using drugs again," Markling wrote. "She said that the only thing in life that he really wanted was his gaming license and that he was severely depressed about being denied. She said that Teddy did this [suicide] on his own and that he was very, very depressed."

Markling said Murphy described Tabish as "my best friend in the whole world," and she suggested that Binion felt Tabish "was the only person he could trust."

She also backed up the story that Tabish had told Nye County sheriff's deputies after his arrest in Pahrump.

"Sandy said that Tabish was given specific instructions by Ted to dig up the silver and to get money for it, and then just put it into a trust for Ted's daughter," Markling wrote. "She said that Ted didn't just want to give her the silver or cash because he didn't want his former wife to get the money and because his daughter wasn't that good a money manager."

Murphy also acknowledged that she and Tabish had the combination to the underground vault in Pahrump.

Then Murphy attempted to steer authorities to other possible suspects in Binion's death, his sister Becky Behnen and her husband, Nick Behnen.

"She said Binion hated his sister and "most of the rest of his family," Markling reported. "She stated that the Behnen family, and especially Becky, are 'treacherous' and 'lowlifes.' "

Murphy blamed the unsolved drive-by shooting at Binion's home three months earlier on Nick Behnen and his son, Benny. She even brought a tape of a caustic telephone message the elder Behnen had left for Binion about the time of the shooting. The Behnens denied any role in the shooting, and when they later heard about Murphy's visit to gaming agents, they described it as an "act of desperation." Nick Behnen referred to Murphy's words as the "absurd rantings and ravings of someone who has a lot of problems."

At the close of her interview with the agents, Murphy complained that she was being mistreated by the Behnens and the media, which was reporting much speculation about her possible participation in Binion's death.

"She stated that she was being kept from going into her house and that she had to sell some diamonds to get enough money to live on," Markling wrote.

Binion's estate later alleged that diamonds were among Binion's missing valuables at his home. And Behnen would charge that Murphy had made "taunting" phone calls to her for weeks after her brother's death.

Markling's report quickly made its way to homicide detectives.

"Her actions there were very suspicious," Petersen later said. "The guys at the Gaming Control Board got the feeling she was trying to manipulate them and build an alibi."

Petersen also was wise to Murphy's hysteria at the hospital.

"The amount of information detectives got from Sandy at the hospital was negligible," he said. "It was all an act. I think it was obvious that Sandy was looking at going from living like a queen to being back out on the streets. Certainly, she had motive and opportunity. That was clear from the start. The hard part was proving she killed Binion."

As Murphy was trying to deflect attention away from her in Binion's death, his family was preparing for his funeral.

Later that afternoon, about 3 P.M., more than seven hundred mourners poured into Christ the King Catholic Church headed by the Reverend Bill Kenny, who had known Binion most of his life. The large group that came to give the colorful gambling figure his final send-off was an odd mixture. There were high-stakes gamblers, politicians, civic leaders, wise guys, casino executives and ranch hands, even a topless dancer or two—all of whom represented the diverse life Binion had led.

Kenny was impressed with the turnout.

"This shows that Ted was a most affable person and that he was a friend to so many people of all different backgrounds," he told the mourners.

Kenny reminded the crowd that Binion's wild streak had begun as a teenager. He recalled the time Binion had thrown ink on a school cinder-block wall and was forced to clean it up with a toothbrush.

Among those on hand for the service was Bob Stupak, the huckster turned casino visionary who had created the Stratosphere Hotel & Tower, the tallest structure in the state, on the far north end of the Las Vegas Strip. Also present was Bobby Baldwin, a professional gambler who had become a fixture in the casino industry by running the Mirage hotel-casino and later the Bellagio megaresort for gaming mogul Steve Wynn, who was a good friend of Binion's legendary father, Benny. And there was Michael Gaughan and his father, Jackie Gaughan, who, like the Binion family, were part of old Las Vegas. Jackie had a knack for turning grind joints downtown into profitable businesses, while Michael had become a pioneer in neighborhood gaming, creating all-purpose casinos with movie theaters and bowling alleys and, of course, plenty of slot machines for the locals.

Las Vegas Mayor Jan Laverty Jones, who had received her $40,000 contribution from Binion the day before his death, stayed loyal to the end, also making an appearance at the funeral Mass.

"He was upbeat," Jones told a *Las Vegas Review-Journal* reporter after the service. "It was a nice last memory. Ted

Binion was really a nice man, funny and bright. It was almost as if he was too smart for his own good."

Doyle Brunson, a good friend and world-famous poker player, called Binion "one of a kind," saying he had the "whole package—the personality, the looks, the talent, the guts and the money."

The person who attracted the most attention, however, was Sandy Murphy, who strolled in crying and shaking just after the Mass had started, arm in arm with two of the more widely known criminal defense attorneys in town, Oscar Goodman and his partner, David Chesnoff. The trio rushed past reporters, most of whom didn't recognize Murphy, without saying a word and found seats in the back row. Family members never acknowledged them.

Murphy, who wore sunglasses and a beige designer pantsuit, cried throughout the forty-five-minute Mass, and just before it ended, she began openly sobbing and ran out of the chapel. Goodman and Chesnoff scurried after her and escorted her to their car before photographers had a chance to take her picture.

"It was like she had just lost her best friend," Horseshoe Club security officer Donald Kershaw recalled. "It was just an act . . . It was too good to be real."

Kershaw had been assigned to drive one of the cars in Binion's funeral procession. He had also been given the task of bringing Binion's favorite brown cowboy boots, white cowboy hat and lariat to the funeral. The Western gear was placed on top of Binion's coffin, which was draped with a beige quilt, in the middle of the chapel. Near the coffin was a large floral arrangement with the word "Ted" written on a white sash across a horseshoe made up of yellow daisies. Attached to the flowers were some playing cards.

Kenny began the Mass by playing an excerpt from The Doors' song "The End," written by Binion's favorite artist, the legendary Jim Morrison, a drug and alcohol abuser who died unexpectedly in Paris in 1971 at the age of twenty-seven.

The eleven-minute pop epic concludes with a vision of violent death: "This is the end beautiful friend. This is the end my only friend. The end. It hurts to set you free. But You'll never follow me. The end of laughter and soft lies. The end of nights we tried to die. This is the end."

The irony of the song's dark lyrics hit home with many of those who knew Binion well and wondered whether he, too, had met a violent death.

Harry Claiborne, the eighty-one-year-old surrogate father of the Binion clan, was given the task of eulogizing Binion. Claiborne, a weathered former federal judge driven from the bench by the government in the 1980s, demonstrated his gift for oratory with a moving tribute to the colorful gambling figure.

"I can truthfully say that Ted Binion was the most unforgettable character I ever knew," Claiborne told the crowd. "Father Kenny said that Ted marched to a different drummer than the rest of us. But I would add that Ted was about a mile and a half ahead of the drummer."

Claiborne described Binion as a complex and intense man with a passion for learning and compassion for those less fortunate than he.

"He was a conversationalist and had one of the highest intellects of anyone I've ever known," Claiborne said. "He also had a big heart. There were hundreds and hundreds of cases of him reaching out to help people, some he barely knew."

Claiborne said Binion felt that he was cheated out of his gaming license, and he was obsessed with getting it back at the time of his death.

"The gaming board frowned on a friendship of his, and I told him it would hurt his chances for the license if he continued his association," Claiborne said. "He looked at me and said, 'Harry, this is an old man. He's sick, and he has no friends. How can I close the door to my house if he shows up to see me?'"

That friend was Herbie Blitzstein, a sixty-four-year-old ailing underworld figure who once was the top lieutenant of slain Chicago mob kingpin Anthony Spilotro. Gaming regulators had revoked Binion's license because of his ties to Blitzstein, who was shot to death in January 1997 in a plot by Los Angeles and Buffalo crime figures to take over Las Vegas street rackets.

Claiborne said Binion had faults like most people.

"But on balance, Ted Binion's good points far outweighed the bad," he said. "None of us is as good as we think we are, or as bad as our public perceptions."

From the funeral, Binion's body was driven to a local mausoleum, where it was entombed in an airtight crypt.

For two of his pallbearers, Richard Wright and James Brown, there was business to discuss at the end of the service. Frustrated by the slowness of the police to crank up a homicide investigation, the two lawyers decided to hire private detective Tom Dillard, a former homicide cop, to probe Binion's death for the estate.

Months later, Wright was asked on the witness stand what marching orders he had given Dillard.

"My instructions to Mr. Dillard were to investigate this thoroughly," he said. "And if Sandra Murphy or Rick Tabish had complicity in causing his death or stealing from Ted, to prove it. If they didn't, to prove it. I told him I hoped he'd prove they did not."

CHAPTER 14

• • • • • • • • • • • • • • • • • • •

The Private Detective

• • • • • • • • • • • • • • • • • • •

TOM DILLARD WAS no stranger to publicity when he was given the task of investigating Ted Binion's death.

As a homicide detective the last ten of his twenty-three years at the Las Vegas Metropolitan Police Department, Dillard had worked many high-profile cases.

But since his retirement in 1993, the fifty-three-year-old Dillard, a Vietnam veteran and father of five children, had gone to the "dark side," as Homicide Lieutenant Wayne Petersen put it. He had set up his own firm, Professional Investigators Inc., with his former homicide partner, Bob Leonard. The two ex-cops spent most of their time getting paid to punch holes in cases Petersen and his detectives had put together.

"I respect him as a private investigator," Petersen said. "But I have a real hard time understanding how somebody goes from career law enforcement trying to put criminals behind bars and then retires and goes to the other side and tries to keep them out of jail. I think it's a very mercenary attitude."

Dillard usually began his day at his cramped downtown office, which was flanked on one side by a shabby motel and on the other by a Catholic church. The windows on the white brick building were barred and visitors had to be buzzed in through a locked iron gate, giving one the impression that he was a man with many enemies.

With his receding gray hair, round face and beer drinker's gut, Dillard fit the stereotype of a former homicide cop who loved to remind friends about his days of glory on the police force. He wore a suit only when he had to and generally ended his workday on a barstool at his favorite neighborhood tavern talking with friends about his latest exploits.

Dillard's talent for prying out the most sensitive information was unparalleled among his peers in the business. He had become adept at cultivating relationships with reporters, lawmen and others on the street who could provide him with valuable information in his competitive line of work. His biggest asset—which sometimes turned into a liability— was his relentlessness. Once he latched onto a case, he rarely could be shaken off, even if conflicting evidence turned up. That trait revolved around his immense ego. Nobody, not even the defense lawyers he worked for, could tell Dillard how to do his job.

The Binion case gave Dillard and Leonard a chance to hook back up with the good guys. Dillard quickly established a working relationship with James Buczek, the less-experienced but dedicated homicide detective Petersen had assigned to play the lead role in the Binion investigation.

"In my opinion, Jim Buczek smelled a rat as early in the case as I did," said Dillard, who brought intensity to the homicide probe.

Together, Dillard and Leonard had worked 225 homicides and boasted of solving 80 percent of them. They participated in some ninety courtroom trials.

One of the biggest cases they broke involved the 1985 slayings committed by Steven Homick, an ex-Los Angeles police officer turned contract killer. Homick was convicted of killing oil heiress Bobbie Jean Tipton, her housekeeper and a deliveryman at Tipton's Las Vegas home. The Las

Vegas investigation led to Homick's conviction in the contract slayings of Gerald and Vera Woodman, an elderly Los Angeles couple whose story was told in the book and made-for-television movie *Family Blood*.

The most notorious case Dillard and Leonard worked on was the 1987 slaying of a seven-year-old California boy named Alexander Harris at Whiskey Pete's Hotel and Casino near the California–Nevada border. The boy's body was found a month after he had disappeared from the casino on Thanksgiving Day weekend. Several suspects had surfaced, but Dillard and Leonard zeroed in on tourist Howard Haupt, then a thirty-eight-year-old computer programmer for the San Diego Fire Department.

Haupt, however, was acquitted following a well-publicized, five-week trial in 1989. Just before the close of the trial, Dillard learned that presiding District Judge Stephen Huffaker planned to give the jurors an instruction informing them they could acquit Haupt because of insufficient evidence. Dillard made an unusual phone call to the judge to voice his displeasure. His tirade, which lasted only fifteen seconds, was enough to persuade the judge not to give the instruction. Later, Huffaker said he felt intimidated by the phone call, and that created an uproar at the police department. Dillard was forced to apologize to the judge and serve a one-week suspension without pay.

Haupt's defense lawyer, Steve Stein, said at the time that he was "sickened" by the phone call.

"When anybody calls a judge and tries to influence him, it's wrong," he said. "If I had done it, I'd be in jail."

Haupt later sued Dillard and the police department over the incident, and in March 1995 he won a $1 million judgment. During the trial, Haupt testified that the investigation had ruined his life, and he recalled a time while riding in a car with Dillard when the detective bragged that he had never lost a case.

"I sort of leaned over and said, 'Well, there's always a first time,' " Haupt testified.

Stein described Dillard as a "very able homicide detective" who was prone to becoming "overzealous" at times.

"I think what happened in this case is that the police department was embarrassed," Stein said. "They had to find someone to pin it on, and they pinned it on Haupt. They tailored it to fit Howard to the case."

Dillard stood by his investigative efforts in the case, but he acknowledged he had erred by calling the judge.

"I'm proud of the entire investigation except for fifteen seconds," he said. "That was totally improper, and I admitted it from the first day. My emotions got the best of me. ''

Since his retirement, Dillard earned a comfortable living doing investigations for criminal defense lawyers and local businesses. The work was steady, but rarely did he attract the kind of publicity he had earned as a homicide detective. All that changed with the Binion case.

By the time Dillard was hired on September 23, 1998, the *Las Vegas Sun,* ahead of the rest of the media pack, had already ferreted out Binion's friends and employees, who, like Binion's sister Becky Behnen, were raising suspicions about his death. The newspaper printed an interview with Barbara Brown, his real estate agent, who talked about that troubling phone conversation she had had with Sandy Murphy at noontime on the day Binion died. Dillard got the same story when he interviewed Brown the next day.

Unknown to Dillard, on September 24, Binion's lawyer Richard Wright had received an enlightening phone call from Linda Carroll, who told him she had information about Binion's death. Wright agreed to meet with the Southern California woman—who once had a work card in Las Vegas as a cocktail waitress at Cheetah's topless nightclub—later that afternoon at a lounge at the Gold Coast Hotel & Casino, one of the popular neighborhood casinos owned by Binion friend Michael Gaughan.

Wright later said the forty-two-year-old Carroll's conscience appeared to be bothering her. She was torn between loyalty to Murphy, her best friend, and wanting to help solve the mystery surrounding Binion's death.

"She said she knew things and that she couldn't live with herself if she didn't talk because she thought Ted was a good person," Wright said.

Carroll, who insisted that her conversation be kept confidential, told Wright she suspected Murphy and Rick Tabish had played a role in Binion's demise but that she hoped they hadn't.

She blamed Tabish for corrupting Murphy, and revealed that the two were lovers. Murphy and Tabish, Carroll said, were having romantic trysts behind Binion's back at posh Beverly Hills hotels. Carroll told Wright that prior to Binion's death, Murphy couldn't go ten minutes without calling Tabish on his cell phone. Afterward, however, she stopped calling him. Carroll also couldn't understand how Murphy was so hysterical the day Binion died, but showed no feelings the day after. She said she saw her walk through Binion's den on September 18, right past where his body was found, without showing any emotion. That evening, Carroll said, she and Murphy ordered takeout from Fellini's, a gourmet Italian restaurant not far from Binion's home, and ate it at the home of Murphy's civil attorney, William Knudson, who later agreed to let her live with him temporarily.

Wright said he happened to be having dinner with his wife at the restaurant, a favorite of Binion's, when the takeout order was placed. He asked the owner how Murphy paid for the order and was told it was taken care of with $100 bills. Later that night, Murphy was able to obtain a $3,000 cash advance on Binion's credit card from an ATM machine at the Desert Inn, where her stepmother was staying. The cash was approved even though Binion had canceled the card more than a week earlier.

Wright's meeting with Carroll at the Gold Coast would lead to a dozen follow-up phone conversations between the two over the next several months. Carroll would maintain her friendship with Murphy but secretly provide Wright with leads to pursue in Binion's death. Wright, without saying where he got it, would quietly pass that information to Dillard and homicide detectives. It was Carroll, for example, who first disclosed that Murphy had been at the Neiman Marcus beauty salon a week before Binion's death and was predicting that he would die of a heroin overdose. Carroll also identified the posh Beverly Hills hotels where Murphy and Tabish had stayed behind Binion's back.

That first week after Binion's death, Murphy and Tabish would not let on publicly that they were deep into a romantic relationship. It was a position they would maintain for the next eighteen months.

Attorney Louis Palazzo, who was hired to defend Tabish on the silver-theft charges in Pahrump, denied that such a relationship existed when pressed by the *Las Vegas Sun.*

"I have no reason to believe that there is anything to support that contention," said Palazzo, adding that Murphy was "devoted" to Binion.

But questions about the relationship and Binion's death continued to mount.

While police waited for the results of drug tests on Binion's body, the *Sun* printed a September 25 story of its interviews with Binion's housekeeper, Mary Montoya-Gascoigne, and his video surveillance expert, Brad Parry. Both pointed to odd events at the casino man's home in the days before his death. They joined a growing list of Binion friends and associates who were convinced that Binion had met with foul play.

"He would never take his own life," Parry told the *Sun*. "He was not a coward."

Montoya-Gascoigne added: "He was really a strong person, a strong man. He once told me, 'Don't worry, I'll never kill myself on drugs. I'm not stupid.' "

Parry said Binion had a keen understanding of a wide variety of drugs and their effects on the body, especially the ones he was using.

Murphy, meanwhile, was continuing her pursuit of Binion's assets. She telephoned his bookkeeper, Cathy Rose, and said that Binion had shown her where he had buried some valuable property on his 125-acre ranch in Pahrump. Murphy offered to split whatever was buried with Binion's brother, Jack. That same week, Harry Ford, a Binion neighbor in Pahrump, reported that he had seen someone using a backhoe on the far end of Binion's ranch. He later noticed a mysterious man and woman dressed in camouflage walking near the backhoe. Police later surmised that the couple was Murphy and Tabish looking for the buried treasure.

As the speculation over Binion's death increased, Dillard kept a close eye on the newspaper stories and began gathering his own evidence. One of the first things he did was visit Binion's home and examine the death scene. Then he went to the homicide bureau and viewed photos of the scene with Detective Buczek and his partner, Tom Thowsen. All three men were in agreement. The death scene had appeared staged.

"I've never seen anybody die in such a pose," Buczek later said. "I've seen overdoses. I've see people who have committed suicide, and they've never been that rigid, just lying on their back looking off to the side."

CHAPTER 15

•••••••••••••••••••

The Drug Results

•••••••••••••••••••

AT LONG LAST, on September 30, Clark County Coroner Ron Flud received the lab results of the drug tests done on Ted Binion's body.

The toxicology report showed that Binion had lethal levels of heroin and Xanax in his system. That included a large amount of both drugs in liquid form in his stomach. At the autopsy, Flud's chief medical examiner, Lary Simms, had taken forty milliliters of what he described as a gray-brown fluid from the stomach. There was nothing else there, not even food particles.

To Flud, the lab results served to heighten the mystery surrounding Binion's death. Flud had grown up in Las Vegas and was very familiar with Binion and his notorious heroin use. It was well known that Binion liked to "chase the dragon," or smoke heroin. There was no way that much heroin would be in Binion's stomach if he had smoked it. But what bothered Flud even more was seeing Xanax in a liquid form in the dead man's stomach, indicating the prescription drug was dissolved before being ingested by Binion. That was odd, indeed.

After consulting with Simms, Flud told homicide detectives James Buczek and Tom Thowsen about the lab results and set up a meeting to review the results with the detectives and Simms at his office.

"Things intensified after that, because now you had evidence that something was wrong," Flud said.

The toxicology report was all that was needed to light a fire under Buczek and Thowsen, who already had their own questions about Binion's death.

"What really raised the suspicion level was the fact that Ted had so much heroin in his stomach," Buczek said. "We didn't think there was any way possible you could smoke that much heroin and have that much in your stomach. That was the flag that went up there."

Added Buczek's boss, Lieutenant Wayne Petersen: "It was very telling when we got the drug results back. Having the heroin and Xanax in his stomach was inconsistent with anything Binion could have done by himself. We knew then it wasn't an accidental overdose or suicide."

Investigators began to suspect that someone had made a fatal cocktail of either heroin or Xanax, or both, and forced it down Binion's throat. The challenge was finding the evidence to prove it.

Despite the bizarre drug results, Flud was reluctant to call Binion's death a homicide. Officially, he told reporters the death would remain "undetermined" pending further investigation.

It was Buczek's cue to step things up. And that was what he did.

At forty-three, Buczek was six feet tall with a medium build. His round face, soft features and bowl-shaped light brown hair made him look more like a Boy Scout who had just come off the farm than a hardened, big-city homicide detective. But like most who made it to the high-profile homicide unit, he had the drive and persistence to stay with the case until the bad guys were caught. He was tougher than he looked and had a strong work ethic, often being forced to leave his wife and young daughter in the middle of the night when called out on a case.

Buczek, soft-spoken and positive in his approach to his

job, began his career in law enforcement with the Georgetown University Police Department. He had been with the Las Vegas Metropolitan Police Department for more than eleven years, the last four in homicide. Buczek had met his wife, local television reporter Denise Rosch, eight years earlier while on assignment. His partner at the time had shot a suspect at close range, and some of the suspect's blood had spattered on Buczek. Rosch, who was covering the shooting for KVBC-TV, noticed the blood, and later that evening, she called Buczek to see how he was doing. He told her he'd feel a lot better if she went out on a date with him. She agreed. As Buczek explained, it was love at first sight. They were married three years later.

Buczek was in Hawaii when Binion died, pursuing leads in a well-publicized quadruple homicide that had occurred a month earlier. Four young men, from ages seventeen to twenty, had been found bound and brutally shot to death execution-style in a home in a quiet neighborhood in southeast Las Vegas. Police believed the killers were looking for drugs and money in the home, but had come away with only $240. The cold-blooded nature of the killings had shocked the city. At the time of Binion's death, the horrifying shootings were the police department's biggest priority. Buczek found himself juggling that case and others with the Binion probe.

After reviewing the toxicology report with Flud and Simms, Buczek persuaded the two men to join him at Binion's home to visit the death scene. Buczek arranged an October 7 tour of the home through James Brown. The day before the visit was to take place, Petersen made it clear to reporters that the homicide unit had stepped up the investigation. He said attorneys for Sandy Murphy and Rick Tabish had refused to allow detectives to talk to their clients, but that the probe was progressing.

"We're not stifled yet," Petersen told the *Las Vegas Sun*. "There are things we're working on."

He suggested detectives were beginning to interview those close to Binion in an attempt to trace his final hours.

Private investigator Tom Dillard, in the meantime, had been given the green light by detectives to conduct his own interviews. He shared everything he picked up with detectives. Among the first people Dillard talked to were Binion's gardener, Thomas Loveday, his housekeeper, Mary Montoya-Gascoigne, video surveillance expert Brad Parry and Binion's longtime bookkeeper, Cathy Rose. All four would later become important prosecution witnesses.

On October 7, the day after Petersen had told the media the homicide investigation was intensifying, all of the key players in the probe—Flud, Simms, Buczek, Thowsen, Dillard and Brown—returned to Binion's home. Buczek and Thowsen brought several crime-scene experts with them to take more fingerprints and photos and collect additional evidence.

Murphy's lawyer, Oscar Goodman, had gotten word of the tour and went there himself to protest, but police refused to allow him inside.

"They went out to get some firsthand knowledge of the physical layout of the house," Petersen said the morning of October 8.

He continued, however, to downplay his unit's interest in Binion's death.

"We still don't have enough evidence to say it's a homicide," he said. "But of course we can't say it's not a homicide, which is our dilemma."

Because Binion's death wasn't treated as a homicide when his body was found, police originally did not collect evidence as if he had met with foul play. Officers also relinquished control of the house to Binion's estate. That left the investigation vulnerable to attacks from defense lawyers down the road. Attorneys could claim that the estate had tampered with the crime scene.

"We knew the crime scene was contaminated from the beginning," Buczek later said. "We had to work off of that.

There was a murder, and we had to investigate it. We couldn't just give up."

Buczek said that had homicide been involved from the very start, the house would have been sealed off and not given back to the estate until detectives were comfortable they had obtained all the evidence they needed.

"We would have made sure the crime scene remained as pristine as we had left it," he said. "But on the other hand, we knew the estate wasn't letting anybody inside the house. It had security officers on duty twenty-four hours a day. The scene was well protected."

As it turned out, the estate had virtually left the scene intact, except for what was impounded initially by police the night of Binion's death.

At the house, crime-scene analyst Jessie Sams made her way from the living room off the entranceway to the southeast den, where Binion's body was found. In a four-page crime report, she described seeing the navy blue sleeping mat on which Binion's body had been lying alongside a sofa. There was one whole Vantage cigarette, which was Binion's brand, on the mat. On one end of the mat was a white pillow and on the other end was a multicolored quilt. Sams found Binion's black jeans and an overturned ashtray with a Vantage cigarette butt underneath to the side of the mat near an end table by the sofa. Across the room on the west wall of the den, which was lined with white bookshelves, Sams saw an opened bottle of Optima Cabernet Sauvignon wine. She also noticed a small trail of stains on the moth-colored carpet that began at the doorway to the den and led to the nearest end of the sleeping mat. The trail was about six to eight feet long.

From the den, Sams went through a door on the south end of the room and entered a garage where Binion had kept his safe. She found more cigarette butts and dozens of coins and keys scattered about the floor safe, which previously had been drilled by the estate and found to be empty. Near the safe was a piece of crumpled aluminum foil with burn spots.

Police had taken similarly looking foil from Binion's bathroom the night of his death. Binion was known to place a chunk of tar heroin on a piece of foil, light a flame underneath and inhale the fumes. It was called the rich man's way of getting high off heroin. Throughout the garage were empty Army ammunition cans and fishing gear. And hanging from the rafters were several sleeping bags.

Sams also toured Binion's secret hideaway in the garage—a small, wood-paneled basement room where he kept a queen-sized bed, a thirty-five-inch Mitsubishi television and plenty of reading material, mainly nonfiction books, such as William Manchester's *Death of a President* and Priscilla Presley's autobiography, *Elvis and Me*. To get to the room, which was no bigger than ten feet wide and twelve feet long, Sams had to open a crude wooden hatch on the cement garage floor and travel down ten unfinished wooden steps. There were wicker nightstands on each side of the bed and game fish posters and fox skins on the walls. This was where Binion often would hang out when he wanted to be alone or come off heroin. The room was dark and musky. Scattered about the carpeted floor were family photos, and on the bed were legal papers from an old racketeering case against Binion.

From the den and garage area, Sams went through the dining room, where she found Murphy's purse on top of a long table. The black purse contained Murphy's passport, $50 in cash, a torn-up $8,000 check from Binion made out to Murphy, a credit card holder and an astrology readout. In the kitchen, Sams discovered a receipt, dated September 16, 1998, from a local pharmacy for a prescription for 120 Xanax tablets.

Moving to the newly remodeled west area of the 8,000-square-foot house, Sams walked through Binion's bedroom, which had French doors leading to his patio on one side and the backyard on the other side. The bed itself was huge—it looked like a king-size—with four whitewashed wood head posts and a headboard. It was covered with a heavy pink quilt and four throw pillows. In the middle of each post by the headboard were two small convex mirrors. Binion was so paranoid his last months that he had installed the mirrors so that he could watch people walking into his room while he was in his dressing area and walk-in closet across from the bed.

Sams noticed what appeared to be dried blood on a small area of the mattress near the headboard and took a sample. But more important, she saw partial footprints on the top of the box spring under the mattress from what appeared to be male work boots or hiking boots. There was one print on the box spring on each side of the bed. Both were cut out and taken back to the police lab for testing. The footprints led police to theorize that Binion's killers were looking for cash that might have been hidden under his mattress.

Inside Binion's walk-in closet was a tall dresser. Sams inspected a small wooden box that had been retrieved from a secret hiding place underneath the drawer. This was the box where Binion had kept his heroin. The lock was broken and there was nothing inside but one photograph. Sams also noticed a large black desk chair in the middle of the closet underneath an opening to the attic. Police later found nothing of value in the attic.

While Sams and her colleagues were collecting evidence, Buczek was walking through the house with Montoya-Gascoigne, the person most familiar with the surroundings other than Binion and Murphy. Buczek took a tape-recorded statement from her as they walked.

Small, soft-spoken and timid, Montoya-Gascoigne had been cleaning the casino man's house almost every day in the year leading up to his death. She had watched Binion smoke heroin and Murphy marijuana and knew most of Binion's secret hiding spots around the sprawling home. One of the first things the housekeeper noticed in Binion's bedroom was that his bed had been made differently from the way she had done it the day before his death. A pink blanket underneath the bedspread was hanging out.

"Okay . . . looking at the bed, is this the way you made the bed that last Wednesday?" Buczek asked.

"No, I changed the sheets and tucked it all in," she responded.

That suggested to Buczek that Binion's killers had gone out of their way to clean up his room. Binion never made his own bed and generally kept his clothes strewn about the floor until Montoya-Gascoigne picked them up. Loveday had previously told Dillard that Binion's room was immaculate when he peered inside the morning of his death. Nothing was out of place.

Montoya-Gascoigne said she had seen the desk chair underneath the attic opening in Binion's closet only one other time, and that had been about two weeks earlier.

A wooden box on top of a nightstand on the right side of Binion's bed was empty, the housekeeper said. Binion normally kept dollar bills and loose change in it. Another box filled with coins and valuable tokens of his father, Benny Binion, was missing inside the nightstand. And gone from Binion's small, dark wooden desk near the doorway to his room was a stack of Canadian currency, two antique gold watches and a cigar box holding small bills. Another container packed with silver dollars also was missing from his closet.

In the living room, Montoya-Gascoigne pointed out to Buczek that Binion's checkbook and other business papers had disappeared from a brown wooden box on a coffee table. And in the den, Binion's prized collection of antique coins and currency dating back to the Civil War was gone as well. The collection was worth $300,000. The housekeeper said she also had seen bags of silver dollars and quarters in Binion's safe prior to his death.

"I got the impression he was cleaned out of all of his valuables," Buczek later said. "The Civil War currency was missing. The Canadian currency was missing. There was no cash, no diamonds and no Carson City silver dollars, the most valuable of all."

Montoya-Gascoigne noticed there was an unusual amount of white pillowcases scattered about the house. Buczek surmised they might have been used by Binion's killers to cart away his valuables. In the bathroom in the den, the housekeeper saw a plunger by the toilet that she had seen in a laundry room on the other side of the house the day before Binion's death. The plunger was thought to have been used to help clean up the death scene.

Buczek never saw the "R.I.P." Halloween sign above the entranceway to Binion's home that day. But after noticing it on a later visit, he said he became disgusted.

"I said, 'What in the heck is that?'" he explained. "I saw it as someone's sick humor."

One thing that stood out in Buczek's mind during the October 7 visit to the home was the patio chair underneath an opened window in Murphy's bathroom. Murphy said she had lost her house key and, after doing some errands around town the afternoon of September 17, made her way back inside through the bathroom window.

"But how do you lose your house key and not your car key?" Buczek asked. "Everyone I know has both keys on the same ring. I surmised that Binion had taken her house key away and booted her out of the house the night before his death or early that morning. He was telling people that morning that he was going to 'kick the bitch out.'"

Buczek's interest, meanwhile, was piqued by the book *Lovers, Killers, Husbands and Wives* by Martin Blinder, which he found in the huge walk-in closet of Murphy's bedroom. The book documents court cases involving crimes of passion. One case in particular stood out in Buczek's mind. It was about a mother who had killed her children by slipping barbiturates into their milk. The mother smothered the children after they were unconscious.

Police ended up leaving Binion's house that day with a wealth of additional evidence. They took most of the relevant items at the death scene that had been left behind on September 17—the navy blue sleeping mat, the quilt that covered it, Binion's jeans, the bottle of wine, the cigarette butts and Murphy's purse containing her passport.

A week later, on October 15, police returned to cut out the strip of carpet that had the stains leading to Binion's body and sent it to a lab for tests. They also requested a copy of Murphy's hysterical 911 call the day Binion died.

By this time, the police weren't the only ones picking up their interest in Binion's death. The national media began making inquiries. *The Wall Street Journal, The Washington Post* and the *Los Angeles Times* all saw the sensational nature of the story. So did such highly rated network news-magazines as NBC's *Dateline* and ABC's *20/20,* as well as the tabloid television shows *Inside Edition, Hard Copy* and *Unsolved Mysteries.*

Binion's family also did its part to keep things stirred up.

Becky Behnen publicly praised police for stepping up the probe, and Binion's estate, overseen by his brother, Jack, of-fered a $25,000 reward for information leading to the arrest and conviction of the people responsible for Binion's death. The reward was later upped to $100,000, as homicide detec-tives pressed on.

CHAPTER 16

• • • • • • • • • • • • • • • • • • • •

Battle Over Money

• • • • • • • • • • • • • • • • • • • •

JAMES BUCZEK WAS in the field investigating a shooting on October 21, 1998, when he received a call from Deana Perry, a local manicurist who said she had information about Ted Binion's death.

Buczek and his partner, Tom Thowsen, had heard that employees at the Neiman Marcus beauty salon were talking up a storm about a bizarre visit from Sandy Murphy and Linda Carroll a week before Binion died. Buczek was anxious to talk to Perry, whose husband was on the police force, but he was tied up on the shooting. So he referred the call to Sergeant Ken Hefner, who quickly arranged to speak to the manicurist.

Perry, a blonde with sharp features and a hard edge to her, gave Hefner a brief tape-recorded statement at the offices of the homicide unit later that afternoon. She insisted that Murphy, while having her nails done on September 10, had predicted Binion would die of a heroin overdose and that she would inherit millions from him. Perry said a friend had persuaded her to step forward after they had heard on the evening news that police were looking into the possibility that Binion was a victim of a homicide.

"I'm not a snitch," she told Hefner. "My friend talked me into doing it, and I guess it's the right thing."

Hefner asked Perry to describe the demeanor of Murphy

130

and Carroll when they arrived for a day of pampering at the salon.

Hefner then asked Perry specifically what Murphy had told her about Binion's pending demise.

"She said that he was gonna OD on heroin within the next—he'd be dead within the next three weeks," Perry responded.

"Did she say he'd be dead of an overdose?"

"Of a heroin overdose."

"Of a heroin overdose?" Hefner repeated. "It's my understanding when she said these things to you, you didn't take it as engaging in risky behavior and [that he] was going to end up dead, but that you took that to mean something more sinister or threatening. Is that true?"

"She was gonna kill him," Perry replied.

"That's how you understood it?"

"Absolutely, yeah."

Hefner steered the conversation to another subject, but a few minutes later, he returned to Murphy's prediction to make sure there was no doubt in Perry's mind about what had been said.

Perry sensed what the sergeant was trying to do.

"Truly, why would somebody come in and tell a stranger you're gonna kill your husband?" she asked. "Why would I take that seriously?"

"Let's talk a little about it," Hefner said, "because, you know, some people might say, 'Well, you know, my husband was a dope addict and he's really abusing drugs. He's gonna die any day if he keeps doing what he's doing.' That's how some people might interpret it . . ."

"Correct," Perry responded.

"But you did not get that impression."

"Absolutely not."

"And what kind of impression did you get? And why did you perceive it a different way?"

"Because she was joking about it the entire time they were there, and she was very adamant that this guy was

going to die of a drug overdose, of a heroin overdose . . . and
she would have gotten $3 million if he died . . . Then she
could proceed with her new boyfriend, who's worth a lot
more than that . . . and she was only twenty-three, twenty-
four years old, and $3 million would get her until the next
guy. So I don't see how anybody else would take it [any
other way]."

Perry went on to tell Hefner that she became more suspicious of Murphy when Murphy started talking about her
plans to attend upcoming social events after Binion's death.

"I also think I got the impression," Perry said, "that Ted
needed to die so she could get the money to help her
boyfriend get out of his marriage because he was in an unhappy marriage . . ."

Then she asked Hefner: "Does that make any sense?"

"To some extent, yeah," Hefner responded.

Perry's voluntary statement gave detectives the break they
were looking for to show that Murphy had a motive to kill
Binion. More important, Perry supported their theory that
Murphy might have staged Binion's death to make it look
like an overdose. Perry led the detectives to other witnesses
at the beauty salon who could corroborate her story.

Five days later, Buczek learned about Binion's rambunc-
tious lifestyle, including his drug use, from his former wife,
Doris, an attractive, physically fit woman who had divorced
Binion two years earlier. The Binions had lived together
since 1966, but weren't married until 1980, the same year
the couple had their only child, Bonnie. Buczek learned
from Doris that Binion's dependency on drugs began with
marijuana and LSD in the 1960s and progressed to heroin
shortly before they had gotten married. She confirmed that
Binion smoked heroin because he hated needles, and he
never mixed alcohol with it. She said her former husband,
however, used Xanax to come off heroin in order to mini-
mize the withdrawal effects.

Doris also confirmed rumors that Binion kept a lot of cash
and valuables around the house. She told Buczek that Bin-

ion generally would have $100,000 to $1 million in large bills there on any given day. As much as $250,000 would be hidden inside the outboard motors of his boats in the garage.

"She said he would put the money around the engine and snap the cowling back on," Buczek later explained.

Doris said Binion was known to hide cash and jewelry on the shelves in his den and in his suit pockets and boots in his walk-in closet. He also kept vials of loose diamonds and other gems around the house.

Binion's paranoia over his safety stemmed from his days as a youth, when he was the victim of a kidnapping, Doris said. He would hide as many as fifteen loaded weapons throughout the home and always have one or two strapped to his body when he was in public.

"He had Army cans of ammunition," she told Buczek. "And he always had plenty of guns that were loaded. He knew which ones were loaded and which ones weren't loaded. I mean, he always had guns ready. He always felt he should be protected."

Doris said it was impossible for her to believe that her former husband did not have a weapon in the den. And she said Binion never slept on a mat.

Then Doris gave Buczek some insight into the stormy relationship between Binion and Murphy.

"I think she was amazingly and unbelievably controlling him the last year they were together," Doris said. "He could not receive calls from friends and family without going through her. They could not come into the house without going through her. She seemed to be very much controlling the situation, because when she was not there, Ted would talk to everybody and would see everyone. But 85 to 95 percent of the time, she was answering the phone or the door, or the recorder was on and she would take all of those calls or screen all of those calls, and she would say he's asleep, or he's not here or he's unavailable. And you just couldn't reach him."

Doris said it was clear Rick Tabish and Murphy were having an affair behind Binion's back.

"I'm amazed that Rick and Sandy have been together for as long as they have been, and I think they've been together probably longer than we realize," she said. "I feel that Rick Tabish was planning on stealing his silver and a lot of things way before this. And it was my belief that Ted and Sandy had broken up and that Ted had broken up with her and was getting her out of his life, and she had come back."

While Buczek was gaining valuable information from Binion's former wife, the casino man's lawyers were stepping up the pending battle with Murphy over his $55 million estate.

James Brown made it clear that the estate was going to fight efforts by Murphy to inherit any of Binion's wealth. Brown filed court papers disclosing publicly for the first time Binion's chilling instructions to cut Murphy out of his will the day before his death.

"Decedent intended by his directions to James J. Brown that decedent's daughter, Bonnie Leigh Binion, take all of the decedent's estate and that Sandra Murphy receive nothing from decedent's estate," Brown said in a four-page petition in probate court.

This came on the heels of a *Las Vegas Sun* story quoting private detective Don Dibble as saying Binion had asked him on September 16 to "put a tail" on Murphy because he thought she was cheating on him.

Binion estate investigator Tom Dillard was busy as well. On October 22, he told the newspaper that he had uncovered a trail of cellular phone conversations between Murphy and Tabish in the months leading up to Binion's death. Those conversations ended with a call from Tabish to Murphy at 3:47 P.M. on September 17, 1998. Just eight minutes later, Murphy dialed 911 from Binion's home to report that she had discovered his body. To investigators, the 3:47 P.M. call was no coincidence. It further tied Murphy and Tabish to Binion's death and heightened suspicions about their romantic involvement. Murphy and Tabish had been seen together October 11 on a Delta Airlines flight from Salt Lake City to Las Vegas, looking very cozy. Flight attendant Denise Wieser had noticed that Murphy appeared to be kissing Tabish's neck at one point during the flight. Tabish always went through Salt Lake City when commuting between Missoula, Montana, and Las Vegas.

Upon their return to Las Vegas, Murphy was seen at the Neiman Marcus beauty salon having her hair done. She arrived with an open bottle of wine and appeared to be drunk. Employees there observed her talking in codes on two different cell phones. She explained to her hair stylist, Michelle Gilliam, that she was actually using three phones because she never knew who might be listening to her. Gilliam overheard Murphy referring to one party as "bear." Police later learned that Murphy often called Binion by the nickname "Teddy Ruxton Bear." Murphy also complained to Gilliam about the Binion family's efforts to block her from receiving her inheritance. She said she was surprised the family was taking such a hard line, because everyone knew her relationship with Binion was merely a "financial arrangement."

The cell phone story in the *Sun*, meanwhile, had made Tabish nervous. He telephoned his friend Steven Kurt Gratzer in Missoula and asked him to check out whether the location of such a call could be determined. Much to the delight of Tabish, Gratzer reported back that calls could only be pinned down to a ten-mile radius.

As November approached, a financially strapped Tabish was in the middle of intense negotiations to sell his trucking company, MRT Transportation of Nevada. A California company, Rubber Technology International, Inc., also was interested in Tabish's mining rights to the Jean, Nevada, sand pit that he had forced Leo Casey to sign over to him. Before the deal was struck, RTI General Counsel Michael Wells voiced concerns to Tabish about whether Casey still had a claim on the mining rights. Tabish assured Wells that he didn't. Then he claimed that Casey had embezzled money from the sand pit, and he had beaten a confession out of him with a telephone book, Buczek later wrote in a sworn affidavit.

"Tabish declared that no one would hear from Leo Casey again," Buczek wrote.

On November 9, Rubber Technology announced that it had acquired Tabish's company and his mining rights in Jean. The company said it paid MRT Transportation $650,000 and assumed its $3.1 million in debts as part of the deal. Tabish was to stay with MRT as a consultant at an annual salary of $96,000 a year.

Shortly after the deal was signed, Buczek said, RTI officials learned that Tabish had misrepresented MRT's financial condition. The company's $200,000 line of credit had been used up, and $100,000 in checks issued by MRT prior to the sale had not been disclosed to RTI. Tabish also had neglected to tell RTI that he owed the Internal Revenue Service $250,000 in back employee taxes.

One week after Tabish closed the deal with RTI, Murphy was again pursuing the $875,000 life insurance policy she believed Binion had left her. Murphy telephoned Binion's longtime accountant, Greg Stuart, inquiring about the policy, but Stuart told her he knew nothing about it. Murphy complained during the conversation that she had to sell her diamonds and Mercedes to pay $250,000 to her lawyers, Oscar Goodman and David Chesnoff. But she told Stuart she still had money left in a safe-deposit box. Murphy called other Horseshoe Club officials as well. And they later determined that Binion had never followed through with his promise to name her as a beneficiary.

The pursuit of Binion's assets was not working as well as Murphy and Tabish had planned. They were in store for some more bad news in December, when the murder investigation stepped up another notch.

CHAPTER 17

•••••••••••••••••

A Prosecutor Takes Charge

•••••••••••••••••

DAVID ROGER HAD just finished his most sensational murder case in early December 1998 when his friend Tom Dillard asked him to look at the evidence in the death of Ted Binion.

Roger, a member of the district attorney's Major Violators Unit, had obtained the conviction a month earlier of Amy DeChant in the 1996 slaying of Bruce Weinstein, a popular Las Vegas sports bettor. DeChant, whose conviction later was overturned, was the forty-six-year-old Weinstein's girlfriend.

Dillard, who had been examining Binion's death for two months, had worked closely with Roger a number of times as a homicide detective. Socially, the two shared a passion for UNLV basketball and football and would attend the games together. Once in a while they would get a drink after work at Dillard's favorite watering hole. Dillard knew that if he could persuade Roger to become involved in the investigation, it would provide much-needed direction and cause homicide detectives bogged down with other cases to make Binion's death a priority. Roger, on the other hand, trusted Dillard's instincts and thought his gut feelings that Binion had met with foul play probably were on target.

As Roger studied the evidence that Dillard had brought him, he noticed similarities in the Binion and Weinstein

137

cases. Both victims were part of the gambling world and allegedly had been done in by their gold-digging girlfriends. And as with Dillard in the Binion case, a local private investigator, Michael Wysocki, played a prominent role in the investigation into Weinstein's slaying. Working with Wysocki in the Weinstein case was a good experience for Roger. He liked the idea of having that kind of help again. Ironically, Wysocki, who also was a good friend of Dillard's, later signed on as a defense investigator in the Binion case opposite Roger.

About the same time Dillard was working to involve Roger in the case, Richard Wright and Harry Claiborne began putting more heat on Roger's boss, District Attorney Stewart Bell, a cautious two-term incumbent who was a respected criminal defense attorney when he was first elected in 1994.

On December 8, Bell agreed to hold a high-level meeting to discuss Binion's death at his seventh-floor office in the county courthouse. It was rare to assign a deputy to a case before charges were filed.

"It became clear that there was a possibility that this was going to gel into a case, and the police would need guidance from us," Bell said. "We wanted to know if we had a prosecutable case—if we had something that was going anywhere."

His top criminal deputy, Bill Koot, a seasoned, hard-nosed career prosecutor, added: "We needed to know whether we were on the road to something or just on a wild-goose chase."

Bell had asked Roger to join Koot and him at the ninety-minute meeting, along with Coroner Ron Flud, Chief Medical Examiner Lary Simms, homicide detectives James Buczek and Tom Thowsen and their boss, Lieutenant Wayne Petersen, and members of Binion's estate—Dillard, Wright, Claiborne and attorney James Brown.

Wright and Claiborne made it clear there was no doubt in their minds that Binion was murdered, and they weren't happy that two months had passed and no criminal charges had been filed in his death. Once more they brought up the chilling phone call Brown had received from Binion the day before he died predicting Murphy was going to kill him.

"What they were trying to do was interest our office in getting more active in putting together this case," Koot said. "We weren't moving fast enough for them."

Homicide detectives were just as eager as the estate lawyers to file a case against Sandy Murphy and Rick Tabish, and even Flud and Simms said they believed Binion had met with foul play.

"The consensus at that point was that everything was pointing to a homicide," Flud said. "But we knew they needed to collect more evidence."

Bell and Koot, however, expressed strong reservations.

Flud said it appeared to him that the case hadn't risen to their comfort level at that point.

"They were the ones who were going to have to prosecute this, and they were the ones who were going to have to stand behind it," he said.

The top prosecutors told everyone that they were going to have to be convinced that Binion was murdered before they would be willing to file a case.

"The manner and means of death was a big concern for us," Koot said. "We had the opportunity and motive, but where was the evidence that they did it? I can remember saying after the meeting that this baby may never be approved during our term. We were looking for a cause of death that could be supported by medicine, not detective work."

Bell said everyone at the meeting was in agreement that there were plenty of suspicions about Binion's death. But at the same time, the state of the evidence still left open the possibility that Binion, a known drug abuser, had taken the heroin and Xanax himself.

"It was pretty clear that the death scene appeared staged and that it could have been a homicide, but we still had a big hurdle to get from there to a case we could prove beyond a reasonable doubt," Bell said.

Still, the district attorney gave police the green light to continue digging. In his mind there was enough evidence against Murphy and Tabish to warrant further investigation.

Petersen later said Flud was prepared at that meeting to publicly call Binion's death a homicide, but it was decided it was premature to do that without more investigating.

"Everyone agreed that it was not in any of our interests yet to go public with it," he said. "It would have just put the suspects on the defensive more than they already were. Why make them even more cautious? We had nothing to gain by going public."

After the meeting, Petersen continued to be guarded in his comments with reporters.

"The investigation is continuing," he said. "There are things that need to be done."

Bell maintained the same cautious attitude in public.

"Obviously, there are some suspicious circumstances that necessitate continuing to investigate," the *Las Vegas Sun* quoted him as saying. "It's a quantum leap from suspicious circumstances to evidence of a crime."

Bell told Roger after the meeting to review every bit of evidence that Dillard, the police and the medical examiner had uncovered and get back to him in a week.

One week later, Roger said he, too, now was convinced that a homicide had taken place and that he was up to the daunting task of collecting the evidence to prove it. He told his boss that it likely would take months of investigating to accomplish that goal. Days later, Koot, who oversaw the Major Violators Unit, formally assigned Roger to the case.

At the time, Roger was regarded as one of the best prosecutors in the office. He had won all but one of his thirty-three murder cases since joining the high-profile unit seven years earlier.

Round-faced, short and a bit on the stocky side, the thirty-nine-year-old Roger presented a clean-cut image befitting of a traditional FBI agent. His dark brown hair was short and neatly parted at the side. Roger had graduated from the California Western School of Law, where he learned to be thorough and meticulous in his presentation of a case and to treat those in authority with respect. His favorite response when given a directive was "Yes, sir." In court, his straitlaced demeanor was enhanced by his intense preparation, well-organized oratory skills and keen knowledge of criminal law. Roger was adept at predicting what sort of defense his opponent would put on to counter his case.

As he embarked on the Binion probe, Roger acted under the guise that the heroin could have gotten into Binion's stomach only by his swallowing it. He later learned that was an erroneous impression—heroin could actually get into one's stomach if it was smoked the way Binion did it. But at the time, the theory that someone had forced Binion to ingest the dangerous street drug was as good as any. Like Bell and Koot, Roger knew the medical evidence would become important if charges were ever filed. The defendants were sure to mount a case that Binion had taken the drugs himself.

"It became very clear that medical testimony was going to be very huge in this case, and the case would probably turn on medical evidence," Roger said.

That meant the prosecution needed to hire top-flight medical experts to supplement the opinion of its own chief medical examiner. Roger pushed to enlist the help of celebrity forensic pathologist, Dr. Michael Baden, the world's expert on heroin overdose cases. Baden, New York City's former coroner, was an expert witness in many of the country's most sensational court cases, including the O.J. Simpson murder trial. He was on Simpson's winning side.

But getting Baden turned out to be difficult. The call was in the hands of Flud, who was not a Baden fan.

Roger had written Flud a letter asking him to seek Baden's services, but Flud killed the idea, saying he thought the New York pathologist had the reputation of being a hired gun and too slick. Flud, a native Las Vegan, didn't want someone with no ties to the community coming into such a high-profile local case and whipping the media into a further frenzy. He thought that had the potential to backfire on the prosecution. So he opted to hire someone closer to home with less notoriety, Dr. Ellen Clarke, a deputy medical examiner in Reno. The decision to snub Baden early on would later have a profound impact on the investigation and strain relations between investigators and the coroner's office.

As the investigation intensified in December, Tabish began to feel more pressure. He sought to meet with Binion's sister Becky Behnen, who was the first to suggest foul play in Binion's death.

Tabish asked a mutual friend, Charlie Skinner, to arrange the meeting. But when Behnen balked, he telephoned her himself, saying it would be to her benefit to sit down with him.

After nearly a dozen calls from Tabish, Behnen finally agreed to meet him at her house on December 16, two months after her brother's death. But afraid to be alone with the man she believed had killed her brother, Behnen asked FBI agents to come to her home and secretly monitor the meeting. Among those listening from a nearby room were John Plunkett, then the supervisor of the FBI's Organized Crime Squad, and his top undercover operative, Agent Charles Maurer, who had played a key role in the murder investigation of Herbie Blitzstein. Present with Behnen was her husband, Nick, who by this time was totally convinced that Tabish and Murphy had killed Binion. Nick Behnen surmised that Tabish, who had the gift of gab, was using the meeting to wiggle himself out of a big-time jam.

The meeting, which gave Becky Behnen an eerie feeling, lasted about two hours at her home in the upscale Scotch 80s development in the heart of Las Vegas.

"He claimed that he was not afraid to be indicted in this murder because he had an excellent alibi and the people were very credible people and at twelve-thirty P.M. he was with these people," Behnen later told Dillard in a tape-recorded interview.

Tabish acknowledged that he had called Murphy from his cell phone eight minutes before Murphy reported discovering Binion's body, but he contended he was merely checking on her welfare, Behnen said.

He told Behnen that her brother was in poor physical condition before his death.

"He gave a very bleak description of Ted and about how bad he looked and how much weight he had lost and how his teeth were black . . ." Behnen said. "And I said to him, 'If Ted looked so bad and if he was in such bad shape, why didn't you call me to come help him?' "

The subject turned to who could have killed Binion, and Tabish suggested her other brother, Jack, could have arranged it. It was an accusation that even Behnen, who was still at odds with her brother, had trouble believing. Murphy, Tabish told Behnen, had been summoned to Jack's office that afternoon.

"He said Jack could have called Sandy over there and while they were out during this period, he could have had someone do it . . . " Behnen recalled.

Dillard had learned previously from Cathy Rose, the bookkeeper to both of the brothers, that Murphy had shown up unannounced.

Tabish also suggested that he and Murphy were looking to strike a deal.

"He indicated to us that he and Sandy both wanted to talk to the FBI and roll over, but he never said what they were going to roll over on," Behnen said.

At the time, however, Behnen was locked in a chip-cashing dispute with Jack at the Horseshoe Club. Hundreds of thousands of dollars' worth of unaccounted-for chips were being cashed at the Horseshoe, by friends of her brother, including the colorful gambling figure Bob Stupak. Behnen was looking for information from Tabish, but he never provided her with any leads. Gaming regulators looked into the disagreement after Binion's estate had turned in $3 million worth of chips Ted Binion had been storing at his ranch in Pahrump, but they never took any action.

At one point during the meeting, tempers flared when Nick Behnen became impatient with Tabish's ramblings and hurled insults at him. Becky Behnen said her husband called Murphy a "cunt" and Tabish a thief, prompting both men to jump out of their chairs and lunge toward each other. After things settled down, Tabish continued talking.

He said Oscar Goodman had sent him there to talk to the Behnens so that they could arrange a sit-down with the FBI. Goodman later denied doing that. Nick Behnen, meanwhile, told Tabish that there was nothing he and his wife could do for him because they weren't in a position to offer him immunity from prosecution.

"And he said, maybe you could lighten the press up off of him, somewhat," Becky Behnen reported.

Most of the media were following developments in the investigation, but the *Las Vegas Sun,* with almost daily reports raising suspicion about Binion's death, was becoming a particular thorn in Tabish's side.

Behnen told the *Sun* a month after the meeting that it appeared to her that Tabish was very familiar with her brother, even though he had known him for less than a year.

"I could tell he had talked to Ted for hours," she said. "He knew intimate details about Ted that only someone who had spent hours with him would know."

Tabish also seemed to know a lot about the death scene, which sent chills up Behnen's spine. He described how Binion's black jeans were rolled up in a wad and his body was on top of the sleeping mat in a position he had seen many times before.

The meeting ended with Tabish promising to follow up with the FBI. Tabish telephoned Behnen after Christmas, telling her he was still looking to deal, but after that, she never heard from him. The FBI never heard from Tabish either.

The end of December saw the battle over Binion's estate heat up.

District Judge Myron Leavitt, who had just been elected to the Nevada Supreme Court, awarded Murphy Binion's home, its contents and $300,000 in cash. The judge found that Binion's discussions with James Brown the day before he died weren't legally binding, because the estate lawyer didn't change the will until after Binion's death. Brown had filed court papers contending Binion had instructed him to disinherit Murphy on September 16. But Binion was found dead before the change could be made official.

"This is the first good thing that has happened to Sandy since her lover died," Goodman said after Leavitt's ruling. "You can't just with a phone call willy-nilly change a will. That's what they tried to do, and it hit them right between the eyes."

Harry Claiborne, however, said the estate now was taking off the gloves in its inheritance battle with Murphy. He said he planned to appeal Leavitt's order at the Supreme Court and file his own litigation seeking to recover assets he alleged Murphy had stolen from Binion. Among the valuable items Claiborne charged that Murphy stole was Binion's $300,000 collection of antique coins and and currency.

The estate's war with Murphy and Tabish was escalating on several fronts.

CHAPTER 18

• • • • • • • • • • • • • • • • •

Taking the Fifth

• • • • • • • • • • • • • • • • •

As THE NEW YEAR BEGAN, Ted Binion's estate increased the pressure even more on Sandy Murphy and Rick Tabish.

On January 11, 1999, Jack Binion, the executor of the late gambling figure's $55 million estate, filed a ten-page affidavit in probate court suggesting that Murphy, Tabish and two associates, Michael Milot and David Mattsen, might have cleaned out Binion's safe and home of valuables after his September 17, 1998, death. Prior to the affidavit, Tabish, Milot and Mattsen had been charged in Pahrump in the theft of Binion's $6 million silver fortune two days after Binion had died.

The media-shy Jack Binion, who had broken a four-month silence about his younger brother's death, also alleged for the first time publicly that Murphy and Tabish had been carrying on a romantic relationship.

"Based on the information available to me at this time," Binion said, "Ted believed Murphy was having an affair, and he intended to sever his emotional and financial relationship with her. The circumstances surrounding Murphy, Tabish, Milot and Mattsen make it highly probable that they either converted Ted's property or have knowledge regarding the whereabouts of Ted's property that is missing."

The affidavit was enough to persuade District Judge Lee Gates to haul all four theft suspects to court. He ordered them to answer questions under oath about the missing valuables on February 4. Binion's estate had determined that the $300,000 collection of antique coins and currency was gone, as well as at least $20,000 in cash, $35,000 worth of gold coins, a bag of diamonds and two gold pocket watches. Additional bags of silver coins were believed to have been stolen from Binion's safe. And still unaccounted for were millions of dollars' worth of rare Carson City-minted silver dollars that Binion had bragged about owning.

In his affidavit, Jack Binion said his brother's safe was "completely empty except for one dime left precisely in the middle of the safe."

Gates also gave the estate the green light to obtain records from the posh Peninsula and Beverly Hills hotels in Beverly Hills, where Binion alleged Murphy and Tabish had embarked on several trysts in the months leading to his brother's death.

Murphy's lawyers, Oscar Goodman and David Chesnoff, told reporters they planned to "fight tooth and nail" any attempts to take away property they believed was rightfully their client's.

"Teddy Binion intended for her to have the house and the contents, and we're going to make sure Teddy Binion's wishes are fulfilled," Chesnoff said.

Tabish's attorney, Louis Palazzo, was even stronger in his comments, calling the allegations contained in Jack Binion's affidavit a bunch of "rubbish."

"I think it's a twisted version of events to paint a picture that suits the estate's interests," Palazzo said. "It's riddled with inaccuracies."

The judge's order, however, put Murphy and Tabish in a jam. For weeks, upon the advice of their lawyers, they had been ducking questions from homicide detectives about Binion's death. If they talked in court now, they would be hurting their own legal strategy. Detectives would be able to review their testimony and look for incriminating statements, the very thing their lawyers were trying to avoid. Be-

cause of the ongoing criminal probe, most expected Murphy
and Tabish would take the Fifth Amendment and not answer
questions if called to the witness stand. But that presented
another problem for Murphy. How could she expect to receive her inheritance from the estate if she was unwilling to
help the family make an accounting of his assets for the
court?

On January 14, three days after the estate had turned up
the heat in probate court, detectives and crime-scene analysts obtained a search warrant to go back to Binion's home
for more evidence. They were looking for items that could
be tested for fingerprints. Detectives took an empty bottle of
wine and a couple of plastic cups from a shelf in the den, an
empty bottle of Heinecken on the dining room table, a wine
glass on an end table in the living room, a drinking tumbler
from an island countertop in the kitchen and a couple of
drinking glasses in Murphy's bedroom. Prints were obtained
on several of these items and later sent to the police lab to
compare with fingerprint samples from Murphy, Tabish,
Milot and Mattsen. The hunt for prints was an indication
that police weren't ruling out the possibility that Milot and
Mattsen were in the home the day Binion died. Detectives
also took the "R.I.P." Halloween sign above the entranceway
to Binion's home, as well as a mysterious handwritten note
taped inside the safe in Binion's garage.

The note read: "Empty of value. No money, and if I get
lucky and catch you stealing my money, I'm going to kill
you, if I get lucky."

Binion's lawyers recognized the handwriting as Binion's,
but they were hard-pressed to understand what it meant.

All of the items police had seized were dusted for prints,
but none were found.

For the first time, Chief Deputy District Attorney David
Roger was on hand to supervise the search. James Brown
and Tom Dillard also were present. Roger wanted a court-
authorized search this time because of Judge Myron Leavitt's order in December awarding Murphy the home. The

prosecutor didn't want to give the defense any opening down the line to suppress the evidence police had seized because of a possible illegal search.

Detectives also made what would turn out to be a fascinating discovery. They found a large bag of coins hidden behind an entertainment center in Murphy's bedroom. At the time, the bag, which was not opened, had little evidentiary value to the detectives, so they didn't bother to take it. Brown later gave the bag to Dillard, who sealed it and put it in the safe of his downtown office. A couple of months later, the bag was opened in the presence of Oscar Schwartz, an independent appraiser Brown had hired to estimate the value of the contents of Binion's home. In the middle of the coins, Schwartz discovered a pair of thumb cuffs and a small knife, which happened to be two items Leo Casey had told police were used by his kidnappers. Brown called Dillard with the startling news, and Dillard promptly notified homicide detectives. Suspecting they now might have evidence linking Murphy to Casey's July 1998 torture, detectives obtained a search warrant to confiscate the thumb cuffs and knife.

A week after police had executed the search warrant at Binion's home, Roger opened another front in the investigation. He quietly issued grand jury subpoenas for records he thought would establish the relationship between Murphy and Tabish, who steadfastly had been denying any kind of love interest between them.

About the same time, Goodman and Chesnoff filed papers seeking to disqualify Judge Gates, who had ordered Murphy and Tabish to court February 4, from the probate case. Under Nevada law, the attorneys were within their rights to exercise one challenge of a judge in such a civil case. Though they never explained why they wanted to bounce Gates, it was obvious to the lawyers that the judge was not sympathetic to Murphy. Gates promptly removed himself, and newly elected District Judge Michael Cherry, who had once represented Binion's sister Becky Behnen, was randomly chosen to succeed him.

Then Murphy's lawyers, with the help of probate attorney R. Gardner Jolley, filed papers asking the new judge to block Murphy's upcoming testimony in the estate case.

"The representatives of the estate are nothing more than a stalking horse for the police and district attorney's office with whom they have met on several occasions regarding the investigation of Ted Binion's death," the lawyers charged. "Therefore, it is the belief of Murphy's attorneys that the information sought is not to determine whether Murphy has property in her possession belonging to the estate, but instead to seek evidence in support of future criminal allegations against Murphy."

At a January 25 hearing, Cherry refused to halt Murphy's testimony, leaving her lawyers no choice but to tell the judge they would recommend she take the Fifth Amendment and not risk incriminating herself.

"She will assert whatever privileges are available to her," Goodman said in court.

Cherry, a bearded former defense attorney with an easygoing personality, pleaded with both sides to find a way to resolve the impasse, even encouraging Murphy to seek immunity for her testimony so that the judge could move on with settling Binion's $55 million estate.

"I want her to come forward," Cherry said. "If she takes the Fifth Amendment, we'll go from there."

This game of "legal chicken" Murphy was playing had the potential to backfire on her in her bid to hold onto her inheritance from Binion.

"She's in a legal box of her own making," estate lawyer Richard Wright, a former federal prosecutor, told the *Las Vegas Sun* after the hearing. "Apparently, she's begging for what we call an immunity bath. That happens when someone who has something to hide wants to be the first one to go before authorities to be cleansed and protected."

Goodman stood his ground, saying: "I'm not begging for anything. I'm trying to protect a client against the estate's greed and aggression."

The piercing rhetoric illustrated how bizarre the Binion case was becoming. It now was pitting some of the most well-known and respected criminal lawyers, most of whom knew little about probate matters, against each other. Wright, Goodman, Chesnoff and Harry Claiborne were brilliant legal strategists on criminal matters and all were very close to Binion. They were used to being on the same side, not fighting with one another.

As word about efforts to seek immunity for Murphy spread, Bill Koot, chief of the district attorney's Major Violators Unit, made it clear that his office had no intention of accommodating the woman they suspected had played a role in Binion's death.

On February 4, Murphy, Tabish, Milot and Mattsen showed up in court for what was expected to be the first bit of high drama in the case. Goodman announced that he and Murphy were at odds and that Murphy was prepared to take the witness stand without immunity against his advice. He asked Cherry for a one-week delay so that he could either settle the disagreement or get off the case. Goodman's remarks were viewed merely as an effort to buy more time for Murphy before she went on the hot seat. But Cherry granted his request.

Then, one by one, in front of a horde of reporters, photographers and cameramen, Tabish, Milot and Mattsen took the witness stand in the crowded fourth-floor courtroom with their lawyers at their sides and refused to answer questions about Binion's missing valuables. Tabish, reading a prepared answer from a yellow legal-size notepad, asserted his Fifth Amendment privilege ninety-eight times as estate lawyers attempted to pry out of him the whereabouts of Binion's cash, coins and jewelry.

In the meantime, a couple doors down the hall, Roger was in his office preparing to step up the criminal case even more. He began putting together an affidavit he could use to obtain search warrants at the suburban luxury apartment Tabish and Murphy were sharing, as well as at Tabish's businesses in Las Vegas and Missoula, Montana.

"I knew that we needed to shore things up a little bit," Roger said. "I wanted the search warrants for a couple of reasons. First, because it was a good investigative tactic, but also because I was concerned that the public and potential witnesses out there thought that this was a case of the big, bad Binion family beating up on a young girl. I wanted to dispel that notion.

"I wanted the public to know that this was a murder case and that the police department and the district attorney were investigating the case, and if anyone had information, they should come forward."

Roger also was looking to obtain court permission to wiretap Murphy's and Tabish's telephones.

"I knew that Sandy loved to talk and they both had cellular phones," he said. "And I thought it would be easy pickings to get some information off of wiretaps."

Roger was able to get permission to install pen registers, which identify calls coming in and going out of a phone line without monitoring the content of the conversations. But the efforts to obtain wiretaps inadvertently were foiled by Goodman when he telephoned Roger prior to Murphy's February 11 court appearance.

"Oscar said, 'I know what your response is going to be, but I have to ask for immunity for Sandy,' " Roger explained.

When Roger responded that he was not going to seek immunity, Goodman then asked the prosecutor whether he had any wiretaps in the criminal probe.

"Nevada law doesn't allow you to disclose a wiretap's existence, and I wanted to play a head-game with him, so I said, 'Oscar, you know I can't answer that question.' He said, 'OK, OK, that's enough for me.' Then he went to court and told Judge Cherry there were wiretaps in the investigation."

After that, Roger said, there was little chance of eavesdropping on the conversations of Murphy and Tabish. Even the pen-register activity dropped off significantly, he said.

When February 11 came, Goodman and Chesnoff were observed escorting a smiling, designer-clad Murphy to Cherry's courtroom.

At the start of the hearing, Goodman stunned reporters when he disclosed that a county grand jury investigating Binion's death had begun hearing testimony against his client. The next day, the *Las Vegas Sun* reported that Murphy's good friend Tanya Cropp was among the first witnesses whom Roger had hauled before the panel. Roger did not believe that Cropp had been truthful in statements she had given Tom Dillard and wanted to put more pressure on her.

"This is simply another investigative tool that we are using to aid the police in trying to sort out the circumstances surrounding the death of Ted Binion," District Attorney Stewart Bell told the newspaper. "We are not at all in a position to determine whether or not charges might be initiated. Ted Binion died as a result of an overdose of narcotics. How he happened to overdose on narcotics remains a mystery."

Lieutenant Wayne Petersen played his cards close to the vest as well about the news of the grand jury probe.

"We're collecting new information all of the time," he said when asked about the significance of the new development in the criminal case.

James Buczek, the lead homicide detective in the probe, later said such ambiguous statements made it easier on him during the probe.

"I think at that point Lieutenant Petersen was protecting us and the investigation," he said. "We had a comfort zone to work in. If we had said we felt it was a homicide right away, the media would have hounded us."

Buczek said downplaying the investigation until enough evidence was gathered also gave Murphy and Tabish a false sense of security.

At the hearing, Goodman told Cherry that the district attorney's office had refused to offer Murphy immunity in the criminal case and that he had resolved his differences with his client. He said Murphy was now prepared to take the Fifth.

And that was exactly what she did more than two hundred times with Goodman at her side. Among the questions she refused to answer were those involving her reported romantic relationship with Tabish, which was a key aspect of the alleged murder conspiracy against Binion.

A week later, detectives would learn the answers to those questions without Murphy's help.

CHAPTER 19

• • • • • • • • • • • • • • • • • • • •

The Raids

• • • • • • • • • • • • • • • • • • • •

THE DAY FINALLY had arrived when homicide detective James Buczek would get a chance to confront Sandy Murphy and Rick Tabish.

It was a chilly February 19, morning, and Buczek had awakened early, knowing that this was the day he'd come knocking on Murphy's door. He was hoping to find Tabish there as well.

After saying good-bye to his wife and baby daughter, Buczek headed to the Henderson, Nevada, apartment that police believed was shared by Murphy and Tabish. Before executing the search warrant, he hooked up with fellow officers at a nearby Smith's Food King to go over last-minute details of the search. The luxury apartment was one of three sites that police simultaneously were raiding that morning. Buczek's partner, Tom Thowsen, went to Tabish's MRT Transportation of Nevada offices, several miles away on the highway leading into Las Vegas. And Sergeant Ken Hefner took sheriff's deputies in Missoula on a search of Tabish's businesses and home there.

For weeks, Chief Deputy District Attorney David Roger had been preparing a forty-four-page affidavit for Buczek documenting the reasons for the searches. The day before the raid, Roger presented Buczek's affidavit to District Judge Gene Porter, who found cause to sign the search warrants.

Buczek told Porter that both Murphy and Tabish had financial reasons to kill the wealthy Ted Binion.

"Affiant is aware that Sandy Murphy is a former stripper who worked at Cheetah's prior to moving in with Ted Binion," Buczek said. "According to a cohabitation agreement signed by Binion and Murphy in January 1997, upon their separation Murphy was entitled to keep her Mercedes and a percentage of the profits from the sale of Rio Hotel stock owned by Binion.

"Aside from those assets, affiant is unaware of any material assets owned by Murphy. Indeed, the only financial benefits that Murphy was entitled to receive were Binion's house, contents and $300,000 under the terms of Binion's former will. Without intending to be glib, Murphy was worth more with Binion dead than she was worth with Binion being alive.

"Today, in light of the civil litigation involving Murphy and the Binion estate, Murphy appears to be in poor financial condition," Buczek said. "According to a surveillance team assembled by Tom Dillard, Murphy works as a receptionist at MRT Transportation."

Buczek added that records showed that the power bill to the Henderson apartment was paid by MRT Leasing of Nevada, one of Tabish's companies.

The detective also pointed out that Tabish's trucking business was running into financial difficulties.

"Affiant believes that it is important to obtain financial information concerning Tabish, his wife, Mary Jo Tabish, and his corporations set forth above," Buczek said. "This information will either prove or disprove that Tabish had a financial motive to kill Ted Binion."

Buczek told Porter that detectives would be looking for Tabish's financial records, as well as for any evidence that would document his romantic relationship with Murphy. Specifically, detectives wanted to find the expensive designer clothing they believed Murphy had bought Tabish on Binion's credit card prior to the gambling figure's death.

On the morning of the raid, Buczek was feeling more comfortable about the murder case he had been putting together. He had talked to several Neiman Marcus beauty salon employees who were with Deana Perry when Murphy predicted Binion would die of a drug overdose. And he had found Binion's drug supplier, Peter Sheridan, who had provided the gambling figure with twelve balloons of black tar heroin the night before his death. Sheridan, who was familiar with Binion's drug habits, had made it clear to Buczek that Binion only smoked heroin. He never injected it or ate it. Buczek also had obtained a strong statement from retiring Las Vegas Mayor Jan Laverty Jones during a February 9 interview. Jones, a longtime Binion family friend, had explained that Binion was not suicidal and was in good spirits the morning before he died when she visited his home to pick up a $40,000 campaign contribution. Buczek knew Jones would make an excellent witness in court.

Still, as the investigation intensified, Murphy and Tabish weren't letting on that they were worried. In fact, they did the opposite. They kept a high profile, and although they supposedly had fallen on hard financial times, their spending habits didn't decrease.

"I was very surprised that they stayed in Las Vegas and were seen in public together," Buczek said. "They continued to lead a flamboyant lifestyle, dining at expensive restaurants and throwing a lot of money around."

Murphy and Tabish, against the advice of their lawyers, also sought to influence reporters from national news organizations. They spent time, for example, with a correspondent working on a Binion article for *Gentlemen's Quarterly (GQ)*. When the piece came out months later, the writer talked about going bungee jumping and hanging out at topless nightclubs with the couple.

On the morning of February 19, Buczek went to their Henderson apartment looking for a big score. Shortly after 7 A.M., with his colleagues in tow, Buczek knocked on the apartment door. There was no answer, so he knocked again.

Then he heard the sound of Murphy's voice asking, "Who is it?"

"It's the Las Vegas police department," Buczek responded. "We have a search warrant."

"Well, I'm going to call my attorney before I let you in," Murphy said.

"Sandy," Buczek explained in a stern voice, "if you don't open the door right now, I'm going to kick it in."

Murphy, looking disheveled in her white "moo-moo" pajamas, then opened the door. As he entered the apartment, Buczek saw an equally rumpled Tabish in gym shorts and a T-shirt sitting on the living room sofa.

"He looked like he had just combed his hair with a pillow," Buczek later said. "It was all matted down."

Buczek knew he had hit pay dirt. The two obviously had been sleeping together and no longer could claim they weren't romantically involved.

"I knew you guys were coming," Murphy blurted out.

"What do you mean, you knew we were coming?" Buczek responded.

"I had a dream this morning that I woke up and you guys were in our apartment."

Buczek found that amusing, because this was the first time he had actually met Murphy and Tabish. Buczek also had to stop himself from laughing as he observed Murphy walking around the apartment in her juvenile-looking white pajamas with patterns of black cows.

Before detectives began the search, they allowed Murphy to call Oscar Goodman to observe them while they collected evidence. There were two rooms upstairs but just one bed, and it was in the master bedroom and unmade. On one nightstand, police found Murphy's personal belongings, including an emotional Valentine's Day card she had received from a still-loyal Tanya Cropp. On the other stand were items belonging to Tabish, among them photos of his two small children, Amanda and Kyle. In the other bedroom, detectives found all of the men's clothing they were looking for—the expensive Gucci jeans and black Armani slacks, the black velvet Armani shirt, the Wilke Rodriguez top and a pair each of hiking shoes and work boots. Detectives had thought the shoes would match impressions taken from the box spring of Binion's bed, but tests later failed to come to that conclusion. Also seized from the apartment was a money clip engraved with Binion's name, as well as a pair of cuff links with his initials. A white Beverly Hills Hotel polo shirt was also taken, providing more evidence of the couple's California trysts.

The most intriguing piece of evidence seized was a crude handwritten map appearing to point to buried treasure at Binion's 125-acre ranch in Pahrump. An "X" was marked and circled near what was identified as a trailer in the middle of the Binion complex. Buczek found it significant, knowing that Murphy had telephoned Binion's bookkeeper after his death offering to split with his brother, Jack, valuable property she knew had been buried at the ranch. The map was taken from the trunk of Tabish's black, four-door Mercedes in the garage.

But the biggest find of all that morning for the police was seeing Murphy and Tabish together.

"That was big stuff," Buczek said. "I remember calling David Roger from the apartment, and he was really jazzed up."

Roger could hardly contain his excitement in an interview with the *Las Vegas Sun* that morning.

"The best evidence of that relationship is Tabish and Murphy in that apartment at seven in the morning," he said.

Roger later said he had been expecting Murphy and Tabish to be at the apartment.

"That's why we did it five days after Valentine's Day," he said. "I wanted them to be there."

Buczek telephoned Roger with the good news just twenty minutes after the search had begun.

"He said we got them together, and we found all of the clothing items we were looking for," Roger said. "They had been denying being part of a romantic relationship, and we knew that was pretty strong evidence of this conspiracy to murder. It they're having this relationship and Ted Binion doesn't know about it, then it makes sense that they're going to murder him and live happily ever after with his money. So that was pretty big. We had achieved our goal."

Indeed, investigators were on a roll.

Nothing of real evidentiary value, however, was found at the MRT Transportation offices that morning because Tabish had down-scaled the business by then. But in Missoula, police found a $436.51 MRT check made out to David Mattsen, who had been managing Binion's ranch in Pahrump. That was the first solid evidence that Tabish had been buying Mattsen's assistance in the conspiracy. MRT records later showed that Mattsen had been paid that amount each week since Binion's death. Witnesses told police Mattsen never actually performed any duties for Tabish's company.

That afternoon, after Buczek had returned to the homicide office, Wayne Petersen told him that he had received a telephone call from Murphy, who was complaining that something was wrong with the power in her apartment.

"She was blaming us for it," Buczek explained. "I told Wayne that something doesn't sound right. I said if I go back I'm carrying a recorder in my pocket. I'm going to play the game. And he said go ahead."

Buczek, with his recorder in his shirt pocket, then drove back across town to Henderson, where once more he knocked on the door of Murphy's apartment.

"Sandy opens the door, and she's all made up," Buczek said. "She's dressed nicely and she's standing there with a glass of red wine. And I'm thinking, maybe this is a setup. Why else would she be standing there with a glass of wine trying to look seductive?"

Murphy immediately told Buczek, standing in the doorway, that she had reset the breakers in the apartment and resolved the electrical problem.

"I was just thinking, God, you know what? It was working until they came and now it's not working, you know," she said.

"That's fine. I understand," Buczek responded.

Then Buczek suggested that it was time she tell her side of the story.

"You know we've been wanting to talk to you," he said.

"I know," Murphy replied.

"You could put a lot of questions aside."

"I wish I could. Let me tell you, because there are so many things I could tell you that you would just go aaahhhh. But if I did, Oscar would drop me as a client and all the money that I've paid—I had to sell my Mercedes—I mean, I'd probably get in trouble for saying that . . . It's just been one nightmare after the next. And I'm just trying to follow their advice, because if they drop me, then I lose everything I have."

Buczek kept nodding his head and saying "Okay" to Murphy as she rambled on.

"And I swear," Murphy continued, "I would love to talk. Oscar and I fight about this all of the time. And he tells me, 'These guys aren't on your team. They hate you. Don't you dare say a word.' You know. I'm in trouble always."

Buczek then noticed a smiling Tabish standing in the loft above him.

"Come on in," Tabish said. "Don't stand out there. Everybody's looking at you."

"All right," Buczek responded as he stepped inside.

"I'm going to Montana for the weekend," Tabish said, looking at Murphy. "Why don't you get a beeper [number] from him. I'm concerned about her safety . . ."

Murphy chimed in: "Well, 'cause you guys publicized where I live now and the Binions had called some of my family members in California."

Tabish told Buczek that Murphy had been getting constant death threats from the Binion family. One threat, Murphy said, was made to her sister-in-law, who was nine months pregnant.

"And [they] threatened to murder me and my whole family, and she called the police and did a whole statement and the whole deal," Murphy said. "Now, it's like they know where I live, And trust me, they hated me when my old man was alive. Do you think that now that he's dead they don't hate me more?"

Tabish then said Nick Behnen, the husband of Becky Behnen, was out to destroy him.

"This Nick is no good," he said. "I mean, this guy's setting me up, wanting me to come over and talk to them at their house and stuff. I mean, this guy's no good. He hates her for whatever reason . . ."

Buczek did not want to give out his beeper number. So he told Murphy that she already had Petersen's number and that she should call him if she needed help.

"Well, get somebody's number if something happens to you," Tabish told Murphy.

Murphy responded: "Well, I'm just gonna have my brother and all of his friends stay here, because I'm not staying here alone, because then he [Behnen] can't come get me."

Buczek again just nodded his head and said, "Sure."

"And you gotta understand my position," Tabish told Buczek. "She's got nobody. I mean, I'm it. We're in this thing together."

Tabish and Murphy continued talking about Murphy's well-being for a few more minutes before the subject was changed.

"Make sure—and don't be shy—you call these guys," Tabish said. "All right." Then he looked at Buczek and said, "Trust me, she and I are delighted you guys are on [this]. I mean, the more you guys dig up, at least it's something legitimate, taking a legitimate statement. And the grand jury questions people on a bunch of hearsay and bullshit . . . That's all we're hoping for."

"Okay," Buczek responded.

Murphy then decided it was time to end the fifteen-minute conversation.

"You're getting me in trouble," she said.

"You ain't in trouble for nothing," Tabish said. "He ain't gonna call Oscar."

Murphy apologized for summoning Buczek to the apartment, and Buczek then said good-bye and left. He was relieved that he had decided to secretly record the strange chat. It was a long day, but he had finally gotten his chance to confront the suspects in Binion's slaying.

But there was more work ahead.

On March 9, with the help of Nye County sheriff's deputies, homicide detectives executed another search warrant at Mattsen's Pahrump trailer home. The raid was aimed at finding financial records and other evidence that would show Mattsen's ties to Tabish and Murphy. The hard-drinking Mattsen was present and made it clear to detectives that he was not happy about his privacy being invaded. Detectives, who had already established a financial link between Mattsen and Tabish during the previous month's searches, nevertheless pressed on. They found a tax form in Mattsen's personal papers that showed he had declared $4,000 in wages from MRT Transportation in 1998. Also discovered was a February 12 termination notice that was given to all MRT employees because of bankruptcy court proceedings against the company. But the most interesting find was a daily 1998 diary that belonged to his wife, Thressa, a devoutly religious woman.

On August 24, 1998, Thressa wrote: "Tomorrow, David meets with Rick about a job with him." The next day, she added: "David came home excited about working for Rick." Mattsen's wife also said in her diary that Tabish had given Mattsen a new pickup truck on September 8. Witnesses had reported seeing Matttsen driving a red pickup prior to Binion's death.

On the day Binion died, Thressa wrote that she had awakened at 7:30 A.M. and found a note from Mattsen asking her to make him breakfast. She said he didn't return until 11 A.M.

"David talked to Rick, fed the animals, got dressed up and

left for Vegas," she wrote. "Everything with him is hush, hush and secret. I don't know, Lord. Reveal to me what he's up to, and if it's not right, sever that relationship with Rick."

Then she added: "Ted's acting crazy, and release him from the drugs."

On October 3, two weeks after Binion's death, Thressa Mattsen still was having reservations about Tabish and Murphy.

"Lord, if Rick and Sandy are on the up-and-up, please let me know cuz I feel they're using David," she wrote.

The next day, she added: "Now Sandy's telling him she's bringing some money. Lord, if that money is not from you, please keep it away."

In November, according to the diary, Thressa's conscience was still bothering her.

"I've seen Sandy," she said. "She's all dressed up, changed her hair and all. I didn't feel good talking to her. I felt real strong that she had something to do with Ted's death. It hurts me to think that someone hurt him."

Detectives also seized seven weapons from the trailer, including one that was registered in James Brown's name. That discovery gave detectives reason to smile. They knew that Mattsen was a convicted felon who was not allowed to possess any guns. Buczek had dug up records that showed Mattsen was convicted of armed robbery and sexual intercourse with a minor in 1972 in Milwaukee. The weapons provided detectives with something to put pressure on Mattsen to cooperate against Tabish and Murphy.

And that was exactly what Mattsen's lawyer, James "Bucky" Buchanan, charged one day after the raid.

"They're putting heat on him to become involved in this investigation," Buchanan told the *Las Vegas Sun*. "They're looking for his assistance."

Several days later, the heat had taken its toll. Mattsen showed up at the office of District Attorney Stewart Bell with Buchanan, ready to deal. Also on hand for the secret meeting were Roger and his immediate supervisor, Bill

A young Ted Binion (*left*) with
his father, Benny Binion.

(Photo courtesy of *Las Vegas Sun*)

Ted Binion before the hearing of the Nevada Gaming
Commission, May 22, 1997.

(Photo courtesy of *Las Vegas Sun*)

The Horseshoe Club on Fremont Street in the heart of downtown
Las Vegas. The hotel-casino has been owned by the Binion family for five decades.

(Photo courtesy of Art Nadler)

Front view of Binion's 8,000-square-foot home at 2408 Palomino Lane.

(Photo courtesy of Art Nadler)

Cheetah's adult nightclub, where Sandy Murphy danced topless and met Ted Binion.

(Photo courtesy of Art Nadler)

Sandy Murphy and Rick Tabish wait for the start of a hearing, October 22, 1999.
(Photo courtesy of Aaron Mayes/*Las Vegas Sun*)

Rick Tabish and Sandy Murphy talk to a member of the courtroom audience during a break in closing arguments of the trial, May 8, 2000.
(Photo courtesy of Lori Cain/*Las Vegas Sun*)

District Judge Joseph Bonaventure questions the defense during an evidentiary hearing, August 16, 2000.
(Photo courtesy of Sam Morris/*Las Vegas Sun*)

Witness Leo Casey reacts during cross-examination of the trial, April 6, 2000. Casey claimed he was kidnapped and tortured by Rick Tabish.

(Photo courtesy of Sam Morris/*Las Vegas Sun*)

Linda Carroll turns to the cameras as she arrives to appear before the grand jury, April 15, 1999.

(Photo courtesy of Sam Morris/*Las Vegas Sun*)

Steven Kurt Gratzer tries to recall dealings with Rick Tabish while testifying at the trial, April 4, 2000.

(Photo courtesy of Sam Morris/*Las Vegas Sun*)

Bonnie Binion pauses during her trial testimony, April 13, 2000.

(Photo courtesy of Aaron Mayes/*Las Vegas Sun*)

Tanya Cropp, a friend of
Sandy Murphy, testifies,
April 25, 2000.
(Photo courtesy of
Steve Marcus/*Las Vegas Sun*)

Expert witness Dr. Michael Baden explains his suffocation theory
to the jury.

(Photo courtesy of Sam Morris/*Las Vegas Sun*)

Defense attorney John Momot looks back at the courtroom audience during the murder trial.
(Photo courtesy of Lori Cain/*Las Vegas Sun*)

Chief Deputy District Attorney David Roger addresses the jury during his opening statement, March 31, 2000.
(Photo courtesy of Aaron Mayes/*Las Vegas Sun*)

Forensic pathologist Cyril Wecht listens as Chief Deputy District Attorney David Wall questions him during the trial, May 3, 2000.
(Photo courtesy of Lori Cain/*Las Vegas Sun*)

(*From left*): Mary Jo Tabish, Frank Tabish and Rick Tabish hug during a break in the penalty phase of the trial.

(Photo courtesy of Sam Morris/*Las Vegas Sun*)

Becky Behnen leaves the Clark County Courthouse after Rick Tabish and Sandy Murphy are found guilty in her brother's murder.

(Photo courtesy of Lori Cain/*Las Vegas Sun*)

Koot. Mattsen made it known he wanted the $100,000 reward that Binion's estate was offering if he reached an agreement with prosecutors.

Roger had been at a court hearing in another case and arrived late to the meeting. Bell briefed him on what Mattsen was willing to say, and Roger didn't like what he was hearing. Mattsen was insisting that he had seen Murphy and Tabish handcuff Binion and take him hostage on September 16, 1998, the night before Binion was killed. That conflicted with the statements of several reliable witnesses who had seen Binion outside and away from his home in the early-morning hours of September 17.

Roger questioned Mattsen's story, and the two got into a heated argument. The prosecutor accused Mattsen of lying and suggested he was wasting everyone's time. Mattsen, in turn, became belligerent, forcing an abrupt ending to the meeting without a deal. At Mattsen's request, prosecutors agreed to tell no one about the meeting.

If nothing else, the meeting served to reinforce to investigators that they were getting closer to breaking open the case.

CHAPTER 20

• • • • • • • • • • • • • • • • • •

Stepping It Up

• • • • • • • • • • • • • • • • • •

BY THE TIME Clark County Coroner Ron Flud assembled
reporters at his office for a late-afternoon news conference,
word had already leaked out about what he was going to say:
Ted Binion did not kill himself.

The *Las Vegas Sun* had reported in its afternoon edition
and on its web site that Flud was preparing to call Binion's
death a homicide. Flud, of course, had known for months
that this was the case. But now he was ready to go public in
the aftermath of the successful police raids on Sandy Murphy, Rick Tabish and David Mattsen.

"It was just a matter of the investigation coming to a point
that everybody involved felt comfortable," Flud said.

The news conference, which was carried live on Las
Vegas One, a local cable news channel, took place in a small
conference room at the coroner's office. Flud had asked
Wayne Petersen and David Roger to join him as he addressed the crowd of reporters and cameramen. Standing behind an American flag, Flud, a career bureaucrat with a
reputation for choosing his words carefully and playing
things by the book, opened the news conference by declar-
ing it was his opinion that Binion had met with foul play.
But he refused to elaborate.

"We're going to change the manner of death to homicide," he
said. "We have no statement about why we made this decision."

Reporters peppered Flud with questions, but he gave few answers.

Later, he would complain: "We spent forty-five minutes answering the same questions over and over."

Some nuggets of information, however, were gleaned from the news conference. It was clear, for example, that investigators were suspicious of the fact that a large amount of heroin and Xanax had been found in Binion's stomach.

"You tell me," Flud said when pressed by reporters. "How do you inhale [heroin] and get it in your stomach?"

Roger and Petersen knew that Sandy Murphy and Rick Tabish were the chief suspects in Binion's death, but they refused to name them at the news conference. But then, they probably didn't have to.

"I think it's fairly obvious to all of us who was present there and who had a motive and opportunity," Petersen said. "We're getting, I think, to some conclusion in this case."

Afterward, Becky Behnen, who had been waiting six months for this day, praised investigators.

"I've always had faith in their ability to follow through and solve this," she said. "It's very saddening, but it brings some closure to my life."

Harry Claiborne was elated. "I said from the very beginning that the murder scene was staged and that I believed that Ted was murdered. And I stand by that."

Roger, meanwhile, left little doubt that investigators planned to turn up the heat even more in the coming weeks.

"Now that the coroner has determined it is homicide, we will be stepping up our efforts to serve justice in a timely manner," he said.

Later, Roger called the news conference a "milestone in our investigation.

"We just felt the time was right," he said. "We were telling the public that this was now a murder and potential witnesses that this was a criminal investigation, and they could feel safe about coming forward and giving us evidence."

At the time, several witnesses, among them Linda Carroll,

were said to have been reluctant to step forward out of fear of Tabish, who had been bragging about his ties to the Chicago mob.

"We weren't in any rush to arrest these people," Roger said. "When you're building a prosecutable murder case, you have to take it step by step and make sure that all of your ducks are in a row before you make any arrests. I wanted to close all of the loopholes in the case before the defense lawyers got involved."

Roger told reporters at the news conference that witnesses in the case had been "intimidated." Though he didn't name her, he was referring primarily to Carroll, the onetime cocktail waitress at Cheetah's.

Carroll was on Roger's mind several days earlier when he attended a court hearing in Missoula on whether to unseal the forty-four-page affidavit used to obtain the February search warrants. Roger had argued that if the affidavit was unsealed and disclosed to Tabish, it would undermine the investigation into Binion's death, but more important, it would compromise the safety of witnesses he said had been "hounded" by the suspects in the case. The contents of Carroll's secret conversations with Binion attorney Richard Wright, it turned out, had found their way into Buczek's affidavit.

"Affiant is aware that one person who is more familiar with Sandy Murphy than anyone else is Murphy's friend, Linda Carroll," Buczek wrote. "At the present time, affiant has been unable to obtain a formal statement from Carroll. Despite significant efforts by your affiant, I have been unable to dispel Carroll's fears of reprisal from Murphy and Tabish."

Buczek said Carroll, through Wright, had "provided investigators with leads that have almost always proved to be fruitful. Unfortunately, Wright has had little success in convincing Carroll to come forward and provide law enforcement with a full account of her knowledge about Ted Binion's death."

Murphy had talked to Carroll about her stormy relationship with Binion and her dislike for Bonnie Binion, Buczek wrote. She also told Carroll that she had maintained control over Binion by recording and listening to his telephone calls.

"At some point, Murphy disclosed that she was having an affair with Tabish," Buczek reported. "Murphy told Carroll that she purchased clothing items at Neiman Marcus for Tabish. Also, Murphy confided that she had gone on a trip to Southern California with Tabish and stayed at the Peninsula Hotel. Indeed, Carroll stated that Murphy possesses a photograph of herself and Tabish together in an affectionate pose.

"Carroll explained that Murphy and Tabish grew closer over time. In fact, Murphy stated, 'Rick is OK. We did something together that would turn your stomach and land us in jail.'"

Buczek said Carroll had told Wright that Tabish frequently stated in her presence that he "hated" Binion and wanted him dead.

"Moreover," Buczek wrote, "Carroll was aware that Tabish was experiencing significant financial difficulties. Prior to Binion's death, Tabish was desperately searching for an investor to contribute funds to his failing business. In fact, Carroll became friends with one of Tabish's potential investors. Even after Binion's death, Tabish continued to solicit the individual's financial support."

Buczek said Carroll had reported that Murphy occasionally discussed aspects of the Binion case with her.

"At one point, Murphy tried to influence Carroll by reminding her that Binion frequently slept on a mattress and a sleeping bag on the floor," he said. "Carroll stated that she knew that Murphy's statement was not true. At another time, Carroll and Murphy discussed reports that Binion was found to have a large quantity of heroin in his stomach contents. Murphy attempted to explain the results by claiming that Binion always licked the aluminum foil that he used to smoke heroin. Carroll found that statement to be comical."

Buczek said Tom Dillard had tried to take a tape-recorded statement from Carroll at her home in Southern California, but Carroll balked at the idea.

"Carroll explained that she felt Tabish was responsible for Binion's death and she feared retaliation," Buczek said.

Following a conversation with David Chesnoff, one of Murphy's attorneys, Carroll telephoned Wright to complain that Chesnoff had been rude to her, Buczek explained in the affidavit.

"She related that Chesnoff stated that if she was truly Murphy's friend, she should 'suck it up' and keep her mouth shut. Shortly thereafter, Murphy called Carroll and left a message on her answering machine. Murphy accused Carroll of perjuring herself for the reward. Carroll told Wright that she was unaware that a reward had been offered . . . Additionally, Carroll told Wright that she has retained a copy of a tape-recorded threat from Murphy and given it to her son for safekeeping."

Buczek added: "Murphy has used her best efforts to stifle Linda Carroll. Carroll told Wright that Murphy warned her that she should not talk to anyone except her attorneys, David Chesnoff and Oscar Goodman. Also, Carroll revealed that she met with Louis Palazzo, who is Tabish's attorney. Palazzo wanted Carroll to sign an affidavit stating that Jim Brown did not act professionally when he was present at the Binion house and that Murphy and Tabish did not have a sexual relationship and that Tabish stated, 'I'm going to Pahrump to save the silver.'

"Carroll refused to sign the affidavit stating that not all of the allegations were true. To this date, Carroll maintains that she knows more information about Binion's death, but has refused to come forward in fear of retaliation."

Several days after the hearing in Missoula, District Judge Doug Harkin issued an opinion declining to unseal Buczek's affidavit.

And one day after Flud's news conference in Las Vegas, investigators disclosed that they had issued a warrant to arrest Carroll as a material witness in the Binion murder investigation. Prosecutors had tried as early as late January to subpoena her to testify before the grand jury, but couldn't find her at her home in California.

"Linda Carroll's attorney, Chet Bennett, spoke with prosecutors and made arrangements to accompany Carroll to Las Vegas to provide a statement to authorities on two separate occasions," Buczek said in another affidavit. "Bennett and Carroll canceled both appointments."

Roger had been extremely anxious to gain Carroll's cooperation.

"We tried awfully hard to get her to come in voluntarily, but her attorney played games with us, and he played games with me," the prosecutor later said.

After word had surfaced publicly that authorities were looking to arrest Carroll, Bennett contacted Las Vegas reporters toward the end of March and promised to bring her to Las Vegas.

"I'm going to produce my client," he said. "I'm trying to get it resolved. I don't want to see her handcuffed, and I don't want to see her in jail."

But Roger and homicide detectives weren't taking any chances. They had asked the FBI's Criminal Apprehension Team (CAT), a ten-member task force that searches for fugitives, and the syndicated television show *America's Most Wanted* to join the nationwide hunt for Carroll.

"She has been elusive and uncooperative," Petersen told reporters. "At this point we don't want to resort to the use of a warrant, but it appears it's the only way we can gain her cooperation."

By the first week in April, after *America's Most Wanted* had shown a photo of the natural brunette to a national audience and asked for help in finding Carroll, talks to bring her in got serious.

Detectives, however, remained convinced that Carroll genuinely feared for her life.

Buczek said in his affidavit that one of Carroll's neighbors in Southern California, Mike Fisher, told a private investigator there that Carroll was saying she felt Binion had been murdered.

Fisher reported that Carroll had described Binion's death as "murder straightaway" and that she was worried that if she was placed in protective custody by police, "these people would kill her," Buczek wrote.

"That's exactly what she said over and over and over," Buczek quoted Fisher as saying. "That's what she was worried about."

Bennett, however, was telling a different story to reporters in Las Vegas. He insisted that Carroll was not concerned about her safety, and he accused Dillard and homicide detectives of harassing his client and putting her through hell.

At the same time, Murphy telephoned a *Las Vegas Sun* reporter and played the tape of a frantic phone message left by a crying Carroll. On the tape, Carroll complained about the way she was being treated by Las Vegas investigators, and she sought guidance from Murphy.

Finally, Bennett agreed to bring Carroll to Las Vegas to testify before the grand jury on April 15. But even then, Roger was skeptical.

Two days before her scheduled appearance, Roger said: "I'll be awaiting her arrival, but I'm not holding my breath. She's made plans to come to meet with me on two prior occasions, and I was stood up both times."

Roger also said he was still looking to arrest Carroll on the material-witness warrant.

"I'm not calling off the dogs," he said.

Bennett, however, said his client was "ready and willing" to voluntarily come to Las Vegas.

On the afternoon of April 15, Carroll and Bennett arrived outside the courthouse in style. Ten minutes before her scheduled appearance, Carroll, now a bleached blonde and wearing a cream-colored pantsuit, stepped out of a white limousine with Bennett and strolled past a crowd of reporters into the grand jury room. About the same time, Murphy and Tabish were seen driving in Tabish's black Mercedes a couple of blocks away. Roger kept Carroll at the grand jury for four hours straight, but her testimony turned out to be a bust for the prosecutor. She gave him nothing of evidentiary value.

"It was a farce," Roger said. "She claimed either ignorance or memory loss throughout the proceeding. I grilled her for four hours and all I got out of her was, 'I don't remember. I didn't say that to Richard Wright. I didn't say that to Tom Dillard. I didn't say that to Jim Buczek.' "

Transcripts of Carroll's testimony showed that she had trouble remembering the most significant aspects of Murphy's life, including her romance with Tabish.

Even some of the grand jurors questioned her lack of candor.

"You say you were very good friends with Sandy . . . and yet when you are questioned, you don't know anything," one panel member said. "You're very evasive. It leads us to believe that there's something wrong here."

Carroll, however, had no trouble talking about Binion's heroin problems at the time of his death.

"I don't think people understand the true drug addiction that Ted was experiencing—that he was in his own hell and he wanted help and wanted to get off of heroin, but was very embarrassed and, you know, didn't want anybody to know or see him in that condition," she told the grand jurors.

She testified that when she saw Binion a week before his death, he looked "extremely thin and sick."

The best thing Roger got out of her was an acknowledgment that she was "very frightened" about being perceived as a witness who could "roll over" on Murphy and Tabish.

After her testimony, Carroll told reporters she didn't believe Binion's death was suspicious. She said she didn't know how Binion had died, but she believed he was "extremely addicted" to heroin and prescription drugs.

Bennett said Carroll had come to the grand jury of her "own free will" and testified truthfully.

"She didn't come here to be on one side or the other," he said. "She has absolutely gone through hell. I wouldn't wish this on anybody."

Roger emerged from the grand jury room looking frustrated.

"I've known Roger a long time, and I've never seen him that upset," said Dillard, who had dropped by to get a glimpse of Carroll. "I don't know what she said inside the grand jury, but in my opinion, something didn't go right."

A couple of days later, Dillard publicly suggested Carroll had deliberately withheld information because of her fear of Murphy and Tabish.

"She has flatly said that Ted Binion was murdered and that she feared she would be killed if she testified against those responsible for his death," Dillard said.

Bennett later called Dillard a "lying SOB."

After Carroll and Bennett had left town, Roger checked their phone records at the New Frontier Hotel & Casino and found that telephone calls were made to Murphy and Tabish before and after Carroll's grand jury appearance. Roger also learned that almost immediately after Carroll had testified, she and Bennett went to a video-clipping service to request newsclips of her entering and leaving the grand jury room.

"I think she wanted her fifteen minutes of fame and glory," Roger said.

But if Carroll was a bust for Roger, Steven Kurt Gratzer, a childhood friend of Tabish's, turned out to be a gold mine.

Ironically, it was Tabish who inadvertently had led Roger and Buczek to Gratzer. In mid-March, while Roger was in court in Missoula arguing to keep the search-warrant affidavits sealed, Buczek, who had accompanied the prosecutor to the hearing, ran into a young man in the rest room at the courthouse.

"He said, 'Church's. You have to go to Church's jewelry store and ask about the coins,' " Buczek recalled.

Then, in a flash, the young man left the rest room. But after the hearing, Buczek and Roger went to the jewelry store and talked to its owner, Mike Church, who told them Gratzer had been talking about wanting to learn how to "move" gold and silver coins. Buczek and Roger knew then that they had stumbled onto something big. They asked sheriff's deputies there to take them to Gratzer's apartment. After identifying themselves, they knocked several times, but Gratzer refused to come out. Eventually, the lawmen returned to Las Vegas thinking they had come up empty-handed.

But a couple of days after Flud's pivotal news conference, Gratzer showed up at Roger's office with two lawyers at his side. He wanted to strike a deal. Roger obtained immunity for the onetime Army Ranger, and on March 19, Gratzer gave Buczek and his partner, Tom Thowsen, a stunning sixty-two-page statement.

Gratzer told detectives that Tabish first mentioned killing Binion during a meeting at Tabish's Missoula office in late August 1998. Tabish described Binion as a "monster" who needed to be eliminated.

"He wanted me to help him commit a murder of . . . Ted, a casino owner, and he explained to me how I'd be paid through insurance settlements of . . . the girlfriend of the casino owner," Gratzer told the detectives. "And he was going to steal the guy's money and silver and a lot of valuables he had in the house."

Gratzer said Tabish told him he was considering several ways to kill Binion.

One idea was to introduce Gratzer to Binion and let him show the Army veteran his handgun collection at his Las Vegas home.

"He'd be handing me a weapon, and [Tabish] suggested that I take one of these weapons and shoot Ted in the head," Gratzer said.

Tabish also suggested that Gratzer could act as a sniper and shoot Binion from afar at his ranch in Pahrump.

But Tabish was most interested in "staging a suicide by means of a drug overdose," Gratzer said. He discussed pumping Binion with heroin and Xanax, maybe forcing it down his throat with a tube. Tabish even asked Gratzer to research how much Xanax it would take to kill a person.

Sometime after Binion's death, Gratzer told the detectives, he ran into Tabish and Murphy in Missoula, and Tabish appeared to be acting as if he had gotten away with something.

Another time in Missoula, Gratzer asked Tabish how he had gone about "getting those chemicals down the guy's throat. "And he said to me, 'I'll tell you, Gratz, when I see you murder somebody. If I ever see you kill somebody.' "

A smiling Tabish then drove off in his pickup truck, Gratzer said, and yelled back, "Xanax, Xanax, Xanax."

Like Carroll, Gratzer also expressed fear of his childhood chum, who more than once had implied that he had ties to the Chicago mob.

"I don't want anything to happen to my family," Gratzer told Buczek and Thowsen. "I don't want anything to happen to me. I've been living in hiding for months, occasionally breaking out and . . . retreating back to my apartment and keeping my shades drawn at all times . . . and I'm not sleeping . . . life's been a living hell for me."

Buczek and Thowsen knew that Gratzer was not the most credible person. He had an alcohol problem and took prescription sedatives. He even had ripped off southern Nevada taxpayers during his brief stay by racking up a large long-distance phone bill at the hotel where investigators had put him up. For the most part, Gratzer had not accomplished much in life since washing out of the Rangers. Tabish, however, had looked out for him over the years, periodically giving him low-level jobs at his companies in Missoula.

"He probably was the craziest person Tabish knew, and Tabish took advantage of that," Buczek said. "Who else could Tabish trust to help him murder somebody?"

Despite Gratzer's downside, Buczek and Thowsen were excited about what he had told them. They knew they would need to corroborate his statement, so they flew to Missoula the next week to question several of his friends. Once more, they came back with pay dirt. Several witnesses confirmed that Gratzer had spoken about the Binion murder plot with them before the story had hit the newspapers.

But the investigation was about to take another bizarre turn.

While Buczek and Thowsen were in Montana, Roger and Dillard flew to Southern California to meet with officials from Rubber Technology International, which had purchased MRT Transportation of Nevada and the rights to the Jean, Nevada, sand pit in November 1998.

"They had reams of documents there," Roger said. "I wanted to get a handle on Rick Tabish's financial situation."

Roger and Dillard talked to Fred Schmidt, RTI's chief financial officer, as well as Michael Wells, the company's attorney. Wells told Roger about a conversation he had with Tabish during the negotiations regarding Leo Casey's role in the Jean sand pit. Tabish had told Wells not to worry about Casey because no one would hear from him again.

That piqued Roger's interest.

"I wondered, is he dead?" Roger said. "I thought this murder investigation was going to turn into a double murder. I wanted to find Leo Casey."

Before leaving, Roger and Dillard were able to get word to Casey through the sister of his girlfriend. The next day, Casey's Las Vegas lawyer, Kirby Wells, telephoned Roger at his office and told him that Casey was in hiding, but alive and well. A date for homicide detectives to interview Casey was then set up.

Several days after Buczek and Thowsen returned from Missoula, they were sent back on the road to Southern California to meet Casey at a hotel near an airport. On March 30, they obtained a statement from Casey, laying out the kidnapping plot against him. Casey also told detectives about statements Tabish had made to him, bragging that he was going to kill Binion and steal his silver.

The investigation now was gaining momentum.

On April 8, Roger decided to put more pressure on Mattsen. His wife, Thressa was summoned to the grand jury to testify about the entries in her diary. David Mattsen accompanied his wife to the grand jury room and waited outside as she testified. Before she went before the panel, the couple chastised homicide detectives for seizing Thressa's diary during the March 9 search at their trailer home.

But inside the grand jury, Thressa wasn't shy about linking her husband to Tabish.

"Did there come a point in time when your husband received some cash from Sandra Murphy?" Roger asked.

"Yes," she responded. "He told me he went and picked up some cash from her. She said she sold her car and felt sorry for us. That's what David told me."

"How much cash did your husband come back with?" Roger asked.

"One thousand dollars," she said.

Thressa Mattsen also confirmed that Tabish had given her husband a new truck and had put him on MRT's payroll, even though her husband had never done any actual work for the company.

Roger also asked Thressa to explain an entry in her diary that indicated, from her talks with Murphy, that Murphy might have played a role in Binion's death.

"I didn't see no remorse, no hurt," Thressa told the grand jurors. "When somebody you love dies, you hurt. And I didn't see any with Sandy."

Throughout the investigation, Roger later said, Murphy was acting as if she didn't have a care in the world.

"From the information I was receiving, Sandy was just a bubbly gal who thought that she'd get away with murder," he said. "It wasn't until after we arrested her that I saw a change."

On May 14, as investigators were closing in on the suspects, Murphy kept up the facade. Even though she had earlier taken the Fifth Amendment when asked on the witness stand about Binion's missing valuables, Murphy let it be known that she wanted more from his estate. She filed a palimony suit seeking $2 million for what she claimed were "unique and extraordinary services" she had provided Binion while living with him.

Murphy said in the suit that she had helped Binion with his "personal, family, social, civic and business activities until his death." She insisted that she had "sacrificed her own personal and financial interests in carrying out" those services.

Binion's lawyers and family members were outraged when they were served with the suit.

"She just is incapable of suppressing her true motives," Wright said. "This lawsuit speaks eloquently to her character."

The criminal investigation, on the other hand, seemed to be taking its toll on Tabish.

"He was having major problems with his ulcers, and he was sucking down Maalox by the bottle," Roger said. "He was very stressed about this. He didn't know what we had, but he knew we were getting closer to him."

Tabish continued to have financial problems, and because of his affair with Murphy, he was forced to try extra hard to keep his family together.

"He also had to keep Sandy real close, too, because if she turned on him, he'd be in deep trouble," Roger said.

As the month of June approached, Roger began putting together the finishing touches on a massive affidavit that would be used to persuade a judge to issue warrants for the arrests of Murphy and Tabish. The affidavit was a compilation of all of the physical evidence that had been obtained and of all the witnesses who had been interviewed over the past nine months.

But even knowing the vast amount of circumstantial evidence that had been accumulated, District Attorney Stewart Bell remained cautious when pressed by reporters to discuss the status of the investigation.

"I don't know whether we'll ever be in a position to file

charges or not," Bell said. "We cannot file charges unless we ethically have an abiding conviction in the truth of the charges, and that means we feel we can prove the charges beyond a reasonable doubt."

Bell acknowledged the case was circumstantial, and he called it "as complex as any case we've had since I've been here."

But he added, "We don't feel like we're spinning our wheels. We're making progress in eventually solving this puzzle."

PART

III

The Arrests

CHAPTER 21

● ● ● ● ● ● ● ● ● ● ● ● ● ● ● ● ● ● ● ●

Busted

● ● ● ● ● ● ● ● ● ● ● ● ● ● ● ● ● ● ● ●

SANDY MURPHY AND Rick Tabish, perhaps sensing that authorities were getting closer to charging them in Ted Binion's death, headed into June with new criminal defense lawyers.

Murphy's attorneys, Oscar Goodman and David Chesnoff, and Tabish's lawyer, Louis Palazzo, had all withdrawn at the end of May. As investigators were turning up the heat, Goodman and Chesnoff decided that it was becoming more and more difficult for them to defend someone accused of killing Binion. Like many other fine lawyers in Las Vegas, Goodman and Chesnoff had been close to Binion for years. Goodman also was locked in the middle of a heated campaign for mayor of Las Vegas. Polls were showing that despite his reputation for defending mobsters and other nefarious characters, Goodman was in the lead. He won the race the first week in June.

Murphy ended up hiring William Terry, a former Goodman partner, and Tabish brought in Steve Wolfson, an ex-federal prosecutor. Both lawyers, with their booming courtroom voices, were regarded as two of the best at getting a client through a preliminary hearing, which was what courthouse insiders were saying Murphy and Tabish were likely to be facing soon.

It had become clear that David Roger was not looking to

indict Murphy and Tabish, but rather, to arrest them on a criminal complaint. Preliminary hearings are conducted after a complaint is filed to determine whether there is enough evidence to force a defendant to stand trial on the charges. The standard of proof favors prosecutors, so generally they play their cards close to the vest, presenting just enough evidence to persuade a justice of the peace to bind over a defendant. But sometimes defense lawyers adept at this kind of proceeding can force a prosecutor to reveal more about his case than he wants to. And that can become invaluable as a defendant prepares for trial. With the homicide task force pressing ahead and public opinion going against them, Murphy and Tabish knew they needed all the help they could get.

Almost immediately after Terry and Wolfson were hired, the Murphy-Tabish camp put the word out that famed Harvard University lawyer Alan Dershowitz had agreed to join their defense team. He supposedly had been given a handsome retainer to associate himself with the case. But Dershowitz, who was part of O. J. Simpson's "dream team," ducked calls from reporters and never confirmed whether he had been hired.

About the same time, Lieutenant Wayne Petersen acknowledged that the decision on whether to file charges against Murphy and Tabish was now in the hands of the district attorney's office.

"They have all of the documentation we've gathered so far," Petersen said. "There's an incredible amount of paperwork."

The buzz at the courthouse was that arrests were imminent.

Following a June 11 probate hearing before District Judge Michael Cherry, the pressure seemed to be getting to Murphy. With reporters all around her, a crying Murphy ran up to Binion lawyer Harry Claiborne in the hallway and repeatedly asked him why he had never bothered to help what she described as a "very sick" Binion in the weeks before his death. Claiborne appeared to be taken aback. But he said little to Murphy as she continued to berate him while he walked to the fourth-floor elevator to leave the courthouse. Murphy remained behind with her lawyers.

Inside the elevator, Claiborne said he never knew Binion was sick and that he had been out of town, as he usually was each summer, in the months before Binion's death. He also accused Murphy of putting out disinformation.

"This is a big act," he said. "She's trying to plant a seed that Ted was really sick and not murdered."

At the hearing, Binion estate lawyer Bruce Judd urged Cherry to allow him to take the depositions of officials at the Peninsula and Beverly Hills hotels as part of the estate's efforts to prove that Murphy and Tabish were romantically involved at the time of Binion's death and had plotted to steal his assets.

Murphy's civil lawyers pressed Cherry to allow their client back into Binion's home, which they continued to insist had been willed to her. But with all of the speculation about the imminent arrests, Cherry delayed the hearing another two weeks until June 25.

That was Roger's cue to get moving.

By the last week in June, Roger's boss, District Attorney Stewart Bell, had signed off on a 109-page affidavit Roger and Detective James Buczek had put together to obtain arrest warrants for Murphy and Tabish.

"As we got close," Bell said, "we wanted them together in Las Vegas. So we decided we wouldn't get the warrant and pounce on them until we knew they both were here."

Added Roger: "I didn't want to do two different preliminary hearings. If we screwed up and caught Sandy down here and Rick up in Montana, he could have tied us up for months fighting extradition."

Roger suspected that Tabish, who still was commuting back and forth between Missoula and Las Vegas, would want to be here for the June 25 hearing on the outside chance the judge would give Murphy permission to move back into Binion's house. Tabish knew Murphy would need help moving in.

On Thursday, June 24, the police department's surveillance squad was quietly given orders to start looking for Murphy and Tabish. Roger, meanwhile, went to Justice of the Peace Jennifer Togliatti with the massive affidavit to get the arrest warrants.

Bell said the plan was to arrest the two on the steps of the courthouse prior to the probate hearing the next day.

But by early evening on June 24, the surveillance squad had located the two suspects going into the Smith's Food King near their Henderson apartment. The squad telephoned Buczek and his partner, Tom Thowsen, who jumped in their cars and sped to the parking lot of the grocery store. Murphy and Tabish were taken into custody before they had gotten to the cash register. Buczek escorted a handcuffed Tabish to his car, and Thowsen took Murphy to his vehicle.

"They weren't surprised one bit," Buczek explained. "They said, 'We heard you were going to arrest us. Our attorneys told us it was going to happen last week.'"

Tabish, remembering his brief chat with Buczek at the apartment in February when the search warrants were executed, struck up a friendly conversation with the detective.

"I'm glad you're investigating this," Tabish told Buczek. "I know you'll do a thorough job. It's Tom Dillard I can't stand. I don't trust him."

Buczek recalled that even then, Tabish was a smooth talker, offering to buy him a beer at his favorite watering hole in Missoula the next time the detective visited his hometown.

"He said he was going to beat this," Buczek said. "He wanted to make this go away and the only way to do that was to go to trial."

Buczek and Thowsen transported the two murder suspects back to the Clark County Detention Center, about ten miles away in downtown Las Vegas, where they were booked on no bail. Reporters were waiting as Murphy and Tabish were escorted inside the jail without saying a word. Sketchy details of the arrests topped the evening news.

Detectives also rounded up four other suspects charged with related crimes in an eleven-count complaint. Charged with Murphy and Tabish in the theft of Binion's Pahrump silver fortune were Binion's ranch manager David Mattsen and Tabish employee Michael Milot. Two other men, California banker John Joseph and Las Vegas contractor Steven Wadkins, were charged with Tabish in the torture-kidnapping of Leo Casey. Tabish was named in all eleven counts, which included charges of murder with a deadly weapon, conspiracy to commit murder, and theft involving the removal of the Pahrump silver and items taken from Binion's Las Vegas home after his death. Murphy was given a pass on the five charges relating to the Casey kidnapping, but she was named in the other six counts involving Binion's death.

That evening, the *Las Vegas Sun* was the first news organization to obtain the 109-page affidavit signed by Buczek that methodically laid out the criminal case against Murphy and Tabish. The next day, the newspaper ran a series of stories disclosing for the first time the intimate details of the nine-month investigation. The affidavit explained the police theory that the death scene at Binion's home had been made to look like a self-induced overdose.

"It is affiant's considered opinion that the scene depicting Ted Binion's death was staged," Buczek wrote. "It is clear to affiant that Ted Binion's killers positioned Binion's body in a manner that is inconsistent with the way decedents are normally found in similar situations."

Buczek also made it clear that he was convinced Binion's accused killers had forced him to ingest heroin and Xanax and that Tabish was the brains behind the murder scheme. Incriminating statements taken from Steven Kurt Gratzer and Leo Casey, who talked about Tabish's plans to kill Binion, were included in the affidavit, as well as statements from other witnesses who recalled that a week before his death, Murphy had predicted Binion would succumb to an overdose.

Tom Dillard, who by now had done interviews with

dozens of witnesses himself, also subscribed to Buczek's theory.

"The evidence certainly suggests that Tabish was the driving force to secure Ted's fortune," he told the *Las Vegas Sun.* "Tabish tried to sweet-talk Ted out of his money, swindle him out of his money and neither method worked. And now Ted is dead."

News of the arrests brought relief from Binion's sister Becky Behnen, one of the first to suspect foul play.

"I feel like a great deal of weight has been taken off my shoulders," Behnen said the next day. "I'm not surprised by this. From the moment I heard about his death and the circumstances surrounding his death, I've always felt it was a homicide."

Petersen, who had been badgered by reporters on a daily basis for nine months about the case, also was in good spirits the day after the arrests.

"No one incident brought us to this point today," he said. "It was a culmination of months of work on a complex case. The file for this case is the largest in the office and the biggest I've ever seen in over two years since I joined homicide."

Petersen praised the work of Buczek, Thowsen and their supervisor, Sergeant Ken Hefner.

"It means something for the officers to be able to go down, put the handcuffs on and make an arrest after so much work," he said.

Murphy and Tabish kept their mouths shut about the charges in jail over the weekend, but they scrambled with their lawyers to come up with a strategy to persuade Jennifer Togliatti to grant them bail.

The following Monday, Roger said he would oppose bail for both defendants at the next day's bail hearing. But Togliatti refused to take any action at the hearing, putting off a bail decision for another week. Murphy and Tabish were escorted into the hearing in chains and navy jail garb. Tabish kept a straight face throughout the forty-five-minute proceeding, but Murphy often smiled at friends and relatives in the crowded courtroom gallery. She once mouthed the words "I love you" to her brother, Michael. The two defendants were forced to spend another weekend in jail, this time over the Fourth of July holiday.

On July 8, a shackled Murphy and Tabish were brought back to Togliatti's court for more discussion about their bail. Murphy wasn't smiling this time. Looking haggard, possibly from the toll of spending two weeks in jail, she cried throughout the hearing as lawyers for both defendants stepped up attacks on the prosecution. Both William Terry and Steve Wolfson asked Togliatti to release their clients on $100,000 bail.

Terry described Murphy as someone who "babied" and cared for Binion.

"He was a heroin addict," Terry told Togliatti. "Is this a big surprise?"

Wolfson argued the prosecution's case wasn't as strong as police were contending, and he insisted that Murphy and Tabish weren't having an affair and even stayed at a posh Beverly Hills hotel the weekend before Binion's death with his permission.

Prosecutors, however, continued to push for no bond, saying both Murphy and Tabish had little ties to the community and were flight risks. They also pointed to Tabish's lengthy criminal history in Montana.

At the close of the hearing, Togliatti refused to grant bail for Tabish, calling him a danger to the community. But she agreed to allow Murphy to post a $300,000 bond on the condition that she submit to house arrest with electronic monitoring, surrender her passport and have no contact with any of the witnesses or other defendants in the case. Murphy was eager to post bail. She already had found another benefactor, William Fuller, an eighty-four-year-old Irish-born mining executive worth millions whom she had met several months earlier while dining at her favorite gourmet restaurant, the Aristocrat.

One day after granting Murphy bail, Togliatti, at Roger's

request, held another hearing to determine the source of the funds that were going to be put up. Prosecutors, aware that cash and other valuables were still missing from Binion's house, wanted to be sure that the bail being posted was not coming from any money stolen from Binion. Fuller, whom Togliatti described as a "good Samaritan," took the witness stand at the hearing. Togliatti earlier had instructed photographers to respect his privacy and not take his picture. The redheaded Fuller, who had trouble hearing and spoke softly in a thick Irish accent, testified that he held dual citizenship in Ireland and the United States. He said he owned a mining company in southern Nevada and previously had given Murphy "pocket money," as well as $125,000 to pay her former lawyers. The $300,000, he said, was wired by his lawyer from a bank in Dublin to the Bank of America in Las Vegas. The cash was part of proceeds of the 1997 sale of the well-known Castle Hotel in Ballybunion, a resort town in southwest Ireland, he said.

Fuller testified that he was helping Murphy because she was a "nice person" and that he believed in her innocence.

Following the hearing, Togliatti said she was satisfied that the source of the bail money was legitimate, and the next day, Terry posted the $300,000 on Murphy's behalf. Murphy, however, remained at the detention center until July 16, while jail officials worked out arrangements for her house arrest. Once released, she returned to her Henderson apartment, where officials had installed the monitoring equipment.

In the meantime, Fuller's involvement in the case had attracted the interest of the Irish tabloids, which published stories recalling his legendary days on the Irish show-business scene in the 1960s and 1970s. It turned out that he also had worked with famed San Francisco rock promoter Bill Graham in the 1970s and had brought a number of well-known Irish entertainers to the United States. One of the groups, Brendan Boyer and his Royal Irish Show Band, had been a mainstay in Las Vegas showrooms for years.

While Murphy was battling for her release, prosecutors

received their first post-arrest break in the case. Two days before Murphy was set free, her good friend Tanya Cropp, once considered part of her inner circle, had decided to cooperate and give a statement to homicide detectives.

Cropp had fallen into the hands of detectives following a tip two weeks earlier from Becky Behnen. At 5:40 P.M. on June 29, Cropp's former roommate, Jeannine Pierce, a thirty-one-year-old secretary, telephoned Behnen's secretary, Lynn Saladino, at the Horseshoe Club, saying she had a list of coins "that would help" Behnen. Pierce, who did not identify herself, was told that Behnen had already left for the evening, and she was asked to call back the next day. Pierce also had told Saladino that she had a suitcase that belonged to Cropp that contained antique guns Binion was known to collect.

"She was really worried," Saladino wrote in a memo to Behnen. "She said she had heard 'a lot of conversations.' "

On June 30, a calmer Pierce turned over the handwritten list to Behnen, who promptly gave it to Roger. While the prosecutor was at Behnen's office picking up the list, Pierce called again.

"I started giving her hand signals telling her what to say, and Becky gets the gal to meet with us," Roger said.

Pierce ended up meeting with Roger and Buczek at a local tavern, where she explained that she had been keeping the list of coins for Cropp, who had gotten it from Murphy. A couple of days later, on July 6, Pierce turned over the suitcase and gave a formal statement to Buczek.

The seven-page list was big for investigators because it was the first real evidence that linked Murphy to items that could have been stolen from Binion. Roger believed the coins on the list, which included circulated and uncirculated silver dollars dating back to 1878 and proofs of half-dollars and quarters from the 1950s and 1960s, had been taken from Binion's safe.

Pierce, it turned out, had provided investigators with another piece of important evidence. Along with the list was a fax cover sheet with a telephone number that came back to Tabish's office in Missoula. That tied Tabish to the theft.

On July 14, Buczek and Thowsen took a stab at interviewing Cropp, who they believed had not been truthful about her knowledge of Binion's death in testimony before the grand jury and in three separate interviews with Dillard.

"She started lying to them, and they pulled out the list, and that's when she laid it out and became friends with us," Roger said. "She never asked for immunity, and I never made her any promises. She was just happy to come clean. After that, she left the state to live with her mother, and she turned her life around."

Cropp told Buczek and Thowsen that Murphy had given her the list about a week after Binion's death at the home of William Knudson, where Murphy had taken up temporary residence. At the time, Cropp, who had lost her job with Binion when he died, had just accepted a job working for Knudson. She said she took the list home with her, and several weeks later, on November 1, Murphy asked her to fax the list to Tabish in Montana.

Cropp then said something that drew smiles to the faces of the detectives. Pierce had reported that Murphy had gotten an abortion in late March of 1999, and Cropp seemed to confirm it. If true, the detectives surmised, Murphy's pregnancy likely was a result of her relationship with Tabish. It was more evidence of their much-denied romance.

"She said that she had to take care of something—had to have some procedure done and she wanted Rick to go with her," Cropp told the detectives. "And I saw her prior to that, and she looked pregnant to me. She had gained a bunch of weight in a very short amount of time, and in my mind, I figured that she was gonna go have an abortion. And she was having Rick go with her, so that just kind of confirmed it to me."

Murphy, Cropp said, first confided in her that she was having an affair with Tabish in August 1998, about a month before Binion's death.

"She had mentioned that she was not getting any sex from

Ted and that she'd gone out and found a significant other named Rick," Cropp said. "I didn't know him at the time, and I didn't know his last name."

Later, Cropp said, Murphy told her that she was afraid of Tabish and that, like Binion, Tabish often beat Murphy.

"She would call me and say that she got her punishment last night," Cropp said. "And I asked her what she meant by punishment, and she'd say Rick would beat her up, you know, hit her or whatever, throw her around and that kind of stuff."

"How many times would you get those telephone calls?" Buczek asked.

"I think I got like only two or three of them," she responded. "It wasn't like a lot. Not like it used to be with Ted."

"And when she would get beat up by Ted, how would she refer to that?"

"Punishment. She always for some reason referred to her being beaten up as punishment. It was her punishment. For what I don't know. But it was her punishment."

"When she would call you up after these punishment sessions with Rick, did you ever see her afterwards?"

"No. She wouldn't let me see her."

Cropp told the detectives that she suggested Murphy get out of the relationship with Tabish.

"What would she say then?" Buczek asked.

"Oh, but I love him so much and, you know, he's such a good guy and, you know, bullshit," Cropp replied.

Buczek asked Cropp if she had ever discussed with Murphy whether Murphy had gone to the Peninsula Hotel in Beverly Hills the weekend before Binion's death.

"Yes," Cropp said. "I read that in the newspaper. And I confronted her with it, and she told me that was a lie—that she'd gone to California for her nephew's birthday party and that Rick was never there."

Cropp added that Murphy accused investigators of "making up" the hotel story to use against her. But Cropp said she didn't believe her friend.

Cropp also said Murphy hated Tabish's wife, Mary Jo, and went out of her way to cause problems for her.

"Do you know if Mary Jo was aware of Rick and Sandy having a relationship?" Buczek asked.

"If she didn't know, she was stupid," Cropp responded. "I'm sure it was apparent, because Sandy used to call Rick all the time when Rick was in Montana, and Rick would have Mary Jo sitting right next to him."

Murphy, Cropp said, even used to stay at Tabish's home in Montana. She said Murphy often told her that Tabish planned to get a divorce from his wife.

Cropp also provided Buczek and Thowsen with the key to some of the most damning evidence of all against Murphy. She said she once asked Murphy about talk around town that Murphy had poisoned Binion.

"She said, 'Well, it's kind of funny. They didn't even take the wineglass. If I supposedly poisoned him, they would have taken it.' "

Investigators had hit pay dirt again.

Unknown to Cropp, Roger and Buczek had previously reviewed the twenty-minute videotape of Murphy touring Binion's home the day after his death. Murphy had been resisting turning over the tape, but District Judge Michael Cherry had ordered her to give it to the lawyers for Binion's estate. Roger had obtained a copy from the lawyers with a subpoena. About midway through the tape, Roger and Buczek saw Murphy take what appeared to be a wineglass from an island countertop and put it in her black shoulder bag.

"We could see very clearly that she had taken something from the counter and put it in her bag," Roger said. "After watching it a couple of more times, we could see the glimmer of the light on the glass."

Roger took the tape to Tom McCracken, a video surveillance expert at the Stratosphere Hotel & Tower. McCracken made a slow-motion version of the tape that clearly showed Murphy taking the glass.

The prosecutor was ecstatic. He was convinced that the glass was used to give Binion a fatal cocktail of heroin or Xanax, or both. Roger knew that even if Murphy had destroyed the glass, the video showing her removing it from the kitchen would provide dramatic evidence at the upcoming August 17 preliminary hearing on whether to bind over Murphy and Tabish for trial. This was the same tape that showed a greedy Murphy callously walking past the death scene in the den, looking to grab whatever material possessions she could. Now detectives had Cropp to corroborate the tape in court.

Cropp also told Buczek and Thowsen that Murphy was concerned that Linda Carroll might be talking to investigators.

"She said that she was worried that Linda was gonna open her mouth, and she would have to go take care of her," Cropp said.

Murphy never explained what she was going to do with Carroll, but Cropp said Murphy went to see her in California a couple of days later. The visit occurred before Carroll testified before the grand jury.

Cropp also acknowledged that Murphy and Tabish had pressured her into giving false statements to Dillard and the grand jury and that they had promised to buy her a new car for her help.

"Why don't we clarify why it is you made those false statements and why you're telling us everything and telling us the truth today?" Thowsen asked. "What has changed?"

"I was scared of Rick, and now Rick can't hurt me," Cropp said. "He's in jail."

CHAPTER 22

••••••••••••••••••

A Media Bonanza

••••••••••••••••••

JULY WAS A big month for the *Las Vegas Sun* in its leading coverage of the Binion murder investigation.

The newspaper had obtained hundreds of pages of documents, mostly transcripts of interviews that investigators had done with witnesses, shedding new light on the most-watched story in Las Vegas. Every day for more than a month leading into the August 17 preliminary hearing of Sandy Murphy and Rick Tabish, the paper ran exclusive Page One stories taking its readers inside the much-talked-about probe. The *Sun's* coverage was coordinated by Managing Editor Michael J. Kelley and Metro Editor Warren Johnston, who early in the investigation recognized the importance of the story to the Las Vegas community.

Among the documents obtained by the newspaper were the autopsy and toxicology reports that suggested Ted Binion had lethal levels of Xanax and heroin in his system at the time of his death. The autopsy report, written by Chief Medical Examiner Lary Simms, further suggested that Binion might have been forced by his killers to drink a fatal cocktail of drugs. Simms had come to that conclusion after finding no particles of food, chunks of heroin or undigested tablets of Xanax in Binion's stomach. All that was present were forty milliliters of what Simms described as a "gray-brown fluid," which later was identified as heroin and Xanax.

In the autopsy report, Simms included a brief synopsis of his October 15, 1998, visit to the death scene at Binion's home. He said he was intrigued by a trail of droplets leading to the den, where Binion's body had been discovered.

As he entered the den from the dining room, Simms said, he noticed "a number of dried drops in the carpeting of apparent gastric contents-like fluid. The drops were arranged in a line stopping in the area where the body was found."

Included in the autopsy papers was a report from Dr. Ellen Clarke, the Reno pathologist whom Coroner Ron Flud had hired to review his medical examiner's findings. Clarke backed up Simms all the way.

"Abrasions and excoriations on the decedent's face are consistent with the face having been vigorously rubbed or cleaned prior to initial viewing of the body by death investigation personnel," she wrote. "Based upon observations that the body and death scene were tampered with, that the drugs which killed Mr. Binion were ingested in atypical fashion . . . it is my opinion that another person or persons were involved in the death of . . . Binion. The manner of death is therefore determined to be homicide."

The *Sun* also reported that it had obtained a twenty-one-page transcript of a February 1999 interview that Binion's longtime heroin supplier, Peter Sheridan, had given homicide detectives. Sheridan, himself a heroin addict, disclosed in the interview that he had sold Binion twelve balloons of crude tar heroin the night before his death. Sheridan told James Buczek and Tom Thowsen that he had been selling Binion heroin three times a week for the last several months of his life. Binion, he said, usually smoked two to three balloons a day, but that night he wanted more than his usual supply because he was planning to spend several days horseback riding at his ranch.

That same month, the *Sun* pieced together another part of the puzzle for its readers. It printed a story detailing an October 1, 1998, interview that Binion's neighbor and physician, Enrique Lacayo, had given Tom Dillard. The seventeen-page transcript of that interview provided new insight into Binion's state of mind prior to his death.

Lacayo said Binion had asked him for a prescription for Xanax the morning before he died, to relieve symptoms of stress brought on by the visit of then Las Vegas Mayor Jan Laverty Jones.

The physician explained that he had prescribed Xanax for Binion in the past, but regretted this one, knowing that it might have somehow contributed to his death.

"I feel bad . . . badly after what happened," Lacayo said. "I have to think that maybe, if I said no . . . you know . . ."

Dillard then interrupted: "I'm not sure it would have made a difference."

"Exactly," Lacayo responded.

The *Sun* also provided its readers in July with more depth to Murphy's relationship with Binion and his family. It published details of an interview Bonnie Binion had given Dillard, as well as the interview his ex-wife, Doris, had provided Buczek.

Bonnie told Dillard that Murphy was jealous of her relationship with Binion and tried to turn her father against her. She described an incident in front of her father in which Murphy was "ranting and raving" about "how she didn't want that little bitch in her house.

"She just, at that point, really wasn't that mentally stable, and she had gotten kind of crazed," Bonnie reported. "I think it was easier for her when my dad and I weren't getting along."

Bonnie also said Murphy would "play silly little games" to turn her friends against her.

"She would have my friends over, and she would tell them horrible things about me," Bonnie said. "I would come home and there were all kinds of rumors and crazy things."

In a fit of anger toward Murphy, Bonnie said, she once broke into Murphy's bedroom, stole her clothes and "distributed" them to her friends. She said she later regretted doing that because it led to a further deterioration of her relationship with her father's girlfriend.

Things had gotten so bad between the women in November 1997 that Murphy once pulled out a weapon and threatened to shoot Bonnie and her father, Bonnie said.

During the month of July 1999, the *Sun* also disclosed that Tanya Cropp had agreed to cooperate against Murphy, and it printed details of Murphy's $2 million palimony suit against Binion's estate. And the newspaper was the first to view and report about the September 18 videotape that showed Murphy touring Binion's home.

As the *Sun* continued to come up with exclusives, other reporters, feeling heat from their editors, worked behind the scenes to find the paper's sources. Prosecutors, defense lawyers, even Dillard, were all peppered with questions in hopes of uncovering the same information. No other news organization, however, was able to obtain the documents.

But as the preliminary hearing approached, the rest of the media were about to get a chance to hear the sensational story firsthand with everyone else in Las Vegas.

Just days before the much-anticipated hearing, prosecutors threw a wrench into the defense. On August 14, they filed five new criminal charges against Murphy, linking her to the torture of Leo Casey.

David Roger, it turned out, had stumbled onto information that formed the basis for the new charges. While prepping Binion's housekeeper, Mary Montoya-Gascoigne, for her preliminary-hearing testimony a week earlier, Roger learned that she had seen Murphy with Binion's thumb cuffs several weeks prior to the Casey incident. Roger suspected Murphy had supplied Tabish with the thumb cuffs that were used to restrain Casey.

On August 16, the day before the hearing, Montoya-Gascoigne told the *Sun* that Murphy had told her in July 1998 that she was going to "lend" the restraints to a friend to get some money back.

Justice of the Peace Jennifer Togliatti accepted the new charges above the vigorous objections of Murphy's lawyer, William Terry.

Togliatti, a former prosecutor in the district attorney's office who had been elected to the bench only several months earlier, also denied a request from Murphy's lawyer, Steve Wolfson, to bar the media from the preliminary hearing, which was expected to last three weeks. Las Vegas One, an all-news channel, was planning to air gavel-to-gavel coverage of the hearing, the first time ever for such a proceeding.

Roger went into the hearing prepared to call as many as thirty witnesses, including Bonnie Binion. He had a partner now, Chief Deputy District Attorney David Wall, who, like Roger, approached the case in a straightforward, methodical manner.

At thirty-nine, Wall had handled numerous murder cases from both sides, as a member of the district attorney's Major Violators Unit and, previously, as part of the county public defender's capital murder team. He had a penchant for heading into a case well prepared, and he was quick on his feet. Wall had drawn the assignment of questioning the important medical witnesses. He also had agreed to handle the potentially troublesome witness, Steven Kurt Gratzer.

When the hearing got under way amid the media hype, the public did not have a flattering impression of Murphy and Tabish. There still were many who thought the two outsiders had been set up, but the vast majority of Las Vegans had little trouble coming to the conclusion that Murphy and Tabish had killed Binion. Defense lawyers, without naming the newspaper, would later chastise the *Las Vegas Sun* for its relentless coverage, much of which they felt had the effect of hurting their clients.

Murphy's negative persona, however, was measured in part by her own actions. On the first day of the hearing, she was observed smiling and flitting around in her designer clothes as if she were hosting an ice-cream social. She showed up in court having spray-painted her electronic ankle bracelet beige to match the color of her outfit. The next morning, the bracelet and Murphy's slim legs made the front page of the *Las Vegas Review-Journal*. The accompanying story did little to dissuade the arrogant, spoiled image Murphy had displayed in court. It also got her off on the wrong foot with jail officials keeping tabs of her whereabouts on house arrest. She ended up having to pay the county $300 for the cost of removing the paint on the black monitoring device.

Tabish approached the hearing with a much different attitude. It was obvious the pressure of the investigation had taken its toll on him. Dressed in his navy blue jail garb, Tabish was quiet and more serious-looking. He appeared to have lost as much as forty pounds off his six-foot, 220-pound frame.

"He conducted himself the way a defense attorney would like a client to conduct himself," Wall said. "He looked intelligent. He looked interested. He wasn't overly emotional."

Tabish was the complete opposite of the flippant Murphy, who wore a different expensive outfit to court each day. Though she was under house arrest, Murphy could come and go as she pleased during the hearing. She often chatted with reporters, friends and family members during breaks, and she would have her lunches catered from her favorite gourmet restaurant, the Aristocrat, which was a couple of blocks from Binion's home.

Throughout the three weeks of the hearing, Murphy also was more animated, frequently whispering in Terry's ear and writing him notes as witnesses testified.

Roger said she appeared out of control to him.

"She was constantly talking," he said. "She was going on and on. There was a point in the hearing when I had just had enough. I was trying to either make an argument or question a witness, and I finally turned to Sandy and said: 'Can you pipe down, please?' And she of course was startled that I had said anything to her. It was just typical Sandy.

"She was out of custody. She thought that this was just a big game. She didn't have to go sit in jail like Rick Tabish."

Wall had a similar opinion.

"Sitting three feet from her, there were times when I was distracted by her talking and whispering," he said. "Tabish chose to maintain some respect and decorum in court. She chose to act."

CHAPTER 23

. . . .

A Change of Theory

. . . .

A COUPLE OF days before the preliminary hearing, prosecutors David Roger and David Wall sat down with Lary Simms to prepare the chief medical examiner for his upcoming testimony.

Simms, who performed the autopsy on Ted Binion's body, had concluded that the former casino boss died of lethal levels of heroin and Xanax. The prevailing theory was that Binion was forced to drink a deadly cocktail of the drugs.

"In that interview, he told us there was a chance the heroin did not go down his throat," Roger said. "It completely threw me for a loop. The impression I had, whether it was the result of tunnel vision or not, was that someone had put it down his throat. But Simms told us it was possible to have that much heroin in his stomach by smoking the heroin.

"I didn't like what I was hearing, and I knew we needed Michael Baden after that. I told Tom Dillard to get Baden out here now. "

Baden, a fatherly, professorial-like man who had been a medical expert in some of the nation's biggest murder cases, was the world's foremost expert on heroin deaths. He had done more than 20,000 autopsies over his forty-year career as a forensic pathologist. As many as 1,000 of those examinations were heroin-related, primarily during his days as New York City's chief pathologist.

Though chief of forensic sciences for the New York State Police, Baden had been spending much of his time testifying in criminal cases across the country, writing best-selling books on his trade and hosting an HBO series, *Autopsy*.

Baden had been a defense consultant during the O. J. Simpson murder trial, even once suggesting that more than one person could have killed Simpson's wife, Nicole Brown Simpson, and her friend, Ronald Goldman.

In her book, *Without a Doubt,* former Los Angeles prosecutor Marcia Clark had described Baden as an adversary, but an "affable, charming man who always went out of his way to be sweet to me." She went on to say, "I have to admit, he had expert witnessing down to a science. A big man with a winning smile, he sat on the witness stand as if he owned it."

Roger sought to add Baden to the prosecution team months earlier, but Clark County Coroner Ron Flud, not wanting to deal with his celebrity status, had refused to hire him. Dillard, however, had given Baden a retainer on behalf of Binion's estate as far back as March. Dillard, it turned out, had gotten to the widely known pathologist a couple of weeks before the defense, which ultimately hired Baden's good friend and equally famed pathologist, Cyril Wecht of Pittsburgh.

Baden flew to Las Vegas from New York a couple of days before his planned testimony early in the preliminary hearing. He spent the day before he was to testify poring over the autopsy records and visiting the death scene at Binion's home. Late in the afternoon that day, Roger and Wall went to Dillard's office and met with Baden.

The prosecutors weren't expecting any surprises. Several weeks earlier, they had received a report from Baden saying he had concurred with Simms that Binion had fatal doses of heroin and Xanax in his system. But Baden had come to that conclusion after reviewing a summary of a report from Ellen Clarke that contained a typographical error. The summary mistakenly had described the amount of Xanax in Binion's body in milligrams instead of nanograms, which had made it look as though his system had one million times more

Xanax than what actually was there. Baden determined that Binion's body did not contain a lethal amount of Xanax and surmised that Binion, a heroin addict, had likely built up a tolerance for the drug and could have survived the high dose of heroin in his stomach. Then, after he reviewed the actual tissue samples of the bruises and abrasions on Binion's body and toured the death scene earlier in the day, signs of suffocation became obvious to him.

"He said to me, 'Dave, Binion didn't die of a heroin overdose,' " Roger explained. "I turned white and wanted to die. We were in the middle of a televised preliminary hearing, and I figured we weren't getting past the hearing. It was going down quickly.

"I asked, 'Well, how did he die?' And he said he was suffocated. He was burked. And then he explained everything."

Baden told the prosecutors that "burking" was a nineteenth-century method of killing someone without leaving a lot of marks. He theorized that Binion's killers had either sat on his chest or held him down with a knee and then smothered him with their hands or a pillow.

"I'm looking at David as Baden is talking, and what he was saying started to make sense," Roger said. "Simms concluded the marks on Binion's chest were the result of bug bites. It never made sense to me that a bug would jump up on Binion's chest, bite him and run off. Simms said the marks on his wrist probably were from a watch, but Binion never wore a watch. And Simms said the redness around his mouth was caused by vomiting. But there was no vomit on his face, nor anywhere around him."

Baden suggested the marks on Binion's wrists were caused by handcuffs or other restraints, and small, ruptured blood vessels under Binion's lower eyelids were the result of suffocation. He also said the marks on his chest could have been impressions from his shirt buttons.

"As Dr. Baden explained his findings, it made perfect sense to me," Wall said. "But I was still trying to absorb it and figure out how we were going to fit this into our theory."

Wall said he was impressed with Baden:

"He was very persuasive and very knowledgeable, and he explained it in a way that I could understand it and reconcile it with all of the medical reports. He was a little reluctant to give us that opinion because he knew it differed with Simms'. But I remember telling him, 'Look, I want to know what you think. Don't worry about hurting anybody's feelings.' "

Still a bit in shock, Roger and Wall asked Baden to meet them for dinner that night to explain things further.

"We walked back to our cars," Roger recalled, "and I looked at David and said, 'You know, I think he's right.' And he said, 'I think he's right, too.' "

The prosecutors decided to go to the restaurant ahead of time to discuss how to proceed with Baden's theory of death.

"We got to McCormick and Schmick's [a seafood place just off the Strip], and had a beer and talked for a while," Roger said. "It really was starting to make sense from our perspective. With Tom Loveday, the gardener, at the house that morning, they had to close the drapes and hasten Binion's death."

Roger, however, said the two prosecutors were still convinced that Murphy and Tabish had first tried to kill Binion by forcing the deadly cocktail down his throat. Baden had told them Binion probably didn't die right away from the drugs and that he most likely had gone into a coma first.

"They called up the maid and told her not to come in, but they forgot about Tom Loveday," Roger said. "They had television monitors in the den, so they could see a suspicious Loveday going around the house trying to open doors, and they knew they had to kill Binion faster, and they suffocated him."

Baden later said he told the prosecutors they didn't have to put him on the witness stand the next day.

"They thought about it and decided that what I had said had merit, and they decided to put it all out there," he explained. "I was very impressed with their professionalism in this matter."

After dinner, Wall went home to prepare for what was going to be stunning testimony the next day.

"Suddenly, one of the most renowned forensic pathologists had taken what was a very difficult conclusion and made it easier to understand," Wall said. "Dr. Baden was the only one whose conclusions took into consideration all of the injuries to Binion's body."

Wall stayed up most of the night rethinking his examination of Baden and Simms, while an excited Roger got in touch with his boss, District Attorney Stewart Bell, and homicide detectives to let them know what was coming.

"Dave called me up and said, 'This is huge. This is big,'" Detective James Buczek said. "It really was a bombshell. But in my mind, everything started to come together. It made sense."

The next day, Wall kept Simms on the witness stand most of the morning, explaining what he had done during the autopsy and allowing him to offer his conclusion that Binion had died of fatal heroin and Xanax overdoses.

Simms had been on the job less than three weeks when he performed the autopsy on Binion's body. He had much less experience than Baden, having done about 2,000 autopsies in his young career.

Early in the medical examiner's testimony, a small drama played out in the courtroom. As Simms was identifying autopsy photos, Sandy Murphy suddenly burst into tears at the defense table and was excused from the courtroom to compose herself. The photos had been passed around the table for defense lawyers to inspect while Simms was testifying, and Murphy had seen them.

Knowing that Baden was going to be called next, Wall steered Simms into an area of inquiry intended to support Baden's testimony. Simms had not been told of Baden's findings.

Wall asked Simms to speculate on what could have caused the red spots under Binion's eyelids.

"What does that suggest to you as a forensic pathologist?" Wall asked.

"When I first see it," Simms said, "the first thing you think about, could the person have been suffocated or strangled? Could that person have been on their stomach? There are a number of different things that can cause that."

Simms also acknowledged that the marks on Binion's chest and wrists could have occurred just prior to his death, which tended to support the suffocation theory.

Next up was Baden.

After spending some time questioning Baden about his extensive credentials and letting him explain what evidence he had reviewed, Wall methodically guided the famed pathologist to his startling conclusions.

He showed him a photo of Binion's chest and asked him to discuss his opinion of the two small marks there.

"What can you tell us about the characteristics of those two particular, I think you called them, abrasions?"

"Yeah," the gray-haired Baden responded in a calm, soothing voice. "I think that, in my opinion, the larger mark is due to some pressure on the skin, rubbing and pressure on the skin in the lower chest area, and the upper one has more the appearance of an imprint from a button or some button-like structure on the shirt . . . My opinion would be that these injuries were caused by some pressure on the shirt that was lying on Mr. Binion prior to death."

Baden testified that it was likely the abrasions could have happened a half hour before Binion died.

At this point, tension began to build in the courtroom. It was obvious that Baden was starting to contradict Simms. Murphy and Tabish, along with their lawyers, William Terry and Steve Wolfson, were sitting on the edge of their seats, riveted to Baden's every word.

Baden calmly went on to describe the injuries to Binion's wrists, suggesting they were caused prior to death by some type of "teethlike" object.

Next, Wall questioned Baden about the redness around Binion's mouth.

As he examined a photo of Binion's mouth with a magnifying glass on the witness stand, Baden was asked to describe what he saw.

"What is the significance to you regarding those particular types of injuries?" Wall asked.

"They look like pressure marks," Baden replied.

"What do you mean by pressure marks?"

"That at some point pressure was put against, there was pressure against Mr. Binion's mouth."

"With what type of object?"

"I can't tell the type of object. It could be a soft object like a pillow with some rubbing against it. It could be, could be a hand. I lean more toward a pillow because of the way the abrasions occur, but it could be any object that can rub the mouth and lip."

"Are you able to make any type of determination as to the age of those injuries relative to death?"

"Just from the appearance, they appeared to have occurred about the time of death. There is no evidence from this photograph of the body's reaction to the injury."

Wall then asked Baden to look at the autopsy report. Simms had concluded that the redness under Binion's lower eyelids were the result of "vascular congestion," a filling of the blood vessels with blood. Simms did not see any ruptured blood vessels.

"Did you have the opportunity to review any photographs that would have shown that particular area of Mr. Binion?" Wall asked.

"Yes," Baden responded.

"And where did you view those?"

"At the medical examiner's office yesterday. I did have a chance to review the Polaroid photographs that were taken after Mr. Binion's body came to the medical examiner's office. Coroner Flud was there. They were in his possession. He showed them to me."

"And did you come to the same conclusions after reviewing those photographs as Dr. Simms?"

"No, no."

"What was your conclusion?"

"My opinions are that the discolorations in both lower eyelids shown on those photographs are what we call petechial hemorrhages—that is a small rupture of blood vessels, the kind that occurs sometimes if somebody coughs violently . . . "

"And what would the fact that there may be petechiae suggest to you as it relates to cause of death or evidence of trauma?"

"Petechiae, ruptured blood vessels in the eye area, are an indicator of some kind of asphyxia, some inability of oxygen to get to the head area and the brain area, commonly seen in strangulation when the blood vessels are compressed, also seen in suffocation . . ."

Reporters and other courtroom observers were stunned.

Wall then asked Baden if he knew how the blood vessels in Binion's eyes had become ruptured.

"Based on the appearance and the surrounding circumstances, including the fact he doesn't have heart failure, including the fact that he wasn't lying facedown for a long period of time, and based on the fact that he has the compression abrasions around the mouth," Baden said, "it would be my opinion that the petechiae are due to some kind of suffocation with the inability to breathe because the mouth and nose area were obstructed."

Later, Wall asked Baden if he was able to determine with a reasonable medical certainty the cause of Binion's death.

"I have an opinion, yes," Baden replied.

"And what is that opinion?"

"The cause of death was asphyxia by suffocation. That is the inability to breathe because of suffocation."

Baden went on to say that the marks on Binion's wrists were the result of being restrained while being suffocated by the method of "burking."

"What is burking?" Wall asked.

"Burking is a means of causing death without leaving marks on the body by interfering with breathing . . . by sitting or putting pressure on the chest and obstructing the nose and mouth by hand or pillow that prevents breathing and prevents the lungs from expanding."

During cross-examination, Baden said burking was invented in Europe in the 1800s by William Burke and an associate out of a need to come up with fresh bodies for anatomy courses.

"They would take old women in bars," he said, "ply them with alcohol, bring them up to a room and one would sit on them on the chest and the other would put fingers over their nose and mouth and cause them to die by suffocation without any marks on the body. And the next day they would then sell them to the medical school."

Baden said Burke and his partner ultimately were caught and charged in the deaths, but their method of suffocation became known as burking from then on.

On direct examination, Baden told Wall he was convinced that Binion was the victim of a homicide, which was the same conclusion Simms had come to in his own way.

"Well, under these circumstances, the suffocation would have to be homicidal because he couldn't do it to himself and it couldn't happen accidentally," Baden testified.

Baden said that from the pattern of lividity (the settling of blood) in Binion's body, Binion had died five to eight hours before paramedics had arrived at his house in response to Murphy's 911 call at 3:55 P.M.

Bell later said he got the impression while observing Tabish and Murphy during Baden's testimony that they recognized prosecutors had finally figured out how Binion had died.

So did Roger.

"I enjoyed watching their faces," he said. "It was like, whoops, you got it."

After cross-examination, Roger asked Justice of the Peace Jennifer Togliatti to allow him to amend the murder complaint to include suffocation as an alternative theory of death to the forced-overdose theory.

Terry and Wolfson strenuously objected.

"It isn't our fault that they have what appears to me to be inconsistent theories of prosecution," Terry said.

Added Wolfson: "We have to have an ability to defend against charges, and they're just throwing everything up on a wall and hoping that some of it sticks."

Togliatti asked Roger to explain whether the state was now going to assert that the heroin and Xanax had been used to prevent Binion from fighting his killers.

"Well, that's interesting, and I haven't thought of that theory," Roger candidly responded.

"I'm here to entertain you," Togliatti joked.

"Doesn't that say it all?" an angry Wolfson responded. "My client is accused of murder, and we're talking like it's all fun here."

Togliatti ended up siding with Roger.

After Baden's testimony, defense lawyers tried to spin the sudden change in course on the part of the prosecution as a sign that its case was in jeopardy. How could the prosecution have any chance of convicting Murphy and Tabish if its own key medical witnesses were at odds?

But in reality, Baden gave the prosecution the exact boost it needed.

"It took the wind out of the defense," one investigator said after the hearing.

The next morning, an upbeat Bell proclaimed: "It's almost impossible to smother yourself."

Later, Bell said Baden's testimony eliminated in his mind the defense's theory that Binion had died of a self-induced drug overdose, either by accident or by suicide.

"It certainly made an easier case to overcome those two potential defenses," he said. "We didn't see our experts as being inconsistent. Both said it was a homicide.

"Our ultimate theory was that there was an attempt to kill Binion with drugs. They poured liquefied heroin and Xanax down his throat, but he was a horse and had built up quite a tolerance to drugs, so they had to make something happen right away."

Bill Koot, the district attorney's top criminal deputy, added: "Baden convinced us that these two people killed Binion. We were looking for a medical basis, and Baden gave us that."

But not everyone on the prosecution's team was thrilled with Baden.

Homicide Lieutenant Wayne Petersen said he wasn't completely persuaded that Binion had been burked.

"I think Baden went out on a limb a bit," he said. "I don't think the physical evidence was as obvious as he had stated it. But either way, it was a homicide."

As Baden's testimony began to sink in, there were rumblings at the courthouse that Simms was not happy about being contradicted. There also was talk that the testimony had caused friction between Simms and some homicide detectives who regarded him as arrogant and hard to work with. Roger, too, was said to be unhappy with Simms.

But Roger, Bell and Petersen all strongly denied that there was any tension between them and the chief medical examiner.

"There was absolutely no friction between our office and the coroner's office," Bell said. "Professional people like Simms and Baden have some pride in their work, and I'm sure Simms had a little bit of a feeling that his nose was pinched when another doctor came in and gave a different opinion. I don't think you can fault him for that. But it certainly didn't have an impact on our relationship."

Flud also publicly defended Simms in an interview with the *Las Vegas Sun*.

"The cause of death we used is one we can back up with scientific facts," he said. "We haven't wavered from that original stand one bit."

At the preliminary hearing, meanwhile, prosecutors had their share of embarrassing moments.

Steven Kurt Gratzer, the Tabish pal who had told prosecutors Tabish had solicited his help to kill Binion, turned out to be a dud.

"He was very evasive and bizarre," Wall acknowledged. "We knew we had a problem, and we went to a greater effort to corroborate him for the trial."

Gratzer was sidestepping so many of Wall's questions that he almost became a hostile witness during his five hours on the stand. At one point, Togliatti had to threaten him with contempt of court charges to gain his cooperation. There were snickers from the courtroom gallery throughout his testimony.

During breaks, Tabish family members tried to exploit Gratzer's unstable demeanor on the stand with reporters, insisting that was his real personality.

But Wall, who questioned the former Army Ranger, later said he had learned that Gratzer had decided to protect Tabish at the hearing. Television viewers once saw Tabish wink at his childhood friend during his testimony.

"I thought that the people around Tabish had gotten to him," Wall said. "It was very frustrating, because he had an agenda not to provide me with truthful answers."

Other witnesses, such as Binion's heroin supplier, Peter Sheridan, came off poorly. Sheridan acknowledged that he was on methadone, a drug used to treat heroin addiction, when he testified. Tanya Cropp, after testifying that Murphy had asked her to throw investigators looking into Binion's death off course, acknowledged that she lied to a grand jury when she was not under any obligation from Murphy to do so. And Leo Casey, who testified that he was the victim of a Tabish torture plot, was branded on cross-examination by defense lawyers as an embezzler and perjurer.

But in the end, Murphy herself became the prosecution's best witness. Prosecutors got a chance to play the twenty-minute video of Murphy touring Binion's home the day after his death in which she appeared manipulative, foul-mouthed and materialistic. The tape showed Murphy emotionless as she walked past the area of the den where Binion's body had been found, and it appeared to catch her taking the wineglass prosecutors believed was used to either mix or feed Binion the deadly cocktail of drugs.

In closing arguments, defense lawyers attacked the credibility of the prosecution's chief witnesses, saying the case was "fraught with immunity, paid testimony, perjury" and the heavy involvement of the Binion estate.

But Roger said Murphy had shown her "true colors" on the videotape, going from grieving to greedy girlfriend in less then twenty-four hours.

He also attempted to solidify the new suffocation theory, telling Togliatti that Murphy and Tabish had to change their game plan when Loveday showed up to mow Binion's lawn.

"Something unexpected happened that day, and it was Tom Loveday," Roger said.

At one point, as Roger was describing what he called the "cruel" nature of Binion's slaying, Togliatti had to instruct Murphy to refrain from "huffing and puffing" at the defense table. Murphy glanced at Roger and apologized.

"The killers had to stage a suicide or accidental overdose to get away with the crime, and that's exactly what they did," Roger said.

Then the prosecutor went on to charge that the killers had left their signature on their crimes by leaving a single silver dollar in the vault in Pahrump and a lone dime in Binion's safe in Las Vegas.

The topper, Roger charged, was planting the "R.I.P." sign above the entrance to Binion's home.

"What a cruel, cruel thing to do to a dead person," the prosecutor said.

In the end, Togliatti ruled that prosecutors had presented enough evidence to force Murphy and Tabish to stand trial. The four other defendants facing lesser charges—David Mattsen, Michael Milot, John Joseph and Steven Wadkins— also were ordered bound over.

CHAPTER 24

• • • • • • • • • • • • • • • • • •

The Judge Takes Over

• • • • • • • • • • • • • • • • • •

AT THE CLARK COUNTY COURTHOUSE, District Judge Joseph Bonaventure was regarded as a hardworking, experienced jurist.

The son of Italian immigrants, he also was considered a personable man with humble, blue-collar beginnings.

He was the perfect judge to preside over the biggest murder case of all time in Las Vegas, a case that was quickly attracting national attention.

The fifty-six-year-old Bonaventure, a native of Queens, New York, was randomly assigned the Ted Binion murder case after Justice of the Peace Jennifer Togliatti had bound over the accused killers, Sandy Murphy and Rick Tabish, for trial.

With his thick silver hair and heavy New York accent, Bonaventure was known for his great sense of humor and quick wit on the bench. At times, however, he also displayed a temper and loss of patience with lawyers slow to make a point in his courtroom.

Such intolerance earned him a reputation as a "no-nonsense" judge during his twenty-two years on the bench. Yet he was considered fair and thoughtful in his decisions.

"He's probably the most experienced in criminal law of all of the judges," fellow jurist Michael Cherry said. "He's very efficient and doesn't like surprises. He'll have complete control over this trial."

To many, Bonaventure was an unlikely judge to draw the high-profile case. He always felt uncomfortable in the presence of reporters and worked hard over the years to keep his name out of the media. At the same time, he recognized the value of the media in society, often ruling on the side of the First Amendment.

One of the first things Bonaventure did in the Binion case was accept the innocent pleas of the six defendants on September 27 in a courtroom packed with reporters. Murphy didn't get off on the right foot with the judge. Looking pale and tired, she showed up fifteen minutes late. Her lawyer, William Terry, told Bonaventure that she had been slowed by food poisoning the night before. After accepting the pleas, Bonaventure set a March 13, 2000, trial date for Murphy, Tabish, David Mattsen and Michael Milot. The two men charged with Tabish in the Leo Casey torture, John Joseph and Steven Wadkins, were granted separate trials after the murder case.

Bonaventure's first crisis came on October 21, when Murphy was arrested and booked into the Clark County Detention Center for violating the terms of her arrest. She was taken back into custody for being away from her Henderson apartment all day without notifying house-arrest officials.

The day after her arrest, Murphy was brought before Bonaventure to explain what had happened.

With a new lawyer, John Momot, at her side, Murphy told Bonaventure that her arrest was the result of a personality conflict with the corrections officer assigned to supervise her.

"I would never do anything to jeopardize or violate the rules in any way," she said in a shaky voice. "If I was rude to her in any way, I apologize. I just didn't want a confrontation."

Murphy contended she was at Terry's office most of the day making arrangements to hire Momot, a former protégé of one of her previous attorneys, Las Vegas Mayor Oscar Goodman.

But her corrections officer, Donna Bryant, said she learned that Murphy also had lunch with her civil lawyer, William Knudson, at her favorite gourmet restaurant, the Aristocrat, while she was AWOL. That offended Bryant.

Bonaventure scheduled a formal hearing to decide Murphy's fate later in the week.

Momot's association with the defense surprised some courthouse observers.

Over the past twenty-five years, the fifty-seven-year-old New Jersey native had earned a reputation as a top-flight criminal attorney while representing a number of underworld figures, including Binion's slain friend, Herbie Blitzstein. Murphy had met Momot through Blitzstein and knew that he was good friends with Bonaventure. Momot, a divorced Vietnam veteran, had started his legal career working under Bonaventure at the county public defender's office, and the judge's wife, Barbara, ended up becoming the godmother of his eighteen-year-old daughter, Roxanne.

Bonaventure informed prosecutors of his long-standing relationship with Momot in his chambers, and no one voiced any concerns.

In Murphy's mind, if anybody knew how to handle Bonaventure in court, it would be Momot. With public opinion stacked against her, she figured she needed any kind of advantage at the trial she could get.

But the laid-back Momot, who hated ruffling feathers within the legal community, also was close to Binion, as well as to his sister Becky. He often had gone out on the town with Binion and Blitzstein. His decision to take Murphy as a client did not sit well with some Binion family members. And he knew it.

"People just need representation," Momot said when pressed about his association with Murphy. "And that's my job as a lawyer."

Murphy wasn't the only one to change attorneys after the preliminary hearing. Tabish's lawyer, Steve Wolfson, had gotten out of the case after the hearing ended, and Tabish brought back Louis Palazzo, who had just helped a reputed Los Angeles mob associate beat a federal murder rap in Blitzstein's slaying. Palazzo was hungry and the same age as Tabish and probably cheaper to hire than other, more mature attorneys in town.

As Murphy tried to wiggle out of her latest jam, prosecutors David Roger and David Wall sat back and smiled. They had expected her to wind up in trouble again.

At the hearing on Murphy's arrest, the prosecutors urged Bonaventure to keep her behind bars.

"What you've got here is a woman who just doesn't get it, or else doesn't care," Wall told the judge.

Bryant testified that Murphy had treated her with indignity, almost as if the officer were there to serve the defendant.

Though he never brought it up at the hearing, Wall knew that police had conducted surveillance on Murphy a couple of weeks earlier, after they had received a tip she might flee to the Philippines. The tip never panned out, but officers had watched her going to a tanning salon a couple of times during the surveillance.

Bonaventure showed little signs of his friendship with Momot during the hearing. He decided, however, to release Murphy back into house arrest, but not before giving her a stern tongue-lashing.

"You think you're something special—you're above the rules," Bonaventure yelled. "Well, you're not, Ms. Murphy."

Bonaventure told Murphy he had been on the case only a couple of weeks, but already he could see what made her tick.

"I just have a feeling about you," he said.

Before ordering her release, Bonaventure told Murphy he was instructing jail officials to keep her at the detention center for another week so she could think about her actions. He also banned her from going back to the Aristocrat.

Momot, appearing embarrassed by Murphy's indiscretion, later told reporters the judge had "instilled the fear of God" in his client.

Jail officials had kept Murphy under a twenty-four-hour lockdown during her week's stay, but when she was released back into house arrest, another controversy arose.

Momot filed a motion complaining that Murphy's black lace panties were missing when jail officials let her go. He asked Bonaventure to bar prosecutors from using the panties as evidence against his client.

The underwear, Momot said, was turned in with the rest of Murphy's clothes, when she was booked on October 21, and placed in a clear plastic bag. But when she was released, the panties weren't in the bag.

Momot's motion didn't sit well with Roger, who thought the attorney was making a mockery of the judicial system.

"The state of Nevada has no interest in Sandy Murphy's panties," Roger told reporters the day after the motion was filed. "It would be an outrageous waste of court time to indulge a hunt for her underwear."

But Momot, though he took some ribbing from his courthouse pals, said he was dead serious about the motion. He said he filed it out of an "abundance of caution." He didn't want investigators winding up with the panties and testing them for body fluids that might somehow be used to incriminate Murphy.

The motion was an example of the new aggressive approach to the case the defense was now taking under Momot's direction.

Bonaventure reluctantly agreed to hold a hearing on the missing panties on November 15. He clearly was not thrilled with having to discuss Murphy's underwear in court before a live television audience. Las Vegas One had planned to cover the hearing.

Jail officials, meanwhile, began searching for the panties. Several that fit Murphy's description actually were found, and Momot and his client were summoned to the detention center to inspect them. But Murphy told officials they weren't hers.

When it came time for the hearing, the panties still hadn't

turned up. All that Bonaventure could do was instruct prosecutors not to conduct any tests on the underwear, if found, without his permission.

Before adjourning, Bonaventure, who was aware that Momot's motion had been the subject of much courthouse humor, made a point of commending his good friend for his "diligence" in representing his client.

The panties never did surface. But Momot went on to more important things—like stepping up the battle in the arena of public opinion.

Tabish was still locked up, but Murphy was free to move about and talk to reporters in her lawyer's office.

"When she spoke, I think she came across in a very good light," Momot said. "We had a lot of things to overcome, and I felt the best way to do it was to let my client speak to the media so they could see and hear her as she really was—a nice person."

Her first television interview was given to ABC correspondent John Miller for the network's *20/20* news magazine. The segment aired the first week in December. In it, television viewers saw a gentle young woman, dressed conservatively in a black pantsuit, describing how distraught she was over losing Binion. It was the complete opposite of her hardened, topless-dancer image that had been playing in the media. That same evening, Momot went on Las Vegas One and described Murphy as a "sweet person" who didn't deserve all the negative publicity she was getting.

Within a day or two, Knudson held a news conference in the presence of his Los Angeles attorney, Arthur Barens, to attack the prosecution.

Knudson, a member of the Nevada Bar for only a couple of years, always seemed to turn up in the case at important times for Murphy and Tabish. And that did not go unnoticed by investigators.

Knudson was at Binion's home the day after his death making the now-infamous videotape for Murphy. Then he let Murphy take up temporary residence at his house for several days, and he helped her bail Tabish out of jail in Pahrump on the silver-theft charges. He also gave Tanya Cropp a job at a time when the defendants were trying to keep her in line.

And cellular phone records showed that Tabish had called Knudson a couple of times in the immediate hours after Binion's death. Through it all, Knudson had refused to talk with prosecutors.

Though the news conference was called primarily to lash out at prosecutors, Knudson ended up tying himself further to the case. He acknowledged that he had lunch with Murphy and Tabish at the Z'Tejas Grill from about 2:30 P.M. until 3:45 P.M. on September 17, 1998. His disclosure left little doubt that he expected to be an alibi witness for the two defendants. Murphy had made her 911 call to police at 3:55 P.M.

Barens told reporters that Knudson had acted in a "professional" and "responsible" manner in his dealings with Murphy and Tabish, and he complained that prosecutors were harassing his client.

Knudson said he was "incensed" at the tactics of prosecutors, who at one point had hauled his mother before the grand jury looking into Binion's death.

A couple of days later, the defense's public relations blitz got another boost. *Gentlemen's Quarterly* published an article on the Binion case in which both Murphy and Tabish proclaimed their innocence. But the story wasn't all flattering.

The couple had been courting *GQ* writer Stephen Rodrick for months, even before they were arrested in Binion's death. Rodrick reported that they had taken him to dinner, a local topless nightclub and bungee jumping at the MGM Grand Hotel/Casino.

"Convinced they're getting a raw deal from the Vegas media, they're enthusiastic to tell their side of things to an outsider," Rodrick wrote. "In a way, they're an archetypal American couple: the ingenue and the handsome jock, skating through life on their cheekbones and white teeth. Both are affable and glib, capable of discussing Ted's gruesome death and their beloved, fat-reducing George Foreman grill in the same conversation.

"Exuding self-confidence, Rick and Sandy speak of their innocence matter-of-factly, as if it's all one big misunderstanding. The thought that I wouldn't be won over by their charm probably never occurred to them."

There would be other prominent interviews for Murphy and Tabish in the coming weeks—*Playboy, Los Angeles* Magazine and *MugShots,* an hour-long documentary for Court TV. The battle was escalating.

In the *20/20* interview, Miller said Murphy had agreed to talk on the condition he not ask her any questions about the charges against her.

Then he turned to Murphy and said: "I would like to ask you a hundred questions. Would you like to answer them?"

"I would love to answer all of your questions," a demure Murphy responded with Momot at her side. "But John is a good attorney, and I respect what he says. And he says there's a time and place for everything legally. And I'm not gonna win anything in the media. We're gonna win it when it's in court, when it counts."

A few moments later, as the piece was about to close, Miller turned to Becky Behnen.

"Based on what you know now," Miller asked, "do you think Sandy Murphy killed your brother?"

"Based on what I know now," Behnen responded, "I think Sandy Murphy and Rick Tabish murdered my brother."

"For the money?"

"For the money."

But it was Murphy who got one last shot at the end of the segment.

"You were living with Ted Binion for three years," Miller said. "Did you love him?"

With a single tear trickling down her cheek, Murphy replied: "Of course I did. He was my man."

"Do you miss him?"

"Very much."

CHAPTER 25

....

Mobbed Up

....

RUMORS OF RICK TABISH'S mob ties were nothing new to investigators. Tabish himself did little to discourage such talk, mostly to enhance his tough-guy image with potential witnesses looking to testify against him.

Detective James Buczek recalled having trouble gaining the cooperation of some witnesses—people like Tanya Cropp and Linda Carroll. That was one reason, he said, a grand jury was asked to assist in the probe.

"Tabish had put the word out about his connections to the Chicago mob," Buczek explained. "Some of the witnesses were afraid to talk to us. They didn't want to be harmed."

Even Sandy Murphy played the wise-guy game. She loved hanging out with the burly Herbie Blitzstein when he was alive, sometimes going to the topless nightclubs with him and Binion. Murphy had always been attracted to tough guys and the aura of danger around them. She certainly knew Blitzstein's reputation as the right-hand man to slain Chicago Mafia kingpin Anthony Spilotro, one of the most feared mobsters ever to walk the streets of Las Vegas. Lawmen regarded Spilotro as a cold-blooded killer. For years, until his brutal 1986 slaying outside Chicago, Spilotro had controlled Las Vegas rackets for his crime family, and Blitzstein was there with him. Even Ted Binion had once been targeted by the FBI because of his ties to Spilotro.

224

"Something always in the back of my head," Buczek said, "was that Ted had friends who were shady characters with mob ties. He was murdered by Rick and Sandy, and Rick and Sandy were never killed. Through my readings about the Mafia, normally if an associate is killed, the Mafia would go after that person unless there was approval to kill the associate."

Buczek said he never ruled out the possibility that Tabish and Murphy had obtained permission from the mob to kill Binion.

"They were never touched," he said.

That theory, he added, helped explain the arrogant attitude of both defendants throughout the investigation.

Buczek also recalled that the same mob associates who had killed Blitzstein in January 1997 also once plotted Binion's death. The scheme was uncovered by FBI agents during the investigation into Blitzstein's gangland hit. Blitzstein was killed as part of a push by the Los Angeles and Buffalo crime families to take over street rackets in Las Vegas. Chicago had given up its control of the streets after Spilotro's slaying.

In early November 1999, the *Las Vegas Sun* disclosed a new mob connection to the Binion murder case. The newspaper reported that another reputed Spilotro associate, Joseph Cusumano, was involved in a movie project on the well-publicized case.

The sixty-five-year-old Cusumano, listed in Nevada's Black Book of "undesirables" banned from casinos, was reported to have been a top Spilotro lieutenant during the heyday of the Chicago crime lord's rackets empire. Cusumano had worked closely with Blitzstein on many occasions in those days.

Charming and good-looking, Cusumano had not been in trouble with the law since his 1987 conviction for trying to divert several hundred thousand dollars from the Culinary Union's insurance fund.

He did, however, attract national attention in 1997, when

60 Minutes exposed his role in an aborted bid to buy the government's troubled Bicycle Club casino in Southern California. The government had taken over the club after seizing it in a racketeering investigation.

Cusumano, it turned out, had also dabbled in the movie industry before. He was a line producer for *The Cotton Club,* a film about organized crime in the 1930s that was directed by Francis Ford Coppola. The film was financed by Cusumano's good friends, colorful Las Vegans Ed and Fred Doumani, the landlords of the Tropicana Hotel & Casino in the late 1970s, when the FBI was investigating allegations of hidden mob influence. Fred Doumani had been involved in the failed Bicycle Club deal.

The *Sun* reported that Cusumano, who had drawn praise for his work in holding *The Cotton Club* together, was using his friendship with Tabish to put the Binion film project together. He was said to have offered to help Tabish with legal fees in return for his movie rights.

Cusumano would not talk to the newspaper, but he had a friend confirm his involvement in the Binion project, which was associated with a Los Angeles company called Edgebrook Productions. The company was run by Michele Berk, the wife of *Baywatch* creator Michael Berk. Neither of the Berks would talk to the newspaper, but Michele left a voice message at the *Sun* confirming she was producing a film about Binion's slaying for the Showtime cable network.

Several months later, KLAS-TV in Las Vegas reported that it had confirmed that Cusumano, Berk and author-screenwriter Nick Pileggi, who co-wrote the movie *Casino* with legendary director Martin Scorsese, had signed on as producers of the Binion movie. Pileggi also later confirmed his involvement.

In the meantime, it was learned that Cusumano had obtained Tabish's and Murphy's movie rights during their preliminary hearing in August. Tabish's former attorney, Steve Wolfson, recalled getting a couple of phone calls from

Cusumano during the hearing, looking for help in securing the rights.

Pileggi, who has written about the mob and Las Vegas for years, credited Cusumano with jump-starting the Showtime project.

"He got the ball rolling," Pileggi said. "He recognized that there was a story in the Binion death. He got the rights to Murphy and Tabish, and sold it to Showtime."

Months earlier, Tabish had bragged to a friend from Montana that he expected to receive $200,000 to $300,000 for selling the rights to his story. The friend, Jason Frazer, later recalled on the witness stand that he had gone to dinner several years earlier with Tabish, Cusumano and Salvatore Galioto, another reputed Chicago mob associate with movie industry ties.

Local reporters already had linked Galioto to Tabish in November.

Records showed that a man identifying himself as Galioto had signed in to visit Tabish with his younger brother, Greg Tabish, at 6:30 P.M. on August 16, the evening before the preliminary hearing. Jail officials had no idea who Galioto was when he showed up to see Tabish. But because he was with Tabish's brother, special accommodations were made for him to meet with the defendant.

Galioto, who, like Cusumano, wasn't talking to reporters, was listed on the Chicago Crime Commission's 1997 Chicago-mob flow chart as an associate. The chart was considered a credible source of intelligence for law enforcement agencies in Las Vegas and across the country. It turned out that Galioto was well known to lawmen in Las Vegas, where he was said to be a frequent visitor. The entire Galioto family was known to authorities in Chicago. Galioto's brother, John Galioto, was forced to resign from a Chicago labor union in 1998 after allegedly embezzling money. Like his brother, he also was listed as a mob associate on the Crime Commission's flow chart.

Salvatore Galioto's name surfaced in Chicago news re-

ports in 1995, when he and his parents, William and Ann
Galioto, were denied a $5.5 million Chicago city loan to
build a video and movie production center. The *Chicago
Sun-Times* reported that city officials had denied the loan because they feared the family had mob ties. At the time,
William and Salvatore Galioto already were involved in the
film industry as owners of the now-defunct Movies in Motion Inc., a Chicago production company that leased vehicles and other equipment to filmmakers in the area.

By December 1999, Binion estate investigator Tom Dillard had managed to link Tabish further to Galioto. Dillard
discovered that Tabish had made several cellular phone calls
to a Chicago area beeper number tied to Galioto in the hours
immediately after Binion's death. The beeper number had
come back to the Melrose Park, Illinois, address of a company called Entertainment Inc. That was the same address of
an adult nightclub run by Galioto's family.

Records showed that Tabish telephoned the number twice
on the evening of Binion's death and three times the next
day, just hours before he drove to Pahrump with an excavator to dig up Binion's $6 million silver fortune. The first call
was made at 5:58 P.M. on September 17, 1998, probably
while Tabish was waiting outside Binion's home with neighbors who had learned of Binion's death on the evening news.
The second call occurred at 8:50 P.M.

The next day, records showed that Tabish called the
beeper number three more times between 10:24 A.M. and
10:26 A.M. Dillard discovered that Tabish had made numerous other calls to the Melrose Park number in the weeks
prior to Binion's death. Despite traveling to Chicago to seek
out Galioto, Dillard never learned why the calls were made.
Galioto wouldn't talk.

But there was speculation that the calls might have had
nothing to do with a movie deal.

Dillard said David Mattsen once told him the mob was
planning to help Tabish fence Binion's silver bars and coins
in Chicago if the thieves had gotten away with stealing the

loot. And prosecutor David Roger reported that he had learned early in the murder investigation, from a friend of Tabish's wife, Mary Jo, that the silver indeed was headed for Chicago.

Still, the talk of Galioto's ties to Tabish intrigued Binion's estate lawyers, who had filed a wrongful-death lawsuit against Tabish and Murphy, alleging that the couple had "engaged in a secret sexual relationship" while plotting Binion's death. In December, Harry Claiborne and Richard Wright informed District Judge Michael Cherry, who was overseeing Binion's estate, that they intended to collect any profits Tabish and Murphy might earn from a book or movie deal.

About the same time, District Judge Joseph Bonaventure became intrigued as well. He hauled Tabish and his lawyers, Louis Palazzo and Robert Murdock, to court for a closed-door hearing December 15 to get to the bottom of whether any mob money had gone toward their legal fees. Bonaventure wanted to know if the movie deal had affected the ability of the lawyers to properly defend Tabish. Both attorneys, however, presented Bonaventure with evidence that they had been paid directly by Tabish's father. They also told the judge that they had not entered into any agreement with anyone from Hollywood about their roles in the defense. And that seemed to quell the judge's concerns.

"The court is convinced," Bonaventure told the lawyers at the secret hearing, "that there is no basis in the fee agreement to undermine the belief that Mr. Palazzo will continue to be a faithful advocate of his client's interest. And I believe the fee agreement that was enumerated here does not violate any Nevada Supreme Court rules. And so I think this puts this issue to rest."

At a subsequent public hearing, Bonaventure stated that the fee arrangements between Tabish and both of his attorneys were proper.

Months later, KLAS-TV reported that both Tabish and Murphy had been cut out of the Showtime movie deal

Cusumano had put together because they were demanding too much money. There also was talk that the *Sun* news reports had attracted too much attention to the agreement and had killed the deal with the two murder defendants.

But there were other mysterious developments in the case worthy of attracting Hollywood's attention—and maybe even the mob's—as 1999 came to a close.

Roger filed court papers disclosing that the IRS was investigating whether a Southern California man who had posted the $100,000 bail for Binion case defendant John Joseph had laundered cash that once might have been buried in Nevada by Binion. The man was a longtime partner of Joseph's in Orange County.

IRS Agent Aimee Schabilion laid out the investigation in a fifteen-page affidavit Roger filed with the court in an attempt to determine whether the bail money had been stolen from Binion.

Schabilion wrote that tellers at a Sunwest Bank in Tustin, California, reported that Joseph's partner had been making suspicious deposits since June 24, 1998, the day detectives began rounding up the suspects in the Binion case. The man, the IRS agent said, had made a series of $9,000 deposits of what the tellers described as "musty and mildewy" $100 bills.

"I personally smelled the majority of the cash deposits within hours to days after the deposits," Schabilion said in her affidavit. "And I agree that these bills have an unusual smell and appearance, as though they had been buried in a moist area and uncirculated for a great deal of time."

Schabilion wrote that Roger told her Binion had once testified in his divorce proceedings that he had buried $2 million near a tree on his property during the savings and loan crisis.

At a bail hearing for Joseph in front of Bonaventure, Roger said investigators didn't know for sure whether the "smelly" money belonged to Binion. But he added: "It's certainly curious when you have these old wet bills turn up."

In her affidavit, Schabilion said Joseph's partner told a

California bank teller when making a June 24 deposit that he had won the cash playing craps in Las Vegas and that the money smelled because it had been in his gym bag.

"One teller told me that the money smelled and looked as though it had been in a cave," Schabilion said. "The teller also noted that all of the deposits had the same smell and appearance like [they] came from one place."

Joseph's Las Vegas lawyer, C. Stanley Hunterton, ultimately was able to persuade Bonaventure that Joseph's bail had come from a legitimate source, and the matter was dropped. But the smelly-money caper added still more mystery to the Binion saga.

Palazzo and Murdock also were doing their share to sensationalize the case. They filed a motion asking Bonaventure to exhume Binion's body, which had been entombed at a local mausoleum, so that they could test Dr. Michael Baden's suffocation theory.

The lawyers wanted scientific tests done to see whether there were any fibers in Binion's nose or mouth that would support the theory that someone had smothered him with a pillow.

The motion, which was filed days before Christmas, was seen as gruesome and a slap in the face to Binion's family, which voiced its objections.

"He's been gone a year," Becky Behnen said. "I believe in letting him rest in peace."

Harry Claiborne added: "To disturb the dead, that bothers me."

And Roger said he couldn't recall such a motion in his thirteen years at the district attorney's office.

At a post-Christmas hearing before Bonaventure, and in the wake of growing criticism, Palazzo and Murdock appeared to back away from their request, asking the judge for more time so they could consult a forensic expert to make sure the exhumation wouldn't be a "futile exercise."

Palazzo said he learned for the first time a few days earlier that Binion's body had been embalmed, making it next to impossible to obtain any meaningful evidence.

"Is it a total shock to you that they embalm bodies?" an angry Bonaventure asked.

"I'm not doing this for kicks and giggles," Palazzo responded.

But the judge was unimpressed. He scolded the attorneys for not including testimony from an expert in their motion. But in the interest of fairness to the defense, he reset the hearing one week later into the new year.

"At that time, I want backup, or, Mr. Palazzo, I want to hear you say, 'Your Honor, I withdraw this motion,'" Bonaventure said.

The following week, the lawyers, failing to obtain the necessary backup, sheepishly told the judge they were withdrawing their motion.

"I'm glad they didn't feel this was necessary," Behnen said afterward. "This gives me peace."

As the year ended, Bonaventure, at the request of defense lawyers, declared Murphy and Tabish indigent and said they could have up to $20,000 apiece in taxpayer funds to pay for legal expenses. The judge, appearing to recognize that his decision could turn into a public relations nightmare for him, said he had no choice but to grant the motion under state law because the defendants had proved that they personally had no money.

His order, as expected, was not viewed well by the public, which knew that both Murphy and Tabish were getting financial help from wealthy third parties. Tabish's father, Frank Tabish, a well-to-do Montana businessman, was paying the legal fees of his son's attorneys, and multimillionaire William Fuller, still captivated by Murphy, was taking care of her lawyer. On top of that, Murphy, though on house arrest, was still being seen around town dining at gourmet restaurants. Almost immediately, calls from angry citizens started pouring into the judge's chambers.

The year ended on a sour note for David Mattsen, too.

Federal authorities, with the help of Binion prosecutors, filed an indictment against Mattsen, charging him with seven counts of being a felon in possession of firearms and ammunition. Mattsen's attorney, James "Bucky" Buchanan, argued that the indictment was handed up to pressure Mattsen to cooperate in the Binion probe.

"They're playing hardball now," Buchanan told reporters.

It was a charge that Binion prosecutors, who earlier had sought to make a deal with Mattsen, didn't deny.

After the first of the year, prosecutors put even more heat on Mattsen and another codefendant, Michael Milot, in the theft of Binion's silver. They filed a motion asking Bonaventure to force Mattsen and Milot to provide them with new fingerprint samples. Investigators wanted to compare the prints with samples recovered from the floor of the bathroom in Binion's den.

The motion suggested that prosecutors still hadn't ruled out the possibility that others besides Murphy and Tabish were involved in Binion's death.

CHAPTER 26

....

The Defense Opens Up

....

WITH THE TRIAL just ten weeks away, the defense started out the new year on the offensive.

Days after Sandy Murphy had been declared indigent in court, her lawyer, John Momot, hired a publicist to increase the public relations battle and deal with the mass of reporters covering the case.

Momot turned to Mark Fierro, a former television newsman turned political consultant. Fierro, a personable guy with good news media contacts, had been a key player in Oscar Goodman's celebrated mayoral campaign a year earlier. But at the close of the campaign, Goodman was forced to drop Fierro after learning that he had tried to parlay his success as a top Goodman adviser into a personal financial windfall. Handling Murphy was Fierro's second chance in the big leagues. Momot used him to cozy up to reporters and cut into Murphy's negative image in the community.

His hiring, however, irked District Judge Joseph Bonaventure because it made the judge's decision to give Murphy taxpayer money for her defense look even worse. If she was so poor, how could she afford a publicist of all things? As a result, Bonaventure was ready to pounce on Murphy if she slipped up again. And many expected Murphy to slip up.

By the end of January 2000, Momot and Rick Tabish's

lawyer, Louis Palazzo, also increased their assault on the case in court. They filed motions seeking to suppress the massive amount of evidence prosecutors had gathered against their clients. As expected, the focus of their attack was Tom Dillard's role in the prosecution.

"Essentially wearing twin hats of state investigator and private detective, Dillard was the primary individual through which the Las Vegas police department and district attorney developed their case," Momot wrote.

He charged that the unusual relationship had resulted in the "contamination" of the death scene at Ted Binion's home.

"Police were just sitting there, and everything was being placed at their doorstep," Momot told the *Las Vegas Sun* after filing his motion. "This is in essence the product of the Binion Money Machine."

Momot was laying the foundation for his anticipated defense at trial—that Binion really had died of a self-induced drug overdose, and prosecutors and Binion's wealthy estate had collaborated to frame his client.

Prosecutors, however, shrugged off the attack.

"This isn't any big deal," District Attorney Stewart Bell said. "We get information from private citizens all the time, sometimes willingly and sometimes unwillingly. But either way, we get it."

Dillard also was prepared to defend himself.

"We have a wrongful-death action," he told reporters. "It's just common sense that evidence applicable to a wrongful-death action is going to be applicable to a homicide. In this instance, the estate's goals and the prosecution's goals were the same—the search for the truth."

On the media front, Fierro arranged for his good buddy and former KLAS-TV colleague George Knapp to do an interview with Murphy in February, about a month before the March 13 trial. Knapp had been cultivating Murphy for months in hopes of getting her on the air. He had even interviewed her father, Kenneth, and stepmother, Sandra. The interview with Murphy took place in Momot's third-floor office in the posh law building owned by Oscar Goodman. The three-story building, with its huge atrium in the center, had sprung up in the late 1970s to accommodate Goodman's steady stream of high-paying underworld clients, particularly Anthony Spilotro. Many called it "the house the mob built." Palazzo's office was on the second floor.

When it came time to sit down with Murphy, Momot imposed a couple of ground rules. He had to be present, and Knapp couldn't inquire about the murder case. As a result, television viewers got a sanitized version of Murphy. They heard her reminisce about her childhood days in Southern California and her happier times with Binion. Her hair was colored red, and she wore it straight, but curled under her cheeks with bangs on her forehead to give her a gentle look. And, displaying what had become customary in her new, managed look, she was dressed in a conservative pantsuit. Murphy wasn't totally candid with Knapp. She lied about her onetime stab at topless dancing, saying she never worked as a stripper at Cheetah's before meeting Binion. She also neglected to talk about her rapes prior to coming to Las Vegas in 1995 and her regular beatings from Binion. She never talked about her love affair with Tabish either. The interview, however, gave viewers a chance to see a different Murphy from the one they had been reading about. That was Momot's goal.

"Sandy, I wanted to start with an interesting conversation we had with your mom and dad about what life was like growing up, but I'd like to hear it in your own words," Knapp said. "It was like your mom said; you were born, not hatched. You were a pretty normal kid."

"Yeah, I was," Murphy responded in a soft voice. "I enjoyed my childhood. I had a great childhood. My house was like the Brady Bunch, you know. I had lots of brothers and sisters and cousins, and everybody lived at my house and it was a good time. I was involved in a lot of extracurricular activities since I was three, up until the day I moved out of the house. So my parents were very, very good parents and always kept us very active."

"Give me a list of the kinds of things you did growing up. The kinds of things you were involved with," Knapp said.

"Oh, I don't know. Before kindergarten, I think my mom enrolled me in tap, jazz, ballet and gymnastics. And then I started, you know, T-ball, softball, baseball . . . Sixth, seventh and eighth grade, I played volleyball, basketball, softball and track. I had given up gymnastics at about age thirteen. I was captain of every team my eighth-grade year and was awarded athlete of the year. I also swam on the city team. God, I did so much."

"Special Olympics?"

"We did Special Olympics. I used to do handicapped swim on Wednesday nights to teach the handicapped children how to swim and then we would do Special Olympics later on that following year. So they would have a good twelve-month period, at least, to prepare before the Special Olympics."

"Student council?"

"Oh, yeah. I did student council in elementary, junior high and high school, and that's when I played volleyball and basketball in high school and swam on the swim team."

"Good grades?"

"Good grades all the way up until my senior year."

Murphy went on to explain that she ended up dropping out of high school because she moved in with an older man she had fallen in love with and started a business with him. She said she was sorry she never graduated.

Knapp then asked Murphy to discuss her relationship with Binion.

"We did a lot of things together," she said. "I think our favorite thing that we did was fishing and horseback riding. We used to go fishing over at Willow Creek or Willow Bay here. Early, early in the morning, four o'clock in the morning, before the sun was up. We'd take our dogs, Pig, Buddy and Princess, and we'd go out and wear our waders. I'd have a fishing hat and all the gear, and we'd start in the morning, and when it started to get real hot in the midafternoon, we'd come back. It was an hour drive."

"And some of those trips, your family was along as well?"

"Oh, absolutely. We went to visit my family probably four or five times a year. We always went for Christmas. Teddy didn't have any family here, and Bonnie used to spend her holidays with her mother. So Teddy would spend Christmas with my family . . . We spent summers together in Laguna Beach at the Surf and Sand Hotel."

Murphy then went deeper into her relationship with Binion.

"I think that everybody tries to paint a real ugly light on my relationship, and the truth of the matter is that when we met, it's like a love story," she said. "He kind of swept me off my feet, and we fell in love and we were a real couple. I think that people lose sight of what our relationship was really about. It was just two human beings that genuinely loved each other and had great affection and had a good time together. It wasn't always good times. There's good and bad in everyone, but I think that no relationship is perfect. Teddy and I genuinely loved each other, and we did the best that we could under the circumstances."

Knapp asked Murphy to explain how they could be together with such an age difference. Binion was almost thirty years older.

"I don't think the age difference had anything to do with it, to tell you the truth," she said. "You know what? Every girl loves an older man. Someone that's handsome, that's a gentleman, that knows how to treat them, that's educated, that's wise to the ways of the world, that's smart. Someone to romance you and charm you. Wine and dine you, and take you out and treat you like a lady. A lot of young guys don't have those qualities. Then the first thirty minutes, I usually get bored with the conversation. They don't know anything about politics or what's going on with the world, and really, they're not mentally stimulating at all."

Murphy then was asked how she felt about the way she

was portrayed in the media as a golddigger and a woman who liked to live in the fast lane.

" . . . I've had so many things said about me in the past year and a half," she said. "Really, most of the time I laugh and everyone gets mad at me downstairs. . . . This stuff is like a comedy . . . They get frustrated because I know what I'm about, and everyone who knows me and loves and cares for me knows what I'm all about, and really, what everyone else thinks doesn't matter to me. If it did, I wouldn't have been with Teddy all that time."

"Let me ask you this," Knapp said. "Did you ever work as a topless dancer?"

"Never," Murphy replied.

He asked it again.

"I was never employed as a topless dancer," she retorted.

"Did you ever work at Cheetah's?"

"No, I never worked or was employed at Cheetah's, ever."

Then Momot interjected: "She was an independent contractor and . . . she sold some costumes in two independent weekends and that's it in total. So she was never a topless dancer at Cheetah's, and she was never employed there."

Knapp looked over at Murphy and quipped, "Like that label is now part of your name—onetime topless dancer Sandy Murphy."

Again Momot came to the rescue.

"Well, that always adds sex appeal to this case," he responded. "That's the problem with the newspaper coverage Sandy receives. That's what grabs the reader's eye to read further, and it's not true."

Weeks later, after courtroom testimony had confirmed earlier *Las Vegas Sun* reports about Murphy's topless-dancing exploits at Cheetah's, Knapp would go on the air and candidly acknowledge that he had been led astray by Murphy and Momot.

In the interview, Knapp asked Murphy what she would like the public to know about her.

"Everyone tries to paint me in a really negative light," she said. "But you know, I'm just an everyday person like everyone else. You know I grew up in an upper-middle-class family. I was a normal kid. I liked to do all the things that regular kids liked to do."

Momot then explained why the defense had taken a new, more aggressive public relations stance.

"Everyone else can throw the snowballs, and I just have to catch them, and we all get tired of it," he said. "We get frustrated, and that's why we find ourselves in these interview-type situations so that you can get an idea of the type of person Sandra really is, and that's the best we can do."

Knapp concluded the interview by asking Murphy about her latest benefactor, eighty-four-year-old William Fuller.

"Do you talk to the guy—the Irish fellow?"

"Oh, all the time," she said. "He's my greatest friend. He comes over like three nights a week, and I make him dinner, and he's out here a lot. He has a house in Malibu, and you know he does a lot of business out of the country."

Murphy was riding high after the interview, but in a few days she would once more become her own worst enemy. The *Las Vegas Sun* ran a story under the headline "Murphy still living the good life: Despite indigent status, defendant continues shopping sprees." The story described how Murphy, with the trial approaching, had moved into an apartment at the upscale Regency Towers on the Las Vegas Country Club grounds. Fuller was reported to be paying her rent. Earlier, Murphy was spotted at a luxury-car dealership with Fuller picking out a new Mercedes. All this had occurred while Murphy was still under house arrest.

Then the newspaper reported something even more amazing. It turned out that before Murphy had moved into the Regency Towers, she had persuaded the power company to transfer the electricity from Binion's sprawling Las Vegas home to her new apartment. She identified herself as "Sandy Binion" when making the request. Power officials had gone to the home to turn off the electricity, but were denied access by security officers stationed there. Estate lawyers ultimately were notified, and they persuaded the power company not to take action.

"It was a pretty brazen thing to do," one estate attorney said at the time.

After the story appeared, Becky Behnen decided to publicly criticize Murphy for accepting taxpayer money for her defense.

"She shouldn't be doing that," Behnen said. "It doesn't endear her to the public."

Momot did his best to defend Murphy, insisting, "She's not living her own life. She's at the hands of others." He complained that Murphy was "living in a fishbowl every minute of the day."

His words did not sway Judge Bonaventure, who had found himself at the receiving end of more telephone calls from vocal residents angry about his decision to declare Murphy indigent. Bonaventure used Murphy's move to the Regency Towers to haul her back to court to grill her about the life of luxury she was leading under house arrest. He told Momot he would require the attorney to put on a full evidentiary hearing if he planned on requesting any more taxpayer funds for Murphy's defense. Bonaventure's stern words landed him back in the public's good graces, and Momot had no choice but to abandon future efforts to obtain taxpayer money.

Bonaventure, however, gave Murphy some reason to smile when he dismissed several charges against her related to the Leo Casey torture. Prosecutors, who had filed the charges late in the game, were not shocked when the judge ruled they had not presented enough evidence to make the charges stick.

Tension, meanwhile, was building during the first week in March, as the city's "trial of the century," expected to last as long as three months, was fast approaching. Las Vegas One was planning to cover it every day, and nationally, Court TV was gearing up for gavel-to-gavel coverage. ABC's *20/20* also was expected in town to keep an eye on the trial, as well as NBC's *Dateline.* All of the country's major newspapers had at one point in the past eighteen months done a piece on the case, and some, like the *Los Angeles Times* and *The Washington Post,* were planning to be on hand for opening arguments. So were a couple of Los Angeles news stations and most of the television tabloid shows. CNN's *Burden of Proof* and CNBC's *Rivera Live* also were anxious to air segments on the trial.

At a March 7 hearing, Bonaventure formally denied key defense motions aimed at suppressing the brunt of the district attorney's case. In so doing, the judge gave Dillard a clean bill of health.

"Mr. Dillard never answered to anyone but to those employed by the Binion family or estate," Bonaventure simply said.

The judge said he would not rule on a previous defense request to move the trial outside Las Vegas unless he had difficulty selecting a jury. But he did give the defense a two-week delay after lawyers complained they had been "bombarded" with last-minute evidence from prosecutors. The new trial date was March 27.

David Roger, who had turned over more than 40,000 pages of documents to defense lawyers since the murder arrests in June 1999, did not oppose the delay. Roger had issued subpoenas the previous week to more than 200 potential witnesses.

On March 16, Murphy wound up in still more trouble with jail officials. She was taken into custody about 4:30 P.M. at her Regency Towers apartment for once more violating the terms of her house arrest. This time, jail officials said Murphy had lied to them a month earlier about her whereabouts. Murphy, they alleged, had told them she was spending the day at her lawyer's office, when in fact she was observed shopping for furniture for her posh new apartment.

Roger made it clear early on that he would oppose any effort by Murphy to regain her freedom.

"She's had too many chances," he said.

Jail officials also said they no longer regarded her as a good candidate for electronic monitoring.

"We don't want to put her back in house arrest," said Sergeant Barry Payne of the detention center. "She's really a challenge."

Even though the trial was getting closer, Bonaventure was in no hurry to hold another hearing on Murphy's alleged indiscretions.

A week later, on March 23, the judge finally brought her back to court. And he left little doubt where he stood.

"The defendant did not commit a crime, did not take drugs, did not become violent and did not try to flee the jurisdiction," Bonaventure said. "However, what the defendant did was prove to this court . . . that she is unsupervisable under the house arrest program."

Bonaventure promised a decision the next morning. Momot still held out hope that the judge would allow Murphy to go free under a higher bail to give her a chance to properly prepare for her trial. But that would not be the case.

When it came time to announce his decision the next day, Bonaventure gave a sullen-looking Murphy another stern lecture from the bench.

"The situation you now find yourself in is a result of your own doing—your own contemptuous actions," he said. "To claim now, on the eve of trial, that you will somehow be prejudiced if you are in custody is without merit."

Bonaventure ordered Murphy held behind bars without bail for the duration of the trial, which was four days away.

CHAPTER 27

•••••••••••••••••

The Prosecution's Push

•••••••••••••••••

DAVID MATTSEN WAS a scared and confused man the first week in March 2000, as his federal firearms trial was about to get under way.

Prosecutor David Roger, who had persuaded federal authorities to file the weapons charges, had made no secret of his desire to gain Mattsen's cooperation against Sandy Murphy and Rick Tabish. Roger believed it was possible that Mattsen was at Ted Binion's home the day of the casino man's slaying and might have helped steal items from the home. With the murder trial just days away, Roger knew he had plenty of witnesses to win a conviction, but he wanted a little insurance. And Mattsen fit the bill.

Talks aimed at reaching a deal between Roger and federal prosecutors and Mattsen and his lawyer, James "Bucky" Buchanan, were occurring that first week in March. Similar discussions had not gone well in the past because Buchanan had offered information about Binion's death that conflicted with what other witnesses in the case had given. Mattsen also wanted the entire $100,000 reward Binion's estate was offering, but the estate was reluctant to give it all to the man it believed had betrayed Binion.

As the negotiations progressed, it was obvious that Mattsen hated Murphy but was afraid of what Tabish might do if he cooperated. At the same time, he was worried about the Binion family, which under legendary patriarch Benny Binion had a reputation for dishing out its own brand of frontier justice in matters affecting its well-being. What Mattsen knew for sure was that he didn't want to go to prison. Serving hard time would not be easy for a man aged fifty-four.

A couple of days before his federal trial, in the middle of negotiations with prosecutors, Mattsen began to feel the pressure. Buchanan reported that his client had disappeared and that negotiations had stalled. Mattsen wasn't totally out of sight, however. The hard-drinking cowboy was spotted in Las Vegas floating from tavern to tavern. Somehow, maybe from the drinking, he had gotten the impression that Nick and Becky Behnen had put a contract out on his life. One day in a drunken stupor, he surfaced at the Horseshoe Club looking for Becky Behnen, but was kicked out by security officers. Eventually, he made contact with the Behnens and met them at their home, where he led them to believe he was present at some point during the murder scheme.

Once Buchanan learned that Mattsen had sought out the Behnens, he took the unusual step of publicly criticizing his client. He told reporters that Mattsen had "gone off the deep end." Later, he described Mattsen as "paranoid." Mattsen's erratic behavior was enough for Roger to proclaim that any hope of a plea bargain had collapsed. In Roger's mind, the former Binion ranch hand had lost all credibility.

"It's over," Roger told the *Las Vegas Sun* on March 5. "I have no desire to speak with David Mattsen anymore."

The next day, Mattsen, looking calm and coherent, showed up in federal court with Buchanan for the start of the firearms trial. During a break, he went up to a reporter who had been chronicling his bizarre exploits and yelled, "Why are you trying to get me killed?"

In court, Buchanan told the jury the charges were brought against his client solely to pressure him into cooperating in the Binion probe.

"This case isn't about guns," Buchanan said in his opening statement. "This case is about the Ted Binion murder case."

Mattsen took the witness stand during the two-day trial to portray himself as a victim of the murder investigation.

"I think they were trying to hang me out for something," Mattsen testified. "All I did was be a good friend to Ted Binion."

The defense worked. The jury took less than two hours to acquit Mattsen of all the charges.

A jubilant Mattsen, his cowboy hat in hand, emerged from the courtroom to tell reporters that he "felt great" about being acquitted and still was interested in telling prosecutors the truth.

Buchanan was more strident.

"I think this is the opening salvo in the Binion murder case," he said. "This is going to put a crimp in what they thought was an impregnable wall."

Tom Dillard responded that he didn't see this as a setback for prosecutors.

"He's still not off the hook," Dillard said. "He's still looking at the silver charges."

In the following days, as the murder trial approached, Mattsen continued to be anxious to tell his story, but prosecutors weren't listening. So he kept up his contact with the Behnens. One Friday evening about 10:30 P.M., a reporter received a telephone call from Nick Behnen summoning him to the Horseshoe Club to meet with Mattsen.

"He wants to talk," Behnen said. "You should be there."

A half hour later, all three hooked up at the casino's main bar and took an elevator up to a suite. Behnen had stationed a Horseshoe security guard outside the room and ordered room service for Mattsen—a thick New York steak, shrimp cocktail and a six-pack of beer over ice. For the next two hours, with a beer constantly in hand, Mattsen talked. He talked about his fondness for Binion and the good old days working at the ranch in Pahrump. And he talked about the murder. He left little doubt that in his mind, Murphy and Tabish had killed Binion. But he kept on insisting that they had taken Binion hostage the evening before his death, a development that did not fit into the prosecution's time line of Binion's last hours. Prosecutors later surmised that Mattsen was trying to put himself in the best possible light by suggesting that Binion was grabbed the night before September 17.

Mattsen told Behnen that Binion had gotten into a violent argument with Tabish the evening of September 16 and that Tabish had thrown him against a wall. Eventually, Tabish and Murphy secured him with rhinestone-studded handcuffs. At that time, Mattsen said, they ordered him—Mattsen—to leave the house or they would harm his wife, Thressa. After telling Binion everything would be all right, Mattsen said he drove back to Pahrump.

The next morning, he met Tabish at the mountain pass between Pahrump and Las Vegas and was told, "It's over." Among other things, Mattsen said Tabish had told him that he and Murphy had sex in front of Binion while the gambling figure was restrained. Mattsen suggested that the couple had used a turkey baster to force a deadly mixture of heroin and Xanax down his throat.

By 1 A.M. and six beers later, Mattsen said he had done enough talking, and he simply went into the bedroom of the suite and collapsed on the bed. The next day, Behnen had Horseshoe security officers kick him out of the room. Mattsen never did strike a deal with Roger before the trial.

But to the prosecutor, it no longer mattered. He had other important witnesses who stepped forward on the eve of the trial.

One was Jason Frazer, a twenty-nine-year-old former Tabish business partner in Montana. Tabish had merged his Montana trucking company with Frazer's following his arrest in Binion's slaying. Homicide detectives had secretly learned months earlier that Frazer was part of a plot by Tabish to pay off alibi witnesses in the Binion case. One day in August 1999, Frazer's wife, Bobbi, a law student, had gone through his briefcase after one of his trips to visit Tabish in jail in Las Vegas and had come across mysterious handwritten notes by her husband.

"These notes were written on stationery from the Rio Suite Hotel & Casino and indicated that defense witnesses in the Binion murder trial are possibly being bribed for their testimony," Detective James Buczek wrote in an affidavit at the time.

Buczek said Bobbi Frazer turned over the notes to Missoula police, who in turn hand-delivered them to Buczek.

Las Vegas police had learned of the plot on August 17, the first day of the preliminary hearing in the murder case.

"It was readily apparent that these notes are notes outlining a false alibi," Buczek wrote. "Also, the notes reflect that the alibi witnesses were to be paid for their testimony."

One of the notes read: "Three guys, $2,000 up front. The rest the day after they take the stand—$4,000 later."

Another note, dated August 12, 1999, said: "Roger and Marty will be here tomorrow night. Final prep and it is done."

Buczek said he learned prosecutors expected that two Tabish employees, Roger M. Davis and Martin M. Frye, would be called as defense witnesses during the trial. Another name on one of the notes was Michael Gary, an associate of Steve Wadkins. Wadkins, who was charged in the Leo Casey portion of the case, ran All Star Transit Mix, a concrete-mixing company that did business with Tabish.

"This was like pennies from heaven," David Roger later said. "It was absolutely wonderful. We knew we had them."

Roger had recently prosecuted another murder trial that included testimony linking the defendant to a plot to bribe alibi witnesses, and that testimony, in his mind, had provided the clincher to winning a conviction.

"I knew that Rick Tabish was going to have an alibi because he bragged about it so much," Roger said. "It wasn't hard to figure out that the witnesses probably would be some truck drivers. We were pretty excited about that.

"We immediately went and put a wiretap on Michael Gary's phone. Midway through the preliminary hearing, I took a day off and called Michael Gary before the grand jury to stimulate conversation for the wiretaps. We subpoenaed him that night at his girlfriend's house. It totally freaked him out. He got on the phone to Wadkins."

The prosecutor said he was able to obtain some "decent information" before the wiretaps ran out, but nothing that was a "case cracker."

"We were going to do another wiretap as soon as the defense filed its alibi notices, and then we planned to interview the alibi witnesses," he said. "But in a shot in the dark, Louis Palazzo filed a motion asking us to reveal whether we had conducted any electronic surveillance in the case. He had no idea that we did, but it forced our hand. I didn't want to lie to Judge Bonaventure, so we decided to go arrest Frazer."

On February 14, Frazer was taken into custody in Missoula as a material witness, and Tabish's alibi plot was exposed. After a $1 million bail was set, Frazer quickly agreed to cooperate and was given immunity from prosecution. He ended up outlining the scheme in a lengthy interview with Buczek in Las Vegas.

Frazer told Buczek the plot was hatched during a series of visits to Tabish at the detention center in the summer of 1999. Frazer acknowledged paying a mystery man known only as "Ishma" $2,000 up front to find three alibi witnesses for Tabish. Those witnesses were to falsely state that Tom Dillard had offered them money to testify in the case.

Palazzo wasn't impressed with Frazer's statement, calling it vague and filled with a lot of uncertainty.

But prosecutors were ecstatic. They knew that Frazer, who also incriminated Murphy, would make an excellent witness at the trial.

Frazer said he believed Murphy knew about Ishma and the alibi plot.

"She was aware of most everything that was going on," he told Buczek. "I believe that she knew about the money situation and that I was going to take care of it after Rick's approval."

Frazer also said William Knudson acted like a courier, passing numerous jailhouse notes, mostly in sealed envelopes, with instructions from Tabish. Knudson strongly denied any knowledge of the alibi scheme.

But Frazer ended up giving Buczek fifty-two pages of notes, written on a legal notepad.

In one note, Tabish appeared to ask Frazer to make sure a Tabish employee identified as Jim Mitchell would be available to help provide him with an alibi on the day of Binion's death.

"I need Roger to get a hold of Jim Mitchell concerning Sept. 17, 1998, at All Star [Transit Mix]," Tabish wrote. "We really need an affidavit from him saying we were working [there] from 7-11:30 A.M. My life is on the line—and we need to fight fire with fire— and I will pay for an attorney for him."

Tabish told Frazer to be guarded in his dealings.

"Everything will be fine," he wrote. "Let's get some stuff handled and pay attention to business."

In another note, Tabish said: "Tell Mitchell we will take care of any legal concerns he has, but his testimony is crucial to me being set free . . ."

Then he added: "This is a slam dunk if everyone sticks in . . . Tell everyone when I owe someone something, the rewards are huge, and I think they know."

Tabish expressed his disdain for Dillard in several of the notes Frazer turned over.

"Half of the 109-page [arrest affidavit] comes from this uneducated moron," Tabish wrote. "This man has no business savvy. Thank God for us he has no ethics either."

After learning of Tabish's words, Dillard described Tabish as a big-time manipulator who had been exposed by Frazer.

"Tabish thinks he's the puppet master, but his strings have been severed," Dillard said.

Palazzo tried to counter Frazer by suggesting that prosecutors really had obtained the notes through a jailhouse informant they had planted next to Tabish. The informant, David Gomez, was reported to have done something similar for Los Angeles prosecutors in the Ennis Cosby murder case.

Gomez, who originally said he was asked to steal

Tabish's confidential notes, had in fact been in the same protective-custody cell block as the murder defendant. But prosecutors, pointing out that Gomez had little credibility, vehemently denied any involvement in such a plot. Judge Bonaventure nevertheless held a hearing on the matter. After Gomez, a three-time convicted felon with reported ties to the Mexican Mafia, took the Fifth Amendment on the witness stand and refused to testify, Palazzo was forced to acknowledge that he had no "smoking gun" to prove the scheme existed. Bonaventure rejected the defense claims, and prosecutors later said they learned that Tabish might have promised to pay Gomez to stir things up for him.

Jason Frazer, meanwhile, wasn't the only eleventh-hour witness to step forward for the prosecution.

In mid-March, Michael Karstedt, an investigator with the district attorney's office, reminded David Roger that he had received information from Missoula that Tabish's thirty-seven-year-old brother-in-law, Dennis Rehbein, had come into possession of a large amount of silver coins. Roger gave Karstedt the go-ahead to ask a Missoula detective to make contact with Rehbein.

"So the detective called Rehbein and said to him, 'I want to talk to you about the silver that you have,'" Roger recalled. "And Rehbein said, 'I need to talk to an attorney.' The detective then told me we had something here—that Dennis Rehbein was just a sweetheart of a guy from a good family whose sister just happened to marry a killer."

Later, Rehbein's Missoula attorney, John E. Smith, telephoned Roger and offered his client's cooperation on the condition he be given immunity. Roger immediately obtained the order from Judge Bonaventure, and on March 15, Tabish's thirty-fifth birthday, Rehbein gave Missoula police 100 pounds of silver coins prosecutors believed had been stolen from Binion. These were believed to be the same coins identified on the seven-page, handwritten list Murphy had once given Tanya Cropp.

The next day, Smith told the *Las Vegas Sun* that Rehbein, the brother of Tabish's wife, Mary Jo, had received the coins on November 1, 1998, as collateral for a $25,000 loan to Tabish. Ironically, Tabish had told his brother-in-law that he needed the loan to help with his legal expenses in the Binion case.

Smith described his client as a "law-abiding citizen" and a victim of circumstances.

"He's stuck in the middle of this only because he accepted these coins from Rick Tabish," Smith said. "This is very difficult for the family."

Once more, prosecutors were elated. Not only did they now have a member of Tabish's own family as a witness, but they actually had some evidence of what had been stolen from Binion's house.

"It was another nail to put in Tabish's coffin," Roger said. "I knew that Jason Frazer was the backbreaker. But Rehbein was the frosting on the case. He had the silver that related to the facts and kind of wrapped it all together."

Rehbein, tall, slender and bland-looking, later would testify that before giving him the coins, Tabish showed him the seven-page list that Cropp had faxed to Tabish. Crime experts had identified the fingerprints of both Tabish and Murphy on the list.

"With the trouble Rick was in, I really didn't want these coins," a stoic Rehbein testified.

Prosecutors also learned that these were among the coins Murphy had brought to Oscar Goodman's law office in the days immediately after Binion's death. Murphy had wanted to pay her legal fees to Goodman's firm with the coins, but ultimately she took them back.

With the murder trial now just days away, everything was starting to fall into place for the prosecutors.

"We had plenty of corroborating evidence," Roger said. "We didn't have to rely upon one particular witness."

PART

IV

The Trial

CHAPTER 28

• • • • • • • • • • • • • • • • • •

Showdown in Court

• • • • • • • • • • • • • • • • • •

THOUGH CONFIDENT AND WELL PREPARED, prosecutors headed into the biggest criminal trial in Las Vegas history with some reservations.

"We had a couple of big concerns," David Roger said. "One was Kurt Gratzer. We didn't know how he was going to respond. The other was the medical testimony."

Gratzer had been a disaster at the preliminary hearing. Roger later learned that the onetime Army Ranger had deliberately muddied his testimony to protect Rick Tabish. At the time, prosecutors, though they later abandoned the idea, were considering seeking the death penalty for Tabish and Murphy, and Gratzer didn't want to see Tabish put to death.

"At prelim, he was trying to help Rick out," Roger said. "But after prelim, Mary Jo Tabish was up North, and she told a barber there that she and Rick were laughing about Gratzer—that he had acted like such a fool. And the barber told Gratzer that, and Gratzer got very pissed. He said, 'Doesn't Tabish realize that I was trying to help him? I was trying to save his life.' And Gratzer stiffened up."

Still, Roger and fellow prosecutor David Wall, who had drawn the assignment of questioning Gratzer at the trial, weren't convinced that Gratzer would be there for them when it counted.

The prosecutors also knew that their key forensic

witnesses—Chief Medical Examiner Lary Simms and famed New York pathologist Michael Baden—had come up with dual theories of death that could give the defense an opening to create confusion in the minds of the jurors.

"I wasn't concerned about the split between Baden and Simms because we had a pretty cohesive theory about how all of this had gone down," Roger said . "I knew that I could explain to the jury that Dr. Simms was a fine doctor but didn't have the experience of Dr. Baden."

What bothered the prosecutors more was that the defense was bringing in its own well-respected medical witnesses, like Baden's close friend, well-known Pittsburgh pathologist Cyril Wecht, to create doubt about the state's medical evidence.

The case appeared to be shaping up as a battle of the experts.

Earlier, Wecht had filed a seventeen-page report, concluding that Binion had died of a "combined heroin and Xanax overdose" as part of a planned suicide.

"I do not find any evidence to support the contention that he was suffocated," Wecht wrote in his report. "I believe that Mr. Binion initially inhaled heroin smoke, as he had in the past, and this led to thoughts of suicide."

Wecht pointed to statements that Sandy Murphy had made to police the night of Ted Binion's death, that Binion would often put a gun to his mouth after smoking heroin. The report fit nicely into the defense's theory that Binion was despondent after losing his gaming license and had returned to using drugs. As the trial approached, Murphy's lawyer, John Momot, insisted, "There is not a homicide in this case."

His words set up the pending showdown between Baden and Wecht. For weeks, both sides had been working hard to come up with dirt on the other's high-profile expert on cross-examination. There was a wealth of information, good and bad, on both professional witnesses, who had consulted on some of the country's biggest murder cases. Baden and Wecht had worked together at the O. J. Simpson murder trial and were involved in the investigation of the death of Jon-Benet Ramsey. Both pathologists also had written popular books on their careers. Baden hosted the HBO series *Autopsy,* and Wecht had appeared on the Fox network's blockbuster, *Alien Autopsy: Fact or Fiction.* Their sparring in court was much anticipated.

Two weeks before the trial, Roger filed court papers listing a whopping 276 potential witnesses, but he told the *Las Vegas Sun* that he actually intended to call less than half that number to the stand.

"It will be a leaner case," he said. "We want to present a relatively simple case to the jury."

The case was anything but simple, and since it was all circumstantial, Roger was concerned that he risked boring the jury if he let things drag on. He privately acknowledged that he didn't want to fall into the same trap as Los Angeles prosecutors in the six-month O. J. Simpson trial. Jurors in that trial had a hard time weeding through the prosecution's evidence. So Roger kept his scaled-down list to a staple of witnesses, many of whom had testified at the preliminary hearing. He planned to bring Bonnie Binion and her mother, Doris, to the witness stand, to show the good and the bad of Binion's personal side. And he expected to call Thomas Loveday, Mary Montoya-Gascoigne, Tanya Cropp, Cathy Rose, Kurt Gratzer, Jason Frazer, Dennis Rehbein, James Brown, Richard Wright, Leo Casey, Peter Sheridan, Dr. Enrique Lacayo and, of course, Lary Simms and Michael Baden.

What Roger didn't tell the defense was that he hoped to avoid calling Tom Dillard and James Buczek so that the defense couldn't get a crack at cross-examining them. Roger wasn't sure that Dillard, who was becoming a media star, was as prepared as he should have been to testify, and he didn't want Momot and Palazzo to have a chance to further their theory that the Binion Money Machine had fueled the investigation. Though they still were good friends, the relationship between Roger and Dillard became strained during the investigation. Roger wasn't happy that the private detective frequently talked about the inner workings of the case with the media, and Dillard often got frustrated with the lawyers telling him how to do his job. Roger also didn't want to give the defense a chance to grill Buczek about problems with the death scene. In hindsight, police privately acknowledged that they would have preferred not to relinquish control of Binion's home to his estate after his death. By giving up the house, they had opened the door for the defense to claim the death scene was contaminated.

Roger had gone to great lengths to ensure that one witness, Linda Carroll, would show up for the trial. He had her arrested in California in January on a material-witness warrant. But as the trial neared, Roger decided not to call Carroll, figuring she would be too much trouble on the witness stand in his new streamlined case. He also decided against calling Becky Behnen and subject her to cross-examination about her warring family members. And Roger was in no mood to bring Nye County Sheriff Wade Lieseke to the witness stand so that the defense could bring up the statements Tabish had allegedly made to him on the night Tabish was arrested for trying to steal Binion's silver fortune in Pahrump. Roger wanted to limit that kind of fallout from reaching the jury.

Defense lawyers let it be known in their witness lists that they planned to make the trial a Binion family affair. They named all of Binion's key surviving family members, including Jack Binion and Becky Behnen and her husband, Nick, as potential witnesses. Jack Binion had maintained an incredibly low profile during the murder investigation, speaking out only once, long before criminal charges were filed. But the defense knew that Binion, as executor of his brother's $55 million estate, was the one who had hired Dillard and signed the checks for the family investigation. The defense also knew that Jack still hated Becky for wrestling away the Horseshoe Club from him in July 1998. Early in the murder investigation, Murphy and Tabish had put the word out that Jack was plotting to undermine his sister and regain control of the downtown casino. The allegations were never proved, but Becky believed them. Jack and Becky did not speak to each other at all during the investigation.

The case, meanwhile, was simplified when District Judge Joseph Bonaventure agreed to give David Mattsen and Michael Milot separate trials at a later date.

A week before the murder trial, Bonaventure, concerned about an increasing amount of media coverage, slapped a gag order on the case. At the time, local television stations, locked in a ratings war, were falling over themselves trying to come up with exclusives for their viewers. One station went as far as showing upbeat home videos of Murphy and Binion during their friendlier days. The two daily newspapers, the *Las Vegas Sun* and the *Las Vegas Review-Journal*, also were running a steady stream of Page One stories.

Much of the information in the days and weeks leading up to the trial was coming from the defense, which was desperately trying to rehabilitate the stained images of Murphy and Tabish in the eyes of the public, but more importantly in the minds of the potential jurors.

In his gag order, however, Bonaventure also rapped the prosecution.

"This court has observed a virtual pipeline of information to particular journalists from both the defendants and the prosecution," he said in court. "Guilt or innocence must be determined in the courtroom—not in the marketplace of public opinion."

Bonaventure said he was concerned that if he continued to allow the defendants, lawyers and investigators in the case to speak with the media, it would hinder his ability to pick a jury. He did not want to be forced to move the trial outside Las Vegas.

Jury selection began with much fanfare under tight security on Monday, March 27. Local and network satellite trucks lined the streets of the downtown courthouse, which was only a couple of blocks from the Horseshoe Club. Court

TV had set up an air-conditioned tent on the lawn outside
the courthouse for its reporter, Mary Jane Stevenson, to conduct live interviews with key Binion players throughout the
trial.

Inside, though both defendants were in jail, Bonaventure
allowed them to wear their street clothes in court to avoid
prejudicing the jurors. Their shackles were taken off before
the jurors entered the courtroom. Murphy came to court
dressed conservatively as usual and wearing her dyed
reddish-blond hair tied behind her nape. It gave her a more
studious look. Earlier, she had caused a stir at the detention
center when her family members showed up with ten different designer outfits for her to rotate wearing during the trial.
Jail officials had no room to store that much clothing, and
after Bonaventure intervened, officials allowed Murphy to
keep three outfits at a time in the jail. Tabish, meanwhile,
appeared in court looking preppy and studious as well. He
wore a navy blue sport coat and glasses.

Despite Bonaventure's concerns, it took less than three
days to pick a twelve-member jury and six alternates from a
pool of 300 citizens, some of whom amazingly said they had
never read or watched anything about the most publicized
criminal case ever in the city. After the twelve jurors were
chosen on the second day, Doug Bradford, an appointed
spokesman for Bonaventure, told reporters that the judge
was very pleased with the way things were progressing.

"He seems to be moving quickly while at the same time
protecting the integrity of the judicial process," Bradford
said.

It sounded as if Bradford had been well briefed by the
judge. Bonaventure's main concern when imposing the gag
order was to protect the integrity of the trial. Now that a jury
had been chosen with ease, he agreed to lift the ban on talking to the media. That freed Momot and Palazzo to go on national television to plead their case almost on a daily basis
throughout the trial. Court TV was doing live shots every
day and *Rivera Live* and *Burden of Proof* were devoting

much airtime to the trial. Roger and Wall shied away from the cameras, opting to do their talking in the courtroom. Bonaventure, meanwhile, was so pleased with the way the jury selection process had gone that he decided it wasn't necessary to sequester the jurors. He estimated that he would save the taxpayers roughly $1 million in the next couple of months by allowing the jurors to go home to their families at night.

"This court," Bonaventure told the lawyers, "has implemented procedures to ensure the defendants get a fair and impartial trial, including the probing interrogation of prospective jurors, providing clear instructions to the jury as to what may be considered in reaching a verdict, cloaking the jury in the highest security ever afforded a petit jury in Clark County, giving them a detailed admonition as to what they can or cannot read or watch and allowing them twenty-four-hour access to the court bailiff in case of any emergency. It is difficult to imagine the situation where all of these safeguards will be inadequate."

The twelve-member panel, whose names were withheld from the public, included nine women and three men. All of the women were middled-aged or older, prompting courthouse observers to speculate that the demographics of the panel were decidedly in the prosecution's favor. The women, it was suggested, would not approve of Murphy's courtroom demeanor and reputation for living in the fast lane with a man nearly thirty years older. Among the jurors were a pharmacist, a wildlife biologist, a retired aerospace engineer, a nurse and a housewife or two, giving the panel a diverse makeup.

On Wednesday, after the jury had been selected, Bonaventure secretly asked both sides whether there was any interest in striking a deal to avoid the upcoming lengthy trial. He held a brief closed-door hearing with prosecutors, Murphy and Tabish and their lawyers to determine whether a plea agreement could be reached.

The judge pointed out that he previously had inquired

about a possible deal in chambers with the lawyers and that Wall had said he'd be willing to consider one.

"And you know me," Bonaventure said in a secret transcript of the hearing. "I always want to [ask], are there any possible negotiations in this case? Do you remember that?"

Wall told the judge he recalled saying: "We'd be in the position to listen to any reasonable offer, take it and assimilate it and determine what to do with it at that time if any was going to be forthcoming."

Bonaventure then asked Momot and Palazzo if they had conveyed Wall's comments to their clients. The lawyers said they had done that, but no one mentioned any interest in a plea arrangement. That ended any chance of averting the trial.

Bonaventure said he called the hearing so that Wall's previous comments could be placed on the record, and at Roger's request, the judge ordered the proceeding sealed.

"Nobody will know about this," Bonaventure said.

Momot then interjected: "Sandy Murphy doesn't want it sealed."

"It's the order of the court," Bonaventure retorted. "It's going to be sealed."

By Friday, after giving both sides a day to prepare, the judge was ready to hear opening statements. First up was Roger.

Over the next three hours, Roger, just as he had done at the preliminary hearing, systematically laid out a case for murder, greed and betrayal.

He began by showing the jurors a photo of a smiling Binion just prior to his death and describing his days under the tutelage of his legendary father, Benny Binion, and how he had become a valuable asset at the Horseshoe's casino because of his mathematical mind and outgoing personality. But Roger also talked about Binion's dark side, his heavy drinking and drug use and his rocky marriage to Doris.

"The marriage with Ted Binion was not easy, and we're not about to paint a picture of a saint," Roger told the jurors in a steady voice. "However, he was a human being. He was a father. He was a brother and a son."

Roger then brought Murphy into the picture, explaining that she had moved in with Binion in April 1995.

"Sandra Murphy led a pretty good life when she lived with Ted Binion," he said. "And I'm not suggesting that it's always a day at the beach living with a drug addict, but she had many material items. Ted Binion bought her a Mercedes convertible, and he gave her a MasterCard with a $10,000 limit."

Next, Roger introduced Tabish into the story and explained how the Montana contractor had come into financial difficulties and schemed to torture Leo Casey into turning over his interests in the Jean, Nevada, sand pit, and how Tabish later needed access to Binion's wealth to keep the pit open.

For the next hour, Roger, in an orderly fashion, described how Murphy and Tabish had fallen in love with each other and plotted Binion's death, and how police found his body at his home in a "classic mortuary pose."

The prosecutor talked about how Simms had concluded that Binion had died of a forced heroin and Xanax overdose.

"He took the stomach contents, and there were forty milliliters of brown fluid in the stomach," Roger said. "However, he found that odd, because there were no particles in the stomach, and if a person took that many Xanax pills, Dr. Simms would expect that there would be particles in the stomach. The stomach would not be able to digest all of those particles before death occurred."

Roger said that concerned Simms.

"He determined, based upon that and based upon the lividity and some of the investigation and the fact that it appeared that this [death] scene was staged, that this was a homicide."

Then Roger built up the experienced Michael Baden and his review of the autopsy findings:

"At the conclusion of his examination, Dr. Baden said that

although there were levels of heroin in Ted Binion's system . . . for a heroin user, those were not lethal levels. He said that the Xanax didn't kill him, although it may have been a contributing cause for Ted to be debilitated.

"Ted Binion was suffocated. He said it was very likely that Ted Binion was restrained by the wrists, that someone sat on his chest, thereby not allowing the lungs to expand, and perhaps because of this pressure on the chest and the buttons on Ted Binion's shirt, it caused those marks at or around the time of death. And he said that the hand or pillow over his mouth would have caused this redness around his mouth.

"It was the state of Nevada's position that Rick Tabish and Sandy Murphy intended to create an overdose. However, the gardener showed up, and they had to put things in progress quicker, and Ted Binion was suffocated."

At the conclusion of his opening statement, Roger confidently told the jurors: "Ladies and gentlemen, the evidence will prove beyond a reasonable doubt that Ted Binion was murdered. That he was murdered for lust, for greed. That he was murdered by someone who he trusted and her new companion. Ladies and gentlemen, the killers are Richard Tabish and Sandra Murphy."

Momot, in his relaxed New Jersey accent, addressed the jurors next.

The seasoned defense attorney cleverly brought up a telephone conversation he said he had prior to coming to court with his teenage daughter, Roxanne.

"And in the brief moments that we spoke on the telephone discussing the upcoming trial, I really felt a sense of the importance of family to her," he said. "Now when I thought of family, I thought about this case and what's really transpiring here today, because what we're doing here today is really looking at a family situation. We're looking at a family that's probably one of the most powerful families in the state of Nevada, the Binion family."

Momot said he planned to put Binion's lifestyle and his

dysfunctional family on trial. Murphy, he said, was merely a victim.

"So what we're doing today and in the next month, couple of months, we're going to virtually take the roof off of their home and look into this family and see how they function with twenty-twenty hindsight."

Momot then went to the heart of his argument.

"This case is not about homicide," he told the jurors. "This case is about heroin. This case is not murder. This case is about money. And I'm going to talk about the Binion Money Machine, as I said to you, from one of the most powerful families in the state of Nevada."

Momot said the Binion family hated Murphy and was bent on "grinding her up." The estate, with Dillard's help, "took over" the police investigation in an effort to frame Murphy.

"This is in effect the Binion Money Machine at work," he said. "This is the power of a gaming family to be able to push forward with an investigation on their own. In a lot of other jurisdictions, you could use the word 'clout.' In this jurisdiction in Las Vegas, you use the word 'juice,' because that's big juice when you talk about the Binion family.

"They took this case from a drug overdose and turned it around and made it a homicide. That's what this family has done. That's what Mr. Dillard has done. Why did they do this? It's because Sandy is not a Binion. That's why."

Momot went on to describe how drugs and alcohol had taken over Binion's life and led him to abuse Murphy.

"The thing that makes Ted Binion so much different than others is real simple," Momot said. "The usual heroin drug addict lives in the gutter, but Ted Binion had the wealth, so he didn't live in the gutter. He didn't have to. He was getting his checks from the family on a yearly income probably in the neighborhood of $3 million. That's his lifestyle. That's Ted Binion's lifestyle. This, ladies and gentlemen, is in a different dimension than what you've lived through yourselves."

Momot called Binion self-centered and a manipulator who cared only about himself and his drugs.

Despite having everything in the world, the defense lawyer told the jurors, Binion was not a happy man, "because there are no happy heroin addicts."

Momot described Murphy as a "nice girl" who had gotten caught up in an overwhelming world of power and money.

"She came here and it was just all glitz and glamour," he said. "That's what you see on the Strip. It's all bright lights, and it's pretty. You have twenty-four-hour liquor, gambling and entertainment. You have everything in this town you could possibly want. It's just there for the taking.

"But you know what? Nothing is free, as she found out. Because there's a dark side to all of this. There's an underbelly to this whole lifestyle. The glitz and the glamour fade away. All the people that you laugh with at night fade away. All the people that are drinking with you and patting you on the back fade away. And what happens? You end up going into a house where the door is shut behind you, and now you're in a different world to live in, because now you're going into a world of a drug addict and how they live. And it's different."

Murphy, the attorney explained, ended up having to take care of Binion when his family wasn't there for him. Binion was unkempt, dirty and a slob. It was Murphy, Momot said, who would clean up his vomit and his body when he soiled himself while in a drug stupor.

And in the middle of all of that, Momot explained, Binion was fighting to keep his gaming license and undergoing a bitter divorce, and his siblings were locked in an equally bitter fight for control of the Horseshoe Club, which their parents had left them.

"This is not a happy household," he said. "There is more litigation going on between brothers and sisters, fighting over what? Money. Money and more money."

Momot then turned to Murphy's relationship with Binion.

"I'll tell you about this relationship," he said. "Ted Binion grabbed her, took her. She wasn't the one that was off chasing after him . . . He went after her, sought her out, and she fell in love with him.

"Did he love her? The drugs became his mistress. They always were his mistress. That's what he loved."

Then Momot revealed the first big surprise of the trial—an acknowledgment after months of denials that Murphy and Tabish indeed did have a romantic affair.

"What do you think, there's some secret about a relationship here?" he asked as he pointed to the two defendants at the defense table. "There's no secret about it. It existed between Rick and Sandy. So what?"

Momot said Murphy turned to Tabish for support as Binion kept pushing her farther and farther away.

"He's talking to her, and she's trying to maintain a relationship with Ted," Momot said. "And then after a while, he's the caretaker of Sandy. That's what happens with Rick. And then affection develops.

"Is that so inhuman to understand that that can happen? Is that against the law?"

Momot went on to attack Baden and the prosecution's dual theories of Binion's death, as well as the "contaminated" death scene and the state's refusal to charge Binion's heroin dealer, Peter Sheridan, with supplying the casino man the drugs that killed him.

Louis Palazzo told the jurors that prosecutors were light on evidence linking Tabish to Binion's death.

"I didn't hear one thing come out of the mouth of Mr. Roger during his long opening statement that in any way demonstrates that Rick Tabish had a hand in murdering Ted Binion," Palazzo said.

He also blasted the state's theory that Tabish had gone to Pahrump to steal Binion's silver.

"They made no secret about what they were doing there," he said. "They made no secret about their presence there. It was very well publicized. There was nothing secretive about it at all."

Tabish was continuing to insist he had gone to Pahrump to fulfill Binion's wishes of protecting the silver for Bonnie Binion.

Palazzo said it was "ludicrous" to think that Tabish would bring in heavy equipment to do the excavation on the busiest thoroughfare in the small town and not expect to be noticed.

At the conclusion of opening statements, what made headlines on the evening news and the next day in the newspapers was Momot's acknowledgment that Murphy and Tabish had been romantically involved. For months, the defendants and their lawyers had been denying the affair to reporters and even many of their friends. Tabish's wife certainly didn't know about it.

Many courthouse observers thought the confession was smart strategy on the part of the defense in the wake of the overwhelming evidence that prosecutors had been planning to present at the trial. By acknowledging the relationship, Murphy and Tabish had overcome one big obstacle that threatened to harm their credibility with the jurors.

But Murphy apparently went along with the strategy reluctantly.

"Sandy didn't want to go for it," one defense lawyer later said. "She kept saying it wasn't true. But we figured it would blow away the prosecution's case."

Well, not exactly.

Roger and Wall weren't dismayed at all by the startling development. To them, the defense was actually bolstering their theory that Murphy and Tabish had wanted Binion out of the way so that they could share his wealth. It also strengthened the credibility of several of their key witnesses—people like Tanya Cropp, Deana Perry and Steven Kurt Gratzer—all of whom had provided investigators with evidence of the affair.

Roger said the confession wouldn't shorten his witness list at all. He said he still planned to present witnesses who would testify about the secret trysts by Murphy and Tabish in Beverly Hills prior to Binion's death.

Momot acknowledged that the defense strategy had the potential to bolster the prosecution's case.

"We felt the better course was to be direct and forthright," he said. "The decision was to be up front about it and let the jury give it whatever weight it wishes."

CHAPTER 29

•••••••••••••••••••

The Sideshow

•••••••••••••••••••

PROSECUTORS TOOK A risk right off the bat by calling Ted Binion's former wife, Doris, as their first witness on the opening day of testimony.

Doris, looking slim and fit, broke into tears early under questioning from David Roger when she was asked to describe how Binion's drug use evolved and how he had come to beat her. Prosecutors knew that getting Doris to talk about her ex-husband's darker side wouldn't help Binion's image with the jurors. They even figured it might bolster the defense, which was contending Binion also had beaten and abused Sandy Murphy. But Roger felt the testimony was necessary to give himself credibility with the jurors. In his opening statement, he had told the panel members that he wasn't going to paint Binion as a saint. Doris was an important witness because she blamed Murphy for her divorce, and she talked about how her husband often kept large sums of cash around the house, cash that had turned up missing after his death. Roger planned to follow up later with Bonnie Binion to humanize her father and explain her soured relationship with Murphy.

Immediately following Doris was her divorce lawyer, Josh Landish, who was present when Murphy acknowledged under oath in a February 15, 1996, deposition that she was dancing topless at Cheetah's adult nightclub when she met Binion in 1995. The *Las Vegas Sun* had obtained the deposition six months earlier and printed a story about Murphy's exploits at Cheetah's, but Murphy still insisted she never danced there. Landish's testimony showed the jurors otherwise, but more important, it showed that Murphy was not the innocent young girl she was making herself out to be in court.

From there, prosecutors slowly began to build their case. They introduced evidence of the secret Beverly Hills trysts between Murphy and Tabish, the tough financial times Tabish was undergoing and the statements both Murphy and Tabish had made predicting Binion's death. Deana Perry took the stand and testified as expected, and then the much-anticipated testimony of Steven Kurt Gratzer took place.

Roger was nervous about Gratzer. Before court that morning, he asked David Wall, who was going to do the questioning, whether Gratzer would come around and fulfill his obligation to prosecutors this time. Wall replied, "He'll be fine."

Gratzer, however, arrived at court twenty minutes late, causing more apprehension on Roger's part. To help Gratzer stay focused, prosecutors put his new girlfriend in the first row of the courtroom.

Once he took the stand, all of Roger's fears subsided. Gratzer gave a stellar performance, delivering precise answers to Wall's questions and leaving little doubt that Tabish had sought his assistance in the murder scheme.

"He wanted to utilize my services in helping him kill this man," Gratzer calmly said.

This time Gratzer was deliberate, not tentative, as he laid out exactly how Tabish had planned to use him.

Under cross-examination from Louis Palazzo, Gratzer acknowledged that his brief career as an Army Ranger was less than outstanding and that he was arrested several times for drunken driving. But he continued to stick to his story.

"[Tabish] said he was going to kill him," Gratzer told Palazzo. "There were no two ways about it. I tried to talk him out of it, but he said he hated him."

Gratzer testified that he had contradicted himself at the preliminary hearing because "from the time I was a little boy, I was taught not to rat on my buddies."

When he learned that prosecutors weren't going to seek the death penalty against Tabish, he said he felt much better about testifying truthfully. Prosecutors presented several witnesses to corroborate Gratzer after he stepped down from the witness stand, and they left court that evening with smiles on their faces.

"David Wall and I were on pins and needles during his testimony," Roger later said. "At the conclusion of direct examination, we were greatly relieved. We knew we had come a long way in securing convictions."

Gratzer was arrested a couple of days later on battery charges stemming from a fight with his girlfriend at the Sahara Hotel and Casino. But even that didn't dampen the spirits of the prosecutors. The Montana man had performed better in court than they ever could have imagined. They also knew the jury, which had been admonished not to watch or read news accounts of the trial, would not have heard about the incident.

Gratzer's arrest was one of many sideshows that occurred outside the courtroom during the trial. Defense lawyers John Momot and Louis Palazzo were doing their part to hype the case in the media. The two made regular appearances on Court TV and *Rivera Live* when the trial was in recess.

Roger and Wall, however, weren't interested in soaking up national publicity. They made no television appearances. With no on-air opposition from the prosecutors, hosts such as Geraldo Rivera seemed to buy into the defense spin. On one show early in the trial, Rivera acknowledged that he hadn't kept totally abreast of the trial's developments. But after listening to Momot state his case, he said: "I like your client's chances."

Roger said he watched Court TV and *Rivera Live* in the evening the first week of the trial, but got so disgusted that he decided to stop watching until the case was over.

"I felt the defense attorneys were creating a circuslike atmosphere," he said. "These shows had invited us on many occasions to interview with them, but we declined because David and I felt it would be unprofessional to discuss our case in the media. We also wanted to focus all of our attention on presenting our case to the jury. We worked from six A.M. until eight P.M. every day."

Some defense-team colleagues of Momot and Palazzo thought the two lawyers had become awestruck at the attention they were getting from the national media.

"They were starting to believe their clips," one colleague said. "They should have spent more time preparing for the case."

But that wasn't the only sideshow.

Shortly after the jury had been selected, a fifteen-second television ad soliciting public opinion about the trial began running on Las Vegas One, which was airing the case live every day. The ad, sponsored by the defense, was the brainchild of William Cassidy, a secretive California private investigator who had been hired as a defense consultant for the trial. Cassidy said he was hoping the ads would generate enough public response to create a "model jury" that mirrored the demographics of the real Binion panel. It was hoped that the defense could then use the model to help prepare its courtroom strategy.

"This is the shadow jury of the information age," Cassidy said after the ad was aired. "This has never been done before. I have already received a number of calls from many attorneys around the country, some quite prominent, who want us to do the same thing for them."

Cassidy, a short, slender man with bad eyesight and a volatile temper, was an intriguing figure in the case. A devout Buddhist, he claimed to have studied under the Dalai Lama, the exiled Tibetan spiritual leader, handled covert assignments for the Central Intelligence Agency and done intelligence work for Philippines President Joseph Estrada. An array of newspaper clippings portrayed him as one of the nation's foremost experts on Vietnamese refugees. He spoke fluent Vietnamese and Tibetan. Years earlier, Cassidy had gotten to know Mayor Oscar Goodman during the mayor's career as a criminal defense attorney. Goodman was so impressed with his work as a defense strategist that he made him part of his campaign team when he ran for mayor in 1999. After Goodman won the race, he decided he still wanted Cassidy close by, so he gave him a $54,000-a-year salary as one of his City Hall aides.

At City Hall, Cassidy was regarded as a restless, atypical bureaucrat who chained-smoked, wore dark sunglasses and sometimes came to work in a white suit. He was low-keyed but intense.

"He's intelligent. He's eccentric. He's mysterious," Goodman once told the *Las Vegas Sun*.

In February, Cassidy already had taken a paid leave of absence from Goodman's side after he had persuaded Murphy's benefactor, William Fuller, that he could be valuable to the defense during the trial. Fuller ended up paying Cassidy a whopping $217,000 for three months' work as a consultant.

Part of that money went toward creating and airing the unprecedented television ad. Cassidy founded a company called Trial Consultants of Nevada with other key members of Goodman's political team to deal with the information gleaned from the ad and work with a local polling firm.

"If you ever wanted to serve on a jury, this is your chance," the ad said, as it asked people to call the polling company, Magellan Research.

Within a week after the ad began airing, Cassidy claimed to have gotten an overwhelming number of phone calls. Soon he released results of the polling that he said showed Murphy and Tabish were being perceived much better in the eyes of the public now that the trial had started. The release of the results irritated Judge Bonaventure, who had been careful to shield the jurors from the media. By coincidence, the judge had run into Cassidy outside his chambers and asked him to stop making public the poll results. Cassidy promised he would stop. Then, on April 13, Bonaventure made a record of his concerns in court in the absence of the jurors. Following a brief discussion with the lawyers at the bench, he read a statement.

"This court has taken every precaution short of full sequestering to ensure that this jury is free from publicity surrounding this case," he said. "And while this court has had no indication to believe otherwise, the court is concerned that the sanctity of the jury may be impinged in the future upon the publishing of the poll results."

Bonaventure said he had asked Palazzo and Momot to make sure that Cassidy would not release any more results until the end of the trial. Then Palazzo set off some fireworks.

"It has come to light at the bench just now — that Mr. Roger has made it clear for the record that he has launched an investigation into Mr. Cassidy," Palazzo said. "And so with that in mind, we believe that that constitutes an obstruction of justice based on Mr. Cassidy's role with the defense."

Roger started turning red with anger as the judge asked Palazzo: "Could you tell me what his role is, by the way?"

"He's been a consultant and has been involved in this case from the inception on behalf of Mr. Goodman, who represented Ms. Murphy early on," Palazzo replied. "And in that regard, Your Honor, I think that it clearly creates a chilling effect because now obviously the DA's office seems to be upset with the activities related to Mr. Cassidy, and so now they've retaliated in their vindictive, vengeful manner to target Mr. Cassidy with a criminal investigation of some type. And I want to make clear for the record that that has an effect on the advancement of the defense."

Prosecutors found it odd that Palazzo, not Momot, was defending Cassidy, who was being paid by Murphy's side of the defense. Momot, it later turned out, did not like Cassidy's role in the defense, but his hands were tied because Murphy wanted him involved.

When Palazzo finished, Bonaventure gave Roger a chance to speak.

"Mr. Palazzo tends to twist words, Judge. And that's not what I said," Roger told Bonaventure. "Let me make a little record here, Judge. Attorneys and their agents are governed by Nevada Supreme Court Rule 177. And this rule provides for the protection of the jury—the protection for a fair trial, not just for the defendants, but for the state of Nevada. All parties are entitled to a fair trial without unnecessary publicity, and I recognize that this court has taken great efforts at making sure that this jury is not exposed to media attention.

"Now they have commissioned a poll, and we've gone around and around. I heard Mr. Palazzo gave an interview just before lunch. He says he doesn't know who's paying Mr. Cassidy—they're just receiving information, but have no control over Mr. Cassidy.

"But [Cassidy] sat right there at that table during jury selection and during this case," Roger said, pointing over to Palazzo. "Mr. Cassidy interviewed witnesses in this case. And so when they say we don't have any control over him, it really is disingenuous, Judge."

Then Roger took aim at Cassidy:

"The fact of the matter is that Mr. Cassidy is talking to the media and leaking these fraudulent numbers about how the jury—or these shadow juries—feel about Sandra Murphy, Rick Tabish and Judge Bonaventure. Gratuitously, they ask questions about Judge Bonaventure and how he's doing in the case. And I can tell you that there is only one reason why they would present those numbers to the media. It's not to help their defense preparation. It's to influence the public. It's to influence the jury through the eyes and ears of the people who are close to them, and it's wrong. It's unethical. It's a violation of the rules. And when I heard about this news media blitz by Mr. Cassidy, I was offended.

"I can just imagine if I had commissioned a poll, or if I had stepped out and talked to Geraldo Rivera or Court TV and told them that I found that 95 percent of the public felt that these two people were guilty. I know exactly what would happen. They would be in this courtroom complaining to you. They'd be complaining to the State Bar because they aren't getting a fair trial. Well, we're entitled to a fair trial. And then I hear this, Well, we don't have any control over Mr. Cassidy. That's baloney.

"They're in charge of controlling him. He works for them. I don't care if it's an Irishman who pays his bill or not. They're in charge of him and ethically they're in charge of controlling this mouthpiece."

Roger continued:

"And when I said up at the bench that I intend to investigate Mr. Cassidy, I did not say that this was a criminal investigation. And so when Mr. Palazzo comes and makes this record, he is misrepresenting what happened at the bench. What I said, and what I'm saying now, is that I am investigating Mr. Cassidy as a potential witness, just like we investigate all witnesses. I want to know what his background is, and if within the rules of evidence there is impeachment material that I can use, I'm going to use it with the court's permission."

Palazzo asked to respond. He did not back away from his claims that such a probe of Cassidy would have a chilling effect on the defense.

"I want to state for the record that again I view that as a very vindictive and vengeful act on the part of the prosecutor," he said. "Clearly, Mr. Cassidy's involvement, as it relates to his involvement in the case from the infancy stages up to now, is cloaked with the attorney-client privilege and attorney work product doctrine, and [Roger] cannot pierce that without any available legal or factual basis.

"So, clearly to me, I see that as a very retaliative effort being undertaken by the DA's office because they are not happy with what they're seeing when they turn the TV on as it relates to numbers and percentages."

After letting the lawyers have their say, Bonaventure again reminded them that he had merely brought up the subject of the polling in an effort to protect the integrity of the trial.

Later that evening, an angry Cassidy rapped Roger and Tom Dillard on the evening news. At a defense-team meeting in the conference room of Goodman's law building, Cassidy still appeared agitated, colleagues said. With a glass of whiskey in his hand, he was complaining about being served with a subpoena by the prosecution to testify at the trial. He also said he had learned that Dillard was secretly investigating him, a claim Dillard said wasn't true. Eventually, Cassidy approached fellow defense investigator Michael Wysocki, a former police detective who was close friends with Dillard.

"You go tell that motherfucker that he should back off of me if he wants to enjoy all of the money that he's made," Cassidy said. "I'm the gorilla on his back that will kill him."

Cassidy repeated the threat several times in the presence of others during the defense strategy session.

At one point, Palazzo reportedly asked Cassidy, "You're speaking figuratively, aren't you?"

Cassidy replied, "No, I'm not."

As the meeting came to a close, Cassidy made a point of telling Wysocki to make sure he passed the message to Dillard.

Wysocki and Cassidy hadn't gotten along from the start. Wysocki thought Cassidy was a braggart and unethical, and Cassidy suspected Wysocki was too close to Dillard. On the way to dinner that night, Wysocki felt an obligation to inform Dillard about what had transpired.

When told, Dillard reportedly sneered, "The gloves are off now."

Wysocki then made his way to Fellini's, a popular Italian restaurant, where he had planned to meet Momot and Palazzo for dinner. While there, Cassidy unexpectedly showed up and asked Wysocki if he had conveyed the message to Dillard. Wysocki said he had done that, and Dillard had told him he wanted to "settle this in the alley."

Cassidy then spat: "Let's go get the motherfucker. Do you know where he is right now?"

"It's nine P.M. He's probably home in bed sleeping," Wysocki responded.

"I don't care. Let's go find him."

Palazzo joked, "Why don't you have another whiskey first?"

"I don't need whiskey for this," Cassidy replied. Then he made a gesture with his hand as if he were firing a gun.

The next day, Dillard met with Wysocki and told his friend that he was filing a threat-to-life complaint against Cassidy with police.

Cassidy later denied making the threat when pressed by reporters, but Dillard filed a complaint anyway and subsequently obtained a restraining order to keep Cassidy away from him during the trial.

A couple of days later, another bizarre incident occurred outside the courtroom. Judge Bonaventure learned from his bailiff that a seasoned Golden Nugget Hotel and Casino bellman had attempted to influence the jurors at lunch one day. The bellman, twenty-year-veteran Richard Sueno, was said to have yelled, "They're not guilty," to the jurors as they entered the downtown casino. Bonaventure was prepared to let the comment slide, but then he learned that Sueno had a reputation as a troublemaker at the Golden Nugget. Word also had gotten back to the judge that three jurors and an alternate had heard the comment, so he questioned them on the record in court to determine whether the remark would influence their deliberations. All four said it would not. But Bonaventure decided to have Sueno brought before him in open court anyway. There, as he leaned forward at the bench, the judge unleashed his anger.

"You knew my jury was coming over there and you made a comment," Bonaventure screamed. "What comment did you make?"

"I said they're not guilty," Sueno responded in a timid, low voice.

"You got a lot of nerve," Bonaventure said, his voice rising even louder. "Do you know I could put you in contempt? I could put you in jail for thirty days. And I'm almost of a mind to do that right now. Don't ever do that again. Now get out of here."

The bellman ultimately was fired.

Bonaventure later said he had gotten his "Sicilian temper" up over the incident and didn't intend to make Sueno lose his job. But he added, "So be it."

Two days after Bonaventure's outburst in court, there was another distraction in the case. The defense sponsored a public seance to reach out to Binion's spirit and ask him directly how he had died. The stunt attracted national attention.

"Mr. Binion, we are calling you to come to us tonight," seance leader Robert Leysen intoned in the incense-filled back room of the Psychic Eye Book Shop. Eleven psychics participated in the seance in front of local and national reporters as Binion's spirit was summoned. Binion was a no-show. But the psychics, amid flashing cameras, took a poll on the outcome of the trial. By an 8 to 3 margin, and no small surprise, they concluded that Murphy and Tabish would not be convicted.

Prosecutors later learned that the seance had been arranged by the publicist of Murphy lawyer William Knudson.

CHAPTER 30

••••••••••••••••••

The Defense Falters

••••••••••••••••••

WHEN MICHAEL BADEN took the witness stand three weeks into the trial, there was a new face glaring at him from the defense table.

James Shellow, a well-known Milwaukee defense attorney, had been hired by William Fuller specifically to cross-examine the celebrity pathologist. Fuller, who was bankrolling Sandy Murphy's defense, wanted to be sure he had someone who understood medicine handling the experienced Baden, who had caught the defense by surprise at the preliminary hearing.

Shellow's hiring came as a shock to John Momot, who had been preparing for weeks to cross-examine Baden himself. Several days earlier, Momot had expressed his unhappiness about being left in the dark during a courthouse conversation with Louis Palazzo and William Cassidy. At a later meeting, Cassidy acknowledged that Fuller had instructed him to hire Shellow, who had come recommended by Oscar Goodman. Cassidy told Momot that he believed Fuller had ties to the Irish Republican Army and that if Fuller wanted something done, Cassidy had no choice but to do it. *Ireland on Sunday,* a Dublin-based newspaper, had just reported that Fuller had bailed out a number of "IRA men" in the mid-1970s. Fuller acknowledged helping the IRA in an interview with the newspaper. Later, it was learned that Fuller had paid Shellow

$130,000 for basically two days in court. Momot was getting a little more than $250,000 from Fuller for six months of work.

At the trial, the charming, easygoing Baden breezed through his direct testimony for several hours in the morning under questioning from David Wall. Shellow got a crack at the pathologist after lunch.

Prior to Baden's testimony, Wall, a Marquette University Law School graduate, had done some checking on Shellow in Milwaukee. Attorneys there said Shellow was a fine lawyer, but had an unusual scientific method of cross-examination and could be abrasive at times.

"We decided to let Baden go head-to-head with Shellow so the jury could see the contrast in the two men," David Roger said.

The strategy seemed to work.

Within fifteen minutes, Shellow was pointing his finger in Baden's face at the witness stand. Baden, who seemed to enjoy the sparring, often would look at the jurors and smile before answering one of Shellow's piercing questions. Sometimes he would place his hand over his forehead in a studious fashion while contemplating an answer.

As the cross-examination moved along slowly, the Milwaukee lawyer seemed out of place. His aggressive, sometimes condescending style was the opposite of the laid-back Momot, whom the jurors had come to like. As he jostled with Baden all afternoon and into the next morning, Shellow frequently drew snickers from courtroom observers, including the jurors, who seemed to connect with Baden.

"You're a slow learner, aren't you, Doctor?" Shellow once asked to groans from the gallery.

At the defense table, Momot and Murphy kept stern faces as Shellow cross-examined the likable, gray-haired Baden. Murphy looked confused and taken aback by Shellow's questions.

"I looked at Sandy during cross-examination, and from my perspective, she looked mortified," Roger said. "Within about fifteen minutes, I knew we had won the battle."

Wall and Roger were so elated at their good fortune that they rarely raised objections during Shellow's cross-examination.

"We knew the more Shellow attacked Baden, the better off we were in the eyes of the jury," Roger said.

Most of the lawyers on the defense team couldn't believe what Shellow was doing.

"No one was happy," one lawyer later said.

"I was shocked. I didn't understand it," said Robert Murdock, who handled several medical witnesses for Tabish.

Murdock said Shellow had agreed, during dinner at Piero's the night before, to keep the cross-examination of Baden to a minimum.

"We wanted it short and sweet," he said. "We knew that Baden would never agree with anything we said. And he was smarter than all of us."

With Baden and Kurt Gratzer out of the way, prosecutors had gone through the toughest part of their case. Leo Casey also had done a decent job of describing his beating and extortion in the desert.

"By the time Baden finished testifying, we had the bulk of our case completed," Roger said. "I felt that we were heading toward the homestretch in good shape."

A couple of days earlier, there had been high drama in the courtroom when prosecutors played the twenty-minute videotape of Murphy touring the casino man's home the day after his death. Prior to that, Roger and Wall had called several Valley Hospital nurses to testify that Murphy's hysterics on the night Ted Binion had died appeared "theatrical."

"By then, they had seen Murphy wail away in court on several occasions, and any sympathy they had felt for her was lost after listening to the nurses and watching the videotape," Roger said.

In the next two weeks, prosecutors would sail through court with damaging witness after witness. They would make their case in the theft of Binion's silver and bring in Tanya Cropp, Dennis Rehbein and Jason Frazer to sew up the murder case.

The defense, meanwhile, continued to be plagued by internal bickering and competing agendas. It seemed clear that Fuller, the moneyman, was calling the shots for Murphy and that Cassidy, who often confided with Goodman during the trial, had won his ear. Momot didn't like Cassidy and tried to stay away from him while preparing for the trial. As a result, the private investigator had built up a rapport with Palazzo. Cassidy's participation in the defense, however, remained a mystery.

"I don't think anyone understood what his role was in the case," a defense-team lawyer said. "I could never figure it out."

Some had suggested Cassidy was there to give Goodman control over the defense. But Goodman said that he was too busy being mayor to get involved and that he even declined a $1 million offer from Fuller to rejoin the defense.

Momot and Palazzo had told District Judge Joseph Bonaventure that they were putting on a joint defense, which meant they were sharing evidence and planning to present witnesses together.

Jail officials had given Murphy and Rick Tabish special permission to meet with each other and their lawyers at the Goodman law building while preparing for the trial. The strategy sessions took place in Goodman's glass-enclosed boardroom.

For Tabish, it meant being furloughed under guard from the detention center a dozen times. While there, Tabish enjoyed other privileges he couldn't get in jail. He was seen eating pizza and gourmet barbecued ribs and smoking cigars with Palazzo and corrections officers on several occasions during the strategy sessions.

But his most enjoyable privilege might have been having sex with Murphy right under the noses of the guards.

At one session, while the lawyers and other defense-team members were talking with the two defendants, Murphy was observed slipping to her knees under the table and giving oral sex to Tabish. Defense-team members could hardly believe their eyes, as other team members continued the discussion as if nothing unusual was happening. The corrections officers, sitting outside the boardroom, apparently never saw Murphy disappear under the table.

During those sessions, Tabish appeared even-tempered and polite. But the emotional Murphy often was observed going ballistic.

"I really thought she was unstable," one defense source said. "She was ranting and raving all of the time. I thought she might come in one day and start shooting."

Some of Murphy's own defenders also didn't think she understood the seriousness of the charges against her.

"She was just enjoying this too much," the defense source said.

At times, the joint defense was anything but joint because the personalities of Momot and Palazzo didn't mesh.

"Neither one of them trusted each other," a defense-team member said. "Louis thought that John wasn't holding up his end, and John thought the same thing about Louis. They only seemed to talk to each other in court when they had to."

Often, the two lawyers never knew what the other was going to do when it came time to cross-examine the prosecution's key witnesses.

The two lawyers also were hampered by their clients. Murphy didn't want Momot to bring out things during the cross-examination of the prosecution's witnesses that might hurt Tabish. And Tabish had given similar orders to Palazzo not to hurt Murphy.

"The defense between the respective defendants is inconsistent at times," Momot told Bonaventure at a secret April 10 conference in the judge's chambers. "Ms. Murphy has indicated to me that I should not go into certain areas . . . and I have abided by her wishes.

"So in other words, I wouldn't want someone to be reading the record later on, or at any time, and say, well, 'I wonder why Mr. Momot didn't go into this fertile area or that fertile area of cross-examination.' And it's basically because

I've been working with Ms. Murphy, and it's at her direction."

"Is that correct, Ms. Murphy?" Bonaventure asked. "You've had discussion with your attorney, Mr. Momot. And he basically said, 'Maybe, Ms. Murphy, it would be in your best interest if I cross-examine such and such a way.' And you stopped him?"

"That's correct," Murphy replied. "I'm not in the business of hurting anybody to help myself."

Palazzo told Bonaventure that he, too, would be limiting his cross-examination.

"Likewise, Your Honor," he said. "My cross-examination of some of the witnesses . . . will be curtailed in order to avoid or exploit the antagonistic or inconsistent defenses presented as it relates to Mr. Tabish."

"And was this at Mr. Tabish's request?" Bonaventure asked.

"Correct," Palazzo responded.

"Mr. Tabish, you heard what Mr. Palazzo just said?"

"Yes, sir," Tabish replied.

"That he might want to go into some cross-examination to pursue your interests, is that correct?"

"That's correct."

"But you don't want him to . . . go into certain areas that might be of benefit to you?"

"That's correct."

Momot and Palazzo later declined to talk about their strained relationship, though Momot described Palazzo as a "fine young lawyer who obviously tried his best."

The lack of communication between the two attorneys reached its peak as the defense was about to present its case.

For weeks, though they never tipped their hand publicly, Murphy and Tabish had been planning to testify on their own behalf at the trial.

"I always wanted Sandy to testify because I thought she would make an excellent witness," Momot said. "She was intelligent, articulate and to me, she was very candid about what had occurred. She had the potential to be my best witness."

Momot was also expecting Tabish to take the witness stand. Three weeks before the trial, Momot had filed a notice of alibi for Murphy on the murder charges. In the notice, he described how Murphy had gone to lunch with Tabish and William Knudson at 2:45 P.M. on the day of Binion's death. It was obvious from the motion that Momot was counting on Tabish's testimony.

But on the eve of the defense's case, both Murphy and Tabish decided not to testify. Murphy figured the medical experts that the defense was calling would be enough to create doubt in the minds of the jurors, and Palazzo had persuaded Tabish that he risked too much, like exposing his criminal record to the jurors, if he took the witness stand. Palazzo had led Tabish to believe that the defense was well in hand without his testimony. Prior to that, Tabish was eagerly awaiting a chance to tell his side of the story, even once telling investigator Michael Wysocki to send a message to the prosecution through Tom Dillard. The message was that Tabish wanted Roger, the man who had built the case against him, to do his cross-examination.

The night before the defense was to open, communication between Momot and Palazzo totally collapsed when Palazzo refused to tell Momot whether he would call Tabish. Momot didn't learn that Tabish wasn't going to testify until the next morning in court.

"It was obvious that communications had broken down at that point," a defense source said.

The next day, on April 27, the defense began calling witnesses. Among the first to take the stand was Murphy's namesake stepmother, Sandra, who had raised her from the time she was one year old. Murphy, knowing there had been much speculation about whether she would be testifying, was in a playful mood. As her stepmother's name was called, a giggling Murphy stood up from the defense table as if to walk to the witness stand. Then she quickly sat down and smiled at her stepmother as the elder Murphy entered the courtroom. Momot, who was sitting next to his client, did not appear to be happy with the stunt.

A couple of days later, Murphy showed the other side of her emotions. Momot wanted to play the garbled tape of a detective trying to interview Murphy at Valley Hospital the evening of Binion's death in an attempt to show the jurors that she really had been distraught. As the thirteen-minute tape was played, tears welled up in Murphy's eyes and she began sobbing. Periodically, she would lay her head down on the defense table and cry. When she picked her head up, tears would be running down her face.

Roger later said it looked to him as though Murphy was poking her eyes with her fingernails while her head was on the table to stimulate the tears.

Despite her table-side antics, Murphy was not the star of the defense. That distinction went to Cyril Wecht, who topped the list of experts the defense had brought in to take apart Baden's suffocation theory.

Wecht, a distinguished-looking man, arrived from Pittsburgh late in the evening on May 2, the night before he was to testify. He was chauffeured to a meeting with the defense team, who wanted to get a feeling for what he would say on the stand. A couple of days earlier, Roger had put the word out to the defense that Wall planned to ask Wecht on cross-examination about his sometimes joked-about performance on the Fox network's *Alien Autopsy* show.

"I wanted Wecht to be on edge," Roger said. "We told the defense we had blown up a poster of the alien and planned to show it to the jury."

The defense attorneys queried a tired Wecht at the meeting about the Fox broadcast, and he became agitated, telling them, "Don't worry, I'll handle it." The lawyers were taken aback and found Wecht to be arrogant and hard to handle.

But on the witness stand the next day, he was polite and graceful, and he did an excellent job of creating questions about Binion's death. He testified as expected that he didn't believe Binion was suffocated, but rather had committed suicide by overdosing on heroin and Xanax.

Wall had brought the alien poster to court, but never used it.

"We were hoping the defense would bring up the subject on its own to maybe soften the blow on the expected cross-examination, but the defense didn't take the bait," Roger said.

As it turned out, Wall never even mentioned the *Alien Autopsy* report.

"We had spent a lot of time being aboveboard and taking the high road during our case," Roger said. "We wanted to look like the good guys, and we felt that if we had pulled out that poster, it would look unprofessional. I don't know whether it would have gotten us very far."

Roger acknowledged that Wecht made a good defense witness.

"He had great credentials, and he came across well to the jury," he said. "I just think his suicide theory was a weak theory. We had so many people who had contact with Ted Binion the week before he was murdered, and no one found him to be suicidal."

Wecht was forced to concede on the witness stand that defense lawyers basically spoon-fed information about the case and did not provide him with the long list of testimony from witnesses who had shed light on the conspiracy to kill Binion.

"He was just looking at the medical findings," Roger said. "But there was a lot more to our case."

On Friday, May 5, the defense rested, ending five weeks of testimony from 115 witnesses on both sides in a murder case that had captivated all of Las Vegas. In a city known for its entertainment, the Ted Binion murder trial had become the hottest show in town. Every morning, courthouse officials held a lottery for the limited number of public tickets to the trial. Court TV's national coverage caused a run on its chat lines, and ratings for Las Vegas One reached an all-time high, even outdoing the daily soaps on the network affiliates.

On Monday, when attorneys were to deliver their closing arguments, all three affiliates planned live coverage.

For his closing, Roger had made arrangements with Las Vegas One General Manager Bob Stoldal to give him selected video clips from the key witnesses he had called to the witness stand so that he could play them back to the jury. Roger knew his closing argument would be at least three hours, and he wanted to hold the panel's interest. This had never been done before because no trial had ever been carried live on television. When Momot and Palazzo heard about Roger's plans, they lodged an objection with Bonaventure. The two lawyers had not sought to use videotape, and they felt it might give Roger an unfair advantage. Furious with the attorneys, Roger blasted them in court in the absence of the jurors.

"It's not my responsibility to help these gentlemen prepare for their closing arguments," he told Bonaventure. "If they didn't spend so much time talking to Geraldo Rivera and Court TV, they would have been prepared for their arguments, and they weren't."

Bonaventure, however, sided with Momot and Palazzo, saying he didn't want to make a precedent-setting ruling on the use of videotapes in this case.

In the end, most legal experts felt that Roger and Wall had presented a nearly flawless case. All of their witnesses, including the shaky ones, had come through with flying colors.

The defense still held out hope that it had presented enough of a case to raise doubts in the minds of the jurors. But clearly the defense was reeling.

Though they had argued that the Binion Money Machine had influenced the investigation, neither Momot nor Palazzo presented any witnesses to corroborate their theory. And like the prosecutors, the defense lawyers never bothered to call to the witness stand some of the key players in the case— Tom Dillard, James Buczek, Becky Behnen, Jack Binion, Linda Carroll and William Knudson.

CHAPTER 31

....

Closing Out the Case

....

ON THE MORNING of Monday, May 8, David Roger set out
to put the finishing touches on his case against Sandy Murphy and Rick Tabish.

His closing argument was long and deliberate, and it
was delivered with the help of dual large-screen computer
monitors set up before the jurors. Roger, looking as if he
were making a high-tech corporate presentation, spent several hours explaining the charges and how the witnesses he
had presented supported his case. He would flash snippets
of testimony on the screens when he referred to each witness.

As he concluded his well-organized remarks, Roger tried
to humanize his case.

"Ladies and gentlemen, there are two people who are responsible for Ted Binion's death," Roger said. "He didn't
commit suicide. This wasn't an accidental overdose. They
did it for greed. They did it for lust. They did it for money.
They are two people who betrayed Ted Binion.

"We heard a lot about Ted Binion. We heard the character
assassination that the defense conducted on Ted Binion's
character. But he was a human being. He trusted a young
lady by the name of Sandra Murphy. She is the person who
came into his life, maneuvered through his life, manipulated
him. She is the person who was in it for money. She's the

former dancer from Cheetah's. She is the person who wanted money, spent money, wanted more.

"She is the person who fell in love with a person [Tabish] known to her as Prince Charming. She is the one who wanted Ted Binion to put her in his will when she was not happy with her cohabitation agreement. She is the person who talked about Ted Binion dying of a heroin . . . She is the person who committed this signature crime.

"And Rick Tabish, the man from Missoula, Montana, he is the person who had financial difficulties. He was in a position where he was going to be ruined financially.

"Ladies and gentlemen," Roger added. "this isn't all a coincidence. The totality of the evidence in this case establishes that Ted Binion was murdered. You have the medical testimony. You have a great number of circumstances that suggest that those two people, Sandy Murphy and Rick Tabish, were the ones who killed Ted Binion for his money.

"The evidence proved beyond a reasonable doubt that the killers in this case are the two people he trusted, the two people who had a secret affair behind his back, the two people who talked about killing Ted Binion, who stole everything Ted Binion had, including his life. That's Rick Tabish and Sandra Murphy."

The next day, John Momot, looking tired from the strain of the high-profile case, addressed the jurors. He complimented Roger for putting on a "beautiful presentation.

"I'm not into the high-tech syndrome of a presentation to you people," Momot said. "What I am interested in is getting to the facts and the evidence that I think is important for you to review."

Momot went on to explain the heart of the defense.

"Six weeks ago, I came before you folks, and I told you that this case is about heroin, and it's not about homicide," he said. "The true fact is Sandy Murphy did not kill Ted Binion. But the real sad fact is Ted Binion did die of a conspiracy, and it was a conspiracy between himself and heroin.

"And I'm not coming here, ladies and gentlemen . . . to

bash Mr. Binion. That's not my function. I don't bash that man. But pardon me if I do bash the use of drugs and heroin and Xanax and some of the people who provided it. Because that's the intolerable situation that prevails in this courtroom today.

"This case is an absolute tragedy for, once again, Bonnie Binion, the daughter. I have a daughter, Roxanne. I could appreciate the loss of a dad and how it could affect a child, and I felt that for Bonnie when she was up here on the stand. She lost a dad, but not at the hands of Sandy Murphy like the state wants you to believe. She lost a dad as a result of drugs. And that's the curse that plagued Ted Binion. But everybody here, including the state, is in denial about it. All they want to do is take this case, and somehow from this Binion Money Machine, they want to grind up this woman and make it her fault."

Momot described Murphy as the "caring partner" in her stormy relationship with Binion.

The lawyer then attacked Binion's neighbor, Dr. Enrique Lacayo, for carelessly giving the gambling figure a prescription for Xanax the day before his death without a physical examination.

And Momot had particularly harsh words for Peter Sheridan, Binion's longtime drug supplier, who had sold him twelve balloons of black tar heroin on the evening of September 16, 1998. Momot chastised the prosecution for not charging Sheridan with crimes of drug trafficking and worse, murder.

"Heroin's a curse. Heroin is bad," Momot said. "Heroin is not good for people, and if you sell heroin to somebody and they die, what happens? You get charged with murder. So now I look over at the table, and I'm still looking for Pete Sheridan over at my table. But I don't see him. I see Sandy Murphy there.

"I know Pete Sheridan did this crime. He's still out there. Who is he selling to next?"

Momot once more highlighted Binion's drug problems.

"The life of this man is a sad situation," he said. "There's a man that had everything you could possibly want in his life. He had a gaming license. He came from one of the most reputable families of the state of Nevada. A famous family. That's not good enough.

"Wealth. There's an exhibit here of what the man averaged on a yearly income. It was millions of dollars. That's not good enough. He had a beautiful home. At one time a beautiful wife, daughter. That's not good enough. He had everything you could possibly want, and all you have to do is one thing. You just don't have to do drugs. But he couldn't get it on. He couldn't stop using heroin."

Then Momot said: "My point is I don't want to let Ted Binion's addiction destroy Sandy Murphy. Unfortunately for Mr. Binion, it became obvious because of his heroin addiction—he went off the brink with this problem into the abyss."

Momot's closing was forceful and more energetic than Roger's. But he concluded it in an awkward way.

He used an anecdote involving Galileo, the Italian astronomer who had discovered the telescope almost four hundred years ago, to summarize his defense.

Galileo, he said, observed for the first time in the history of mankind that the planet Jupiter had tiny moons around it. But his discovery conflicted with the established order of the day, and he was told to stop talking about it. Galileo, Momot continued, asked his colleagues to look at Jupiter's moons themselves through his telescope, but they refused.

"They saw no need to look for that which they knew did not exist," Momot told the jurors. "We know now that Galileo was right. Jupiter has moons, and it always had moons.

"So what happened to Galileo, the man who saw and spoke the truth? He was charged. He was tried and condemned by the ones who would not look and see the truth.

"Four hundred years later," Momot said, "the state of Nevada refuses to look in the telescope and see the moons of

Jupiter. It would rather condemn Sandy Murphy than see the truth."

If Momot ended on a strange note, Palazzo was even more bizarre in his closing argument.

He had a glaze in his eyes as he approached the podium to address the jurors. His talk was disjointed and appeared to lack focus. It also was too combative and strident for a jury that had spent weeks hearing so many witnesses from the prosecution.

Palazzo told the jurors that prosecutors had not presented "one scintilla" of physical evidence linking Tabish to Binion's death. And he said it was ludicrous to think that Tabish had wanted to steal Binion's silver fortune in Pahrump.

"All we've got is a bunch of talk by ninety-some witnesses that the state provided," he said. "Well, talk is cheap."

While rapping Tom Dillard's role in the investigation, Palazzo said: "He is just on his own with no oversight, no judicial intervention with regard to subpoenas, records, anything like that. This is—it's just like— it's like being in Nazi Germany. OK?"

Another time, Palazzo described the prosecution's case as "sick." And when he referred to the police reliance on Dillard later in his argument, he asked: "Doesn't that stink?"

Toward the end of his argument, Palazzo spent some time on the charges relating to Leo Casey's beating with a telephone book at the Jean sand pit. Witnesses, he said, saw no marks on Casey's body after the beating.

Then Palazzo did something that startled the judge, his fellow lawyers, the courtroom observers, the television audience and even Tabish.

"Your Honor," Palazzo said. "With the court's permission, I'd like to have Mr. Tabish come forward. I want basically to illustrate to the jury what happens to you when you get slammed with a phone book upside the head and what kind of bruising and swelling you're gonna get. And redness, so that it clearly belies anything that Mr. Casey's claiming."

"You want to do what to who?" Judge Bonaventure asked as laughter roared through the courtroom.

"I want to beat him with the . . ." Palazzo said.

There was more laughter.

"I've got his permission."

At that moment Tabish turned red and had to be physically held back by others at the defense table. Then he looked over to Palazzo's partner, Robert Murdock, and out of earshot of the judge asked, "What the fuck is he doing?"

Bonaventure, with his customary quick wit, then joked: "I heard you were a hard-charging attorney, but not a hard-hitting attorney, now, Mr. Palazzo."

"I'd like—I'd like him—I'd like to illustrate for the jury. I've gotten his consent to basically hit him with the phone book several times," Palazzo said.

"Well, let me . . . What does the state want to do?" a puzzled Bonaventure asked the prosecutors.

Before they could respond, the judge looked over at the jurors and continued: "You know, I think it's time for a ten-minute recess, ladies and gentlemen. You need a little break, don't you? And Mr. Palazzo needs a little break, too, I think. So let me resolve this one issue."

After the jurors left, Bonaventure expressed his befuddlement to Palazzo.

"I got a bench book up here. This is a new one on me. Mr. Palazzo," the judge said. "You want to beat the hell out of your client now, is that—"

"Just to make a point," Palazzo interjected. "I'm illustrating that if you get hit with a phone book even half the time that this guy claims he was hit, you're gonna be a hurtin' gator."

Bonaventure said he needed time to research Palazzo's request.

"What you want to do in front of the jury is hit Mr. Tabish," the judge said. "How many times?"

"Maybe six or eight."

"Not hard, though. Just easy."

"As hard as I can."

"All right. Do you have the consent of Mr. Tabish . . . . ?"

"I do."

"Do you have a doctor or nurse present in case we have blood . . . ?"

"We'll get some tissues here, and we can wipe him down."

"Is there any medical personnel here?"

"No."

Bonaventure then said he wanted some questions answered about the liability of performing such a stunt in court. He wanted to know how court-administration and detention-center officials felt about it.

"What is the state's position on this?" he asked Roger.

"It's a new one on me, too, Judge," Roger responded. "I'd like to confer with Mr. Wall."

"We'll all confer," Bonaventure said as he began to leave the bench. "How's that? I'll be back . . . I've got a few notes on closing arguments. I'll look in my bench book and see if this fits in. And we'll come right back before the jury comes back in ten minutes."

When Bonaventure returned, he said he had spoken to jail officials in his chambers, and they were concerned about having one of their inmates being hit about the head. Then he asked Roger for input.

Roger said he objected to the demonstration as well.

"What Mr. Palazzo is attempting to do is to provide the functional equivalent of testimony in this case by having Mr. Tabish stand firm and take the blows the best that he can," he said. "There's no doubt in my mind that what this demonstration would show would be inconsistent with what happened out at the Jean sand pit. Mr. Casey is some sixty years old. He was thumb-cuffed. It is very unlikely that Mr. Casey was standing there firm, trying to take the blows without moving. Mr. Casey, in all likelihood, was moving with the blows, not being a solid object.

"What Mr. Palazzo is attempting to do is have Mr. Tabish

stand firm and take these blows to show what injuries might occur. What is happening to this case, Judge, and I know you won't allow it, is that this case is turning into a circus, a Hollywood drama, and our criminal justice system cannot afford to take that type of black eye."

Palazzo, however, insisted he still wanted to do the demonstration. That forced Bonaventure to politely agree with Roger and deny the request.

" . . . with all due respect to you," Bonaventure told Palazzo, "and I know you're advocating for your client, and I'm not in any way disparaging you . . . I can't allow that, because, as Mr. Roger said, we've had nice, tight control over this case, and I'm not about to lose it now. In all due respect to you, I'm not gonna allow it. All right?"

"Very well, Your Honor," Palazzo responded.

When the jurors were brought back, Palazzo finished up his argument ripping into Casey. Several times while asking for an acquittal, Palazzo addressed the jurors as "you guys."

When he was done, observers could only shake their heads in bewilderment at his disjointed performance.

"He just lost it," one fellow defense-team lawyer said. "The pressure got to him."

Palazzo later acknowledged to reporters that he had blown his closing arguments, though he insisted he had done a good job of defending Tabish.

The next morning, on Wednesday, May 10, David Wall got a chance to wrap things up for the prosecution.

Wall decided to rebut the defense's Binion Money Machine theory right away. He told the jurors that he felt the need to reintroduce himself.

"My name is David Wall, and I work for the district attorney's office," he said. "I don't work for the Horseshoe. I don't work for Jack Binion or Becky Behnen, though they seem like interesting enough people."

Then Wall addressed Momot's claim that Murphy was the caregiver in her relationship with Binion.

"Let's look at Sandra Murphy the caregiver," he said.

"What do you know about her? You know that she met Ted Binion at Cheetah's while dancing topless for money on stage and in the VIP room in 1995. Made over $13,000 in less than two weeks. Tempt them, tease them, and they'll give you money, lots of it. In short order, she hooked up and moved in with Ted Binion at his home, a much older multimillionaire, perhaps the envy of all of the others at Cheetah's."

Wall said Murphy never worked during her three years of living with Binion.

"Her job was to spend Ted Binion's money, and she had a certain talent for it."

And then for months prior to Binion's death, he claimed, she deceived Binion by carrying on a romantic relationship with Tabish.

"Sandra Murphy the caregiver, whose performance in that audiotape at the hospital, I submit to you, is pure manipulation, but whose performance in the videotape, the inventory, is pure Sandy Murphy," Wall said. "Not exactly the caregiver side of her, was it?

"And note this about that videotape. There was an hour or so between the time that she got into that house and the time that James Brown came back with a court order and kicked her out. In the meantime, there's a bottle of wine open in the den. When you see the videotape, you'll see that the television set is on. At one point, you can see a picture. Later in that video, you see sort of the credits, like the end of a movie. So during that hour, she went into the den, popped open a bottle of wine and turned on the television. A toast, perhaps, to getting away with it?

"And on that videotape, when she directs Mr. Knudson into the den and she backs in with that ice in her veins. Right there is the spot where Ted Binion died."

Wall suggested that Murphy really was in love with Tabish and thought that he ultimately would leave his wife and marry her.

"But love or not, it was still about the money," he said. "She wanted her share of the $55 million estate."

Murphy knew that if Binion found out about her affair, he would kick her out of his house, he said.

"She wouldn't have the money, and I submit to you that perhaps she knew that if she didn't have the money, she wasn't gonna get Rick Tabish," he added. "And Rick Tabish wasn't going to leave his family for a poor Sandra Murphy because Rick Tabish was in it for the money. Everything Rick Tabish does is for the money."

Wall then offered his theory of what happened on the day of Binion's death.

"Now we know that Sandra Murphy was at home at 12:04 P.M., because that's the time she gets the call from Barbara Brown, the real estate agent," he explained. "You'll recall that conversation. Sandy Murphy is upset, saying Ted can't come to the phone. Nobody knows what it's like to live with a heroin addict. Don't come over. Ted Binion may not be able to make your meeting tomorrow. Whatever you do, don't come over."

Wall reminded the jurors that Murphy's car was parked on the east side of his house, under a canopy by the kitchen, and was observed there from 11 P.M. on September 16, 1998, until police arrived to take charge of the death scene late in the afternoon of September 17. Murphy usually parked her Mercedes in the southwest garage.

The prosecutor said Murphy herself left the biggest clue to solving the case. She told Binion's neighbor Janis Tanno that she had left her purse in Tabish's car after having lunch with Tabish and William Knudson at Z'Tejas Grill on the afternoon of September 17.

"There are no calls between Sandra Murphy and Rick Tabish that day," Wall said. "There are no calls to set up this lunch. The more logical explanation . . . is that he's there with her. His car is in the garage where hers is normally parked. That's why hers is on the side so that Ted Binion's silver collection, his coins, the valuables, the cash can all be loaded into Mr. Tabish's car. I submit to you that Ted Binion is already dead or dying at 12:04 P.M. when Barbara Brown calls.

"Sandra Murphy's upset. Is she upset because she's stuck in that house with dead or dying Ted Binion because the gardener's still making his rounds until 1:15 P.M.? She can't leave because Tom Loveday is still there. She is trapped inside the house with Rick Tabish and with Ted Binion.

"There were no calls between Sandra Murphy and Rick Tabish on September 17 to set up this lunch because they're there together. She leaves her purse in Rick Tabish's car at lunch and only gets there because she's riding with him. And we know she's in the house when Barbara Brown calls, so the only way she gets into Rick Tabish's car is if he's either already there or he comes by at some point after Tom Loveday leaves.

"And whether it's Mr. Tabish or Mr. Knudson that drops her off back at the house after lunch, shortly before the 911 call, her purse is still in Rick Tabish's car, and likely her keys as well.

"So when she gets back from that lunch, before the 911 call, she has to go through that open window in the back. And remember that there was a chair underneath that window when the detectives got there and the crime-scene people got there on September 17. But Tom Loveday said that chair wasn't there when he was there.

"It means in order for her to climb through that window before the 911 call, she's gotta move the chair to a point where she can climb through the window and get in the house, because she doesn't have her keys because her purse is still in Rick Tabish's car."

Then Wall added: "Rick Tabish was at that house on September 17, because you know Sandra Murphy didn't do it on her own."

Wall told the jurors they didn't have to be unanimous in how Binion died to convict Murphy and Tabish of first-degree murder.

"Let's simplify this issue a little," he said. "If you find that Ted Binion was suffocated and that the drugs they gave him played a part in making it easier to kill him, or even that they tried drugs first, they didn't work and perhaps because Tom Loveday was there, they suffocated Ted Binion, then the verdict is first-degree murder with use of a deadly weapon, because those drugs are considered weapons under the law."

Wall then cut to the heart of the prosecution's case, explaining how the conspiracy to kill Binion had taken place and how his accused killers blamed everyone but themselves for his death.

And he returned to the Binion Money Machine.

"Their position is there's no conspiracy to rob. There's no conspiracy to murder. There's no conspiracy to commit the larceny or kidnapping or to steal silver," he said. "There's only one conspiracy in this case, and that's a conspiracy to frame poor Sandra Murphy and Rick Tabish. The Binion Money Machine conspiracy apparently was masterminded by the estate or Ted Binion's family, along with the police, apparently in Las Vegas and Nye County, the district attorney's office and a whole host of other people."

Wall pointed to a blown-up list of the ninety-plus prosecution witnesses who had testified and with a tone of sarcasm said: "I guess all of those people were influenced by the Binion Money Machine and are lying.

"All of those witnesses had pieces of the puzzle that's presented to you. Either they're all part of the grand conspiracy to frame Richard Tabish and Sandra Murphy, or these two before you are guilty of the crimes that have been charged."

As he closed his remarks, Wall couldn't resist taking one last shot at the money-machine theory

"If this case didn't involve a murder, a tragic murder, the irony in that would be almost laughable because it's the Binion money that these two wanted more than anything else," he said. "It is the whole purpose of all of these crimes. The Binion Money Machine framed us? They would have given anything to be part of the Binion money. She had it for a while and was getting kicked out. He didn't. They wanted it and each other enough to kill an eccentric, wealthy heroin addict."

With that backdrop, Bonaventure read a long admonition to the jurors and sent them off with their instructions to deliberate.

The day after the jury got the case, however, questions arose about Palazzo's health. He reportedly checked himself into a local hospital briefly that day. Friends said he went to University Medical Center after noticing that the left side of his face had become droopy. Al Lasso, Bonaventure's law clerk, recalled that there was a twenty-four-hour period immediately after the jury had received the case when no one from the judge's office could get in touch with Palazzo. Talk of the hospital trip was the buzz among those associated with the Binion case at the time because of Palazzo's lackluster closing argument. But Palazzo would not confirm the rumors. He appeared fine in court the next day, but some said he looked as though he was in a haze.

CHAPTER 32

••••••••••••••••••

The Verdicts

••••••••••••••••••

ON TUESDAY, MAY 16, the fifth day of the jury's deliberations, the county courthouse and all of Las Vegas were stuck
in a waiting game when District Judge Joseph Bonaventure
received an unusual letter from the panel's foreman.

"This jury, after taking a few hours getting organized and
setting a course, is a cohesive unit," wrote the foreman,
Arthur Spear Jr., a retired aerospace engineer from New
York. "We have grasped the seventy instructions, verbalized
and understood the eleven counts, are reviewing the hundreds of pieces of evidence and have extrapolated from all
of the jurors' notes the most credible information of the testimony given in the courtroom.

"This case arguably, unlike most, has a great deal of conflicting testimony, a good portion given by 'experts' in their
field. Nevertheless, we've reviewed the notes on the testimony of over seventy witnesses and the associated evidence.
We're dedicated, working an eleven-hour day, including a
working lunch hour, but getting a much-appreciated restaurant dinner break.

"We feel we're moving in the right direction, taking the time
required to give the defendants a fair and just trial by this jury."

Bonaventure was surprised to receive the handwritten letter, which courthouse spokesman Doug Bradford described
as "unprecedented."

After showing the letter in chambers to the lawyers, Bonaventure released copies to the news media, which immediately began to speculate. The consensus was that the letter was a positive sign for the prosecution. It seemed to suggest that the jury was well organized and being methodical in its deliberation, which meant it was paying close attention to the prosecution's witnesses.

Two days later, Spear sent Bonaventure another note requesting a read-back of portions of Mary Montoya-Gascoigne's testimony.

On Friday, May 19, the jury tied a record in southern Nevada, stretching its deliberations into an eighth day. At that point, Bradford estimated the trial had cost taxpayers $227,000, which wasn't an overly high amount for a case of this magnitude.

By 4 P.M., Bonaventure was considering forcing the panel to deliberate over the weekend when he received another note from Spear. The jury had reached its verdicts. Bonaventure's staff began calling the lawyers while Bradford was given the task of contacting the media. Bonaventure scheduled the reading of the verdicts in court at 6 P.M. Almost immediately, all three local network affiliates and Court TV went live with continuous coverage leading up to the verdicts.

At 6 P.M., tension was everywhere as reporters, family members on both sides of the case and a few lucky spectators jammed the courtroom. Rick Tabish showed no emotion when he was led into the courtroom. Sandy Murphy smiled at John Momot and several faces in the gallery and drew a wink from William Fuller. Both defendants stood up when the stern-faced jurors walked in. Four were wearing sunglasses and none looked directly at the defendants. It was not a good sign for Murphy and Tabish. Bonaventure asked both defendants to remain standing while Spear read the verdicts.

The foreman, in a firm voice, began with Tabish, reading off guilty verdicts on all eleven charges. Tabish stood expressionless as Spear kept reading, but he hung his head when "guilty" was announced on the first-degree murder charge. There were tears everywhere. On one side Becky Behnen was weeping, while Tabish's mother, Lanni, cried across the room. Tears even flowed from some of the jurors. Like Tabish, Murphy showed little emotion while Spear rattled off the six guilty verdicts against her. At one point, Tabish grabbed Murphy's arm to console her, but she stiffened and quickly pulled it away.

Bonaventure then set Tuesday for the penalty phase of the trial. Under Nevada law, the jury can recommend a sentence on a first-degree murder conviction. The Binion jury had the option of life in prison without parole, life with the possibility of parole after twenty years, or fifty years with the possibility of parole after twenty years. Prosecutors weren't seeking the death penalty.

As she was led away from the courthouse, Murphy turned around, glanced at her family members and said confidently, "I'll be out in nine months."

Becky Behnen was greeted outside the courthouse with a hero's welcome by a crowd of friendly onlookers who had gathered around her. She was quickly hustled into a Horseshoe limousine by her husband, Nick, and driven to the nearby casino, where celebrations were occurring. Cheers were heard throughout the casino as loyal patrons fond of Binion watched the guilty verdicts on large-screen televisions in the sports book. Asked there by a *Las Vegas Review-Journal* reporter what she thought her brother would say about the verdicts, Behnen quipped: "He'd be saying, 'The bitch got what she deserved, and she's the most evil, devious, deceptive person I've ever met.' "

Back at the courthouse, David Roger and David Wall walked through the crush of reporters without saying a word. They had vowed to maintain their code of silence until after the penalty hearing.

A dejected John Momot told reporters: "There is no homicide here. This young lady is strong, and she's going to continue to fight until she is vindicated."

Louis Palazzo seemed in shock. "He [Tabish] should not have been convicted," he said.

Before being whisked away from the courthouse, the jurors had told Bonaventure that they were too emotionally drained to grant interviews to the media or the lawyers. But they agreed to talk with District Judge Michael Cherry, who was serving as Bonaventure's spokesman, after the penalty hearing.

On Monday, May 22, the day before the penalty hearing, the *Las Vegas Sun* reported that there was upheaval within the defense team. Sources close to the defense had told the paper that Tabish was upset with Palazzo's handling of the case. Tabish also reportedly was angry at defense consultant William Cassidy, who he believed had run "interference" within the defense and harmed his case. Palazzo and Cassidy denied any misconduct and said all was fine inside the defense. But word surfaced that Harvard University law professor Alan Dershowitz was close to joining the defense to work on the appeal. Dershowitz, who declined to talk to reporters, reportedly was asking for $1 million to take the job. He was rumored to have been given a retainer early in the case to serve as a defense consultant.

Bonaventure, in the meantime, had received a big jolt on Monday morning. A letter from attorney Charles Lobello, who was not involved in the Binion case, was hand-delivered to the judge. The letter suggested there was possible jury tampering in the case.

Lobello wrote that he had been discussing the Binion case during breakfast with his family at a local restaurant on Sunday morning when a bus girl clearing a nearby table decided to join the conversation. The bus girl told Lobello's group that her older sister was a juror in the trial and had informed her family after the verdict that the four female jurors who wore sunglasses to court had been paid to deliver a guilty verdict.

"The group at my table sat literally stunned by what it had just heard," Lobello said in the letter. "I do not know whether any of this is true, but I felt compelled to advise the court. I would prefer to remain anonymous. I will, however, be calling your secretary later today to inquire whether anything further is necessary, in which case I would be willing to meet with your honor privately."

After reading the letter, Bonaventure summoned the defense lawyers and the prosecutors, as well as defense investigator Michael Wysocki and district attorney investigator Michael Karstedt, to his chambers for a closed-door hearing.

According to a secret transcript of the hearing, Roger proposed sending Wysocki and Karstedt to do a joint, tape-recorded interview of the bus girl to determine the legitimacy of her story. Bonaventure liked that idea and recessed the hearing until the investigators had a chance to interview the girl.

By Tuesday afternoon, after the penalty hearing had gotten under way, Wysocki and Karstedt had talked to the eighteen-year-old girl. During the lunchtime break, Bonaventure called both sides back to his chambers. There, Roger gave the judge a report of the interview.

"In front of her parents, she acknowledged making the statements," Roger said. "However, she said that they were false. She does not know any of the jurors in this case, nor is she related to any jurors in this case. She was a young girl making some very stupid comments, trying to make herself an important person related to this case."

Roger said the girl expressed remorse over her comments and apologized.

A relieved Bonaventure then told the lawyers there was no reason to take the matter any further.

"This is a non-issue, and we'll just put it to rest. And that's it," he said. "So that will be the end of that."

The incident was never made public after the trial.

At Tuesday's penalty hearing, prosecutors spent most of their time bringing out Tabish's lengthy criminal background in Montana in the hope of persuading the jurors to give him the harshest possible prison sentence. They also called Bonnie Binion to the witness stand to give a tearful explanation of her happy days growing up with her father. This was designed to once more show the human side of Binion.

But the real drama unfolded on Wednesday, as the defense presented its case for the lightest possible sentence.

Momot dropped a bombshell when he called Murphy's stepmother, Sandra, to the witness stand. Mrs. Murphy, armed with a scrapbook and photos, spent the first half hour sobbing while describing her daughter's active days growing up as the girl next door in Bellflower, California.

Then Momot asked: "Tell me, during the course of this time, especially in the younger teens . . . did something unusual occur?"

"Yes," the elder Murphy replied in a hesitant voice.

"What happened?"

"I don't even like to talk about it, but when she was fourteen years old, we got a call from the school . . . We went up there, and they asked us, 'Did you know that your daughter was raped?' And I didn't know. She didn't tell us. She told a girlfriend."

The disclosure, a still-crying Mrs. Murphy said, explained why her stepdaughter was having nightmares and declining grades. The rape, she said, was done by a neighborhood youth who was tried and convicted as a juvenile.

But the terror in the younger Murphy's life didn't stop there.

Mrs. Murphy testified that her stepdaughter was raped again after she had dropped out of high school. The younger Murphy, the stepmother said, was on the freeway driving home from work one night in 1994 when the hood of her car flew up and smashed the windshield.

"And she couldn't shut it," Mrs. Murphy said. "It wouldn't stay down, so she started walking by herself to a call box, and a van with two men pulled over and asked her if she needed help, and she said no. She kept walking, and they followed her down the off-ramp . . . and they got out and they started chasing her and they raped her."

Mrs. Murphy said the two men, who were never caught, also physically harmed Sandy enough to send her to the hospital. From then on, her stepdaughter was a changed person, who ended up getting arrested for driving with a suspended license and driving under the influence of alcohol. The elder Murphy testified that the last rape was the reason why Sandy left California.

"I think she just needed to get away," Mrs. Murphy said.

After a short pause, Sandy Murphy, looking drained and beaten, followed her stepmother to the witness stand to make an unsworn statement.

With tears streaming down her face, Murphy read the statement she said she had cranked out the night before. She told the jurors she was anxious to "share the truth" about what had happened to Binion.

"Regretfully, I did not testify, and now I can see that was a mistake," she said. "But instead of looking at what could have been, I can only look at what will be. So this will be the first and final time we get to know each other."

Murphy, as she continued crying, said she saw a lot of pain around the courtroom. And she professed her love for the man she had just been convicted of killing, the man she called "my Teddy Ruxton."

"I thought he was my fix-it man," she said. "I thought he would fill the hole in my heart.

"I know you heard some ugly things about Teddy during these proceedings," she continued. "But that was Teddy the heroin addict. There are trials and tribulations in every relationship and sometimes we get lost and go astray. But that doesn't mean that we love each other any less.

"I loved Teddy with all my heart, and I know he loved me just as much. You may have taken away my freedom, but no matter what goes on in these proceedings or what anybody ever says about us, you could never take away the love we had for each other."

Then Murphy concluded: "Last night, I laid in bed thinking of what I wanted to say here today, and there was one thing that stuck out in my mind. There was something that I needed to do for me. I want to say that I'm sorry to the Binion family, but most of all I'm sorry to Bonnie. And I'm sorry for the day I walked out that door on September 17 and left him there alone. And I'm sorry to Teddy for not being there when he needed me the most."

Murphy's statement irked prosecutors, who saw it as an attempt to profess her innocence, something she was prohibited from doing at the penalty phase of the trial.

Roger stood up and objected, and told Bonaventure that Murphy had "crossed the line" by suggesting to Bonnie Binion that her father had died of a drug overdose. Bonnie had given her father's convicted killer a cold stare from the first row when she spoke those words.

After Murphy's dramatic performance, Palazzo called members of Tabish's family to the witness stand, including his wife, Mary Jo, who was making her first appearance ever in court, for more emotional testimony.

Mary Jo, who weeks later would divorce Tabish, brought photos of her two young children to show the jurors. She described her husband as a great father who had many friends.

"He's very positive," she said. "He's very outgoing. He's a very likable person. In my opinion, the only people who don't like him are jealous of him."

Mary Jo, a tall, attractive woman, pleaded with the jurors to give Tabish a chance to one day see his children again as a free man.

Palazzo also called Tabish's parents, Frank and Lanni Tabish, who had attended much of the trial. Both appeared devastated.

Frank Tabish choked up several times on the stand as he talked in glowing terms about his son.

"There's not too much bad I can say about him," he said. "He's been a fun kid to raise. We had a lot of fun with him over the years. The obstacles that he had to go over with his early life—that he had to jump over—he did an absolutely excellent job with himself."

Tabish, his voice cracking, described his son as a "humanitarian" who probably had the "biggest heart in him that you could find."

The father, who believed his son was railroaded, still seemed in shock over his son's conviction.

Palazzo asked the elder Tabish if there was anything else he'd like to tell the jurors.

"There's a lot I'd like to tell them, but I can't," he said. "And it's an absolute shame. It really is . . . that I can't do more for my son. I'm just so mad about it. I can't believe it."

A teary-eyed Lanni Tabish went next, telling the jury the only other time she had seen her husband cry was when the couple had lost an infant son years ago.

"I'm heartbroken for everyone in this courtroom," Mrs. Tabish said. "It's a sad day when you have to beg for your child's life. We're very proud people . . . Rick has won awards in football. He was the captain of the football team. He's part of the puzzle of our family, and he is part of our hearts. And without him, two generations are going to suffer, and I don't know how we're going to [handle] it. And I would give my life for him if I could."

Mrs. Tabish acknowledged that her son probably had gotten away with too many things over the years because he had received too much love from his family.

"They painted him as this bad person, and he's not," she said. "The mistake can't be that big to take a life forever."

Before his mother left the stand, Rick Tabish was seen shedding tears in court for the first time.

He was next to face the men and women who had convicted him.

"Your mom's always the one that can get to you," he said as he began his unsworn testimony. His voice was calm and smooth.

After proclaiming he had the "greatest family in the world," Tabish singled out his affection for Murphy before mentioning his wife.

"This little gal sitting over at the defense table, I think the world of her," he told the jurors.

He went on to express his sorrow to Bonnie Binion and her family.

"My heart is out to the Binion family," he said. "I mean that sincerely. I can look everybody in that front row in the eye and tell you I am sorry. And please take that from the heart, because that's where it's coming from. I hope someday something can get rectified."

Then he looked at the jurors.

"The prosecution did their job," he said. "I almost feel like raising my hand and swearing in and letting me and Mr. Roger go, but I know you guys had a big burden and you did what you had to do based on the evidence presented to you. And I applaud you."

Tabish talked about his past troubles with the law, but insisted he had learned from his mistakes.

"I have no real regrets for anything I did except for getting involved in this situation," he said. "My heart is broken because everybody else is destroyed."

Looking lovingly at his family in the courtroom, he added: "What I'm putting these people through, it disgraces me. I'm humiliated for every time I held my head up, for every time I smiled in this court, for every time I smiled for the news cameras. For every bit of cocky attitude I had during this whole case, I'm ashamed of myself. I'm disgusted to have put good people through this."

Then he glanced back at the jurors.

"You guys have returned a verdict on me," he said. "That's your decision. I'm going to live with that decision. I'm man enough to live with that decision. I've just got to try to help my family have some peace."

Tabish closed by telling the jurors he believed he still had a lot to offer society.

"Please give me my life," he begged. "All I ask is I'd like to get out of prison twenty years from now, so I can at least see my children when they're married, try to get back into society and get started again."

After closing arguments from the attorneys, the jurors returned to the deliberation room to decide how much prison time to give Murphy and Tabish. They came back in less than three hours. Arthur Spear stood up and told Bonaventure that the jurors were recommending life with the possibility of parole after twenty years, a decision that prompted Tabish to mouth the words "Thank you" to the panel members.

Bonaventure also thanked the jurors for their hard work and dismissed them, but not before giving them high praise.

"Your performance as jurors is to be commended," he said. "For you withstood endless days of testimony, hundreds of exhibits and hours of confinement. You followed this court's admonition, and you respected the parties' right to a trial based upon the evidence in the courtroom."

The jurors once more were whisked away from the courthouse without talking to the media.

As darkness fell, Judge Cherry approached the microphones and cameras set up on the grass of the courthouse and told reporters he was able to chat briefly with jurors before they left.

"This is an exhausted group of people," he said. "I think that they were happy that they were able to reach a final conclusion in this case as a jury."

Cherry called the jurors a "very dedicated, committed group of people" who had a difficult time sitting in judgment of a fellow man and woman. He said the four women who had worn sunglasses to court on Friday did it to cover up tears in their eyes from the strain of their deliberations.

"They just were upset," he said. "They had red eyes. They had tears, and it was a tough deliberation for them."

Four months later, the sixty-six-year-old Spear looked back at his experience.

"We worked very hard to do the right thing," he recalled. "We tried hard to make the deliberations fair."

He said the jurors were firmly convinced that Murphy and Tabish killed Binion. They just weren't sure who had the most culpability, which was why they opted to recommend the same penalty for both defendants.

"We didn't know how much one was more involved than the other," he said. "We didn't know whose idea it was."

Spear had put together a handwritten time line of the events surrounding Binion's death for his fellow jurors to consider while discussing how much prison time to dish out to Murphy and Tabish.

In the time line, he said he agreed with the prosecution's theory that Murphy and Tabish were trapped inside Binion's home with the casino man's body on September 17, 1998, while Thomas Loveday was working outside.

"Meanwhile," he wrote, "the $20,000, silver collection and possibly other valuables are stolen from the house by Sandra M. and Rick T."

Spear surmised that Binion had smoked some heroin between 10:30 P.M. the evening before his death and 5:30 A.M. the next morning. During this time, he said, Tabish probably arrived at the home and hid his car inside Binion's garage. Tabish might have entered the home sometime after 5:30 A.M. while Binion had gone to a nearby convenience store to buy some cigarettes. Binion probably continued smoking heroin in his den or bathroom upon his return.

Then Spear wrote: "Ted is given Xanax, some possibly of his own free will. Sandra M. and Rick T. take liquid Xanax and Valium, pouring into his mouth, and then covering his mouth and nose until he passes out. Their force upon him gives multiple injuries to mouth area, chest . . . back of shoulder, knee area, wrists."

Binion, Spear said in the time line, probably collapsed by the entryway to his den.

"If not murdered by means of suffocation and forced Xanax ingestion [right after heavy heroin ingestion] by Sandra M. and Rick T.," he wrote, " then they murdered him by just watching and letting him die no matter how he ingested the Xanax right after heroin use."

Spear described the latter scenario as "depraved indifference," a legal term used in murder cases in a handful of states, but not Nevada. Defense attorneys later would seize upon the use of that term in a bid to win a new trial.

After Loveday left Binion's home about 1:30 P.M., Spear speculated that Binion's body was dragged across the den to a sleeping mat on the floor. The previous ninety minutes, from about the time of the 12:04 P.M. phone call from Barbara Brown, was spent cleaning up the "mess" Murphy had talked about in her conversation with the real estate agent.

The "mess," he wrote, was "still evident" in the den entryway on the tile and carpet, where there was a "linear trail of body fluids to the mat where Ted B.'s body lay."

Recalling the trial, Spear said the jurors found the testimony of New York pathologist Michael Baden, the prosecution's star medical witness, the most credible.

"I think just listening to him and then listening to the others, he had just a little more credibility," Spear said.

The jurors began their deliberations by taking up the lesser charges first and saving the murder for last, he reported.

"We knew we had a big job to do," he said. "We had to go through all of the testimony, and we compared our notebooks with each other."

Spear said that, going into the final day of deliberations, there was one holdout, Joan Sanders, who didn't believe that Murphy and Tabish were guilty. No one, he added, put pressure on her to change her mind, but at lunchtime, she told him she had decided the defendants had killed Binion.

"She said, "I don't know how they could have done this awful crime,' " Spear recalled.

Spear said that he felt the two lovers had killed Binion for a variety of reasons.

"Rick was in a lot of trouble as far as coming up with

money to pay for his trucks and salaries at the various sand pit locations. He needed a lot of money.

"Sandy was upset with her life with a person who took drugs. Binion's love was keeping himself happy on heroin. She wasn't leading a happy life, so when Rick came along, the conspiracy started there. He was a hard worker, an entrepreneur, and he was closer to her age. He was probably a real catch."

Spear reported that he was influenced a great deal by Murphy's demeanor on the twenty-minute videotape at Binion's home the day after his death. He said he was awestruck by the fact that she could walk past the blanket on the floor of the den that had been covering Binion's body and show no emotion except to question why something was missing from a bookshelf.

The jury foreman also said he found it interesting to listen to Tabish at the penalty hearing.

"He thanked the jury for a job well done and said he was ready to take his licks," Spear explained. "That, to me, sounded like a person almost really admitting guilt."

CHAPTER 33

••••••••••••••••••

A Shot in the Dark

••••••••••••••••••

DISTRICT JUDGE JOSEPH BONAVENTURE had scheduled the sentencing of Ted Binion's convicted killers for September 15, which was two days shy of the second anniversary of the casino man's death.

In the next three months, the defense had plenty of work to do as it sought to persuade the judge to overturn the jury verdict and give Sandy Murphy and Rick Tabish a new trial. The first thing Tabish did was find a new lawyer. He dumped Louis Palazzo for the second time and hired William Terry, an aspiring candidate for district attorney who had represented Murphy during the preliminary hearing. Terry's hiring was further evidence of unrest within the defense.

On July 26, Terry gave credence to the media accounts when he filed a sixty-nine-page motion seeking a new trial for Tabish in part because of "ineffective assistance of counsel." Terry questioned the loyalties of Palazzo and William Cassidy, the Murphy defense consultant who Terry alleged had called the shots for the entire defense team. Cassidy had returned to his City Hall job after the trial.

Murphy's benefactor, William Fuller, had paid Cassidy $217,000 for his work, but Cassidy never followed through with a number of promises he had made during defense strategy sessions, Terry said. Cassidy, for example, guaranteed that Tom Dillard and Leo Casey would be indicted prior to the trial. That never happened. He also promised that Oscar Goodman would either play a role in cross-examining witnesses at the trial or testify himself, but that never happened either.

Terry never mentioned it in his motion, but the *Las Vegas Sun* reported a week later that Cassidy, during defense strategy sessions, had suggested breaking into the homes of key prosecution players to plant listening devices and gain access to their computers. Defense sources told the paper the idea was never carried out, and Cassidy vehemently denied making such statements.

According to Terry's motion, Cassidy also discouraged Palazzo and Tabish from bringing up the time Murphy had taken bags of silver coins to Goodman's office within days after Binion's death. Tabish, in an effort to weaken the theft charges against him, wanted to show the jury that those coins were removed the day after Binion's death, not the day of his death, as prosecutors alleged at the trial. If that were the case, Tabish and Murphy could claim she rightfully thought the silver was hers because she knew she would inherit Binion's home and contents.

Terry suggested that Palazzo, through Cassidy's prodding, was trying to protect Goodman from embarrassment. Terry charged that Palazzo's loyalties were divided between Tabish and Goodman, who was his mentor.

"It is submitted that Mr. Palazzo made certain choices based on a conflict of interest, real or imagined, and a misapplication of the law," Terry wrote.

John Momot and his new co-counsel, Gerald Scotti of California, made headlines of their own in their motion for a new trial. They suggested that prosecutors should have provided them with an April 1999 FBI report that alleged the mob once planned to overdose Binion on heroin. Had lawyers seen the report, they said, they might have changed their trial strategy and pursued the angle that organized crime associates had killed Binion.

Scotti had obtained the seven-page report, written by Las

Vegas FBI agent Charles Maurer, after the trial. In the report, Maurer disclosed that he received details of the Binion murder plot from Antone Davi, one of Herbie Blitzstein's killers, after Davi had pleaded guilty to the shooting. Davi told Maurer that Alfred Mauriello, another reputed mob associate who pleaded guilty to killing Blitzstein, had proposed the hit on Binion. Mauriello, Davi reported, wanted Davi and Blitzstein's other convicted shooter, Richard Friedman, to participate in the Binion killing.

"Mauriello told Friedman and Davi that Binion will be robbed, and a door to his house would be left open so Davi and Friedman could kill him," Maurer wrote. "Mauriello said Binion was a heroin user, and he gave Binion's address to Friedman and Davi. Friedman came up with a plan to use a tazer [stun gun] on Binion and give him an overdose of heroin while he was under the influence of the tazer."

Agents had recovered a stun gun from Freidman's apartment when they arrested him for Blitzstein's slaying in 1997.

Defense lawyers also asked Bonaventure to consider possible misconduct on the part of the jurors. Terry charged that the jurors had referred to "depraved indifference," which was not part of the judge's deliberating instructions, and made use of several documents that weren't introduced as evidence during the trial. Those documents included a summary of the charges and jury instructions that one of the jurors had put together. All of this, the lawyers claimed, had "infected" the deliberating process.

Terry and Momot had learned of these allegations from juror Joan Sanders, who had stepped forward a couple of weeks earlier to say she no longer believed Murphy and Tabish had killed Binion. A hearing on the defense motions was set for August 11.

In the meantime, Murphy had wound up in more trouble at the detention center. The *Las Vegas Sun* reported on July 24 that Murphy no longer was housed in the same cell with two other high-profile inmates. Jailers had placed Murphy in the same protective-custody cell with Margaret Rudin, charged in the 1994 slaying of her husband, and Jessica Williams, a twenty-one-year-old former topless dancer accused of plowing her car into a group of teenagers on Interstate 15, killing six of them.

Rudin, the paper said, had complained that Murphy and Williams were engaging in an intimate relationship. Lawyers for both Murphy and Williams, however, denied that such a relationship existed. And jail officials said they had investigated allegations of "inappropriate conduct" between the two inmates, but failed to substantiate the assertions. They nevertheless decided to separate all three inmates. In that same story, the *Sun* reported that Palazzo and Robert Murdock had terminated their longtime partnership. Within the legal community, it was well known that differences over the handling of the Binion case had contributed to the breakup.

As the hearing for a new trial approached, Tabish gave off-camera interviews to television reporters, predicting big things were going to come out. His lawyer was pushing to reopen the issue of David Gomez, who had once claimed to be part of a prosecution conspiracy to steal Tabish's confidential trial notes.

On August 11, just prior to the start of the hearing, Bonaventure granted Palazzo, Cassidy and other former defense-team members an "absolute waiver" of their attorney-client privilege with the two defendants so that they could answer the charges that Terry had raised. Prosecutors, now in the position of having to defend the former defense-team members to preserve the convictions, had asked for the total waiver. Bonaventure's ruling meant that Palazzo and Cassidy and even Goodman, if called to the stand, could talk about the defense's innermost secrets on cross-examination by prosecutors. It forced the defense to abandon the ineffective assistance of counsel allegations. Bonaventure also sided with prosecutors by striking from the record most of what Sanders had alleged, saying it went to the heart of the mental processes of the jurors, which the defense by law was barred from bringing up.

When it came time for the hearing, much of the predicted fireworks never happened. Sanders stood alone in her misconduct allegations. She was rebutted by her eleven colleagues, who testified that none of the items Sanders mentioned, including the use of depraved indifference, figured prominently in their deliberations. Most jurors said they never even heard the legal term. Gomez was called to the stand and once more took the Fifth Amendment, shutting down the defense in its efforts to expose the so-called conspiracy to steal Tabish's notes. Prosecutors had maintained all along there was no such plot.

That left the defense with the organized-crime angle, which Roger described in court as "absurd."

For starters, Roger said he never even had possession of any of the FBI reports. He also said the defense attorneys knew about the mob plot to kill Binion long before the latest FBI report surfaced, and should have tried harder themselves to get more information about it.

"The fact that some mobsters were sitting around talking about murdering Ted Binion in 1997 is not exculpatory to Ms. Murphy and Mr. Tabish," Roger said. "All along, their defense was that Mr. Binion was not murdered and instead died of an accidental overdose or a suicide."

Roger said that if the defense had switched to the theory that the mob had killed Binion, it merely would have dragged the defendants into a broader conspiracy. Murphy, he said, had acknowledged being at the home on the day Binion died, and Tabish had been bragging about his mob ties.

Bonaventure gave himself until September 8 to issue his ruling.

In the meantime, the judge received some startling news that prompted him to haul the defense lawyers and their investigators to a secret hearing in his chambers on August 22.

Summoned to the closed-door hearing were Roger,

Momot, Terry and defense investigators Jim Thomas, Michael Wysocki and Robert Maddox.

"On Friday, August 18, while on duty, my bailiff, Hank, received a telephone call in chambers from a certain individual asking to speak to me," Bonaventure said in a transcript of the hearing. "At the time of the call, I wasn't available, and in substance, it was relayed to Hank that Mr. Tabish, the father of defendant Richard Tabish, was upset by the apparent result of court proceedings during the recent hearing on the motion for a new trial for his son, Rick."

Bonaventure said the caller indicated that Tabish's father had hired Thomas to "dig up dirt" on him to influence his decision because he felt that Bonaventure was in the "pocket" of the prosecution.

The judge added that he was told the defense planned to slowly leak derogatory information about him.

"I talked to the individual myself, and he confirmed that," Bonaventure said. "And this individual—I'm not going to name his name— seems to me a very reliable person. And it seems to me, the one he talked to had access to the defense camp. So I received this information about some, perhaps, investigation being undertaken against me in order to influence the outcome of my decision. And that certain threats were made.

"I don't have any reason to believe this is happening," the judge added. "But I wanted to make a record of it. That's basically why we're here . . . And it's not affecting at all my partiality in this case."

Bonaventure then put the defense team on notice that Nevada laws make it a felony to threaten or try to influence a public official.

"There could be federal crimes involved," he said. "I don't know. But this is what I'm receiving from this inquiry. And this is where we're at. Does anybody want to say anything?"

"I do, sir," Thomas said. "Your Honor, that's the most ridiculous thing I've heard this week. I was hired on this

case in May 1999 to do an investigation for the defense of
Rick Tabish. I have at no time been hired to do an investigation into you. I have not done an investigation into you. I
have not investigated you in any way."

"OK," Bonaventure responded.

"I don't know who your source is, but he needs to get better information," Thomas added.

"I've got some questions," Bonaventure replied. "Are you
aware of any ongoing or planned investigation of myself?"

"No, I'm not. You know, the only thing I heard there that
was true was that Mr. Tabish was upset."

"Has anyone approached you with the idea of investigating me?"

"No, sir."

"Are you aware of any other parties who have been approached about the possibility of investigating me?"

"No, sir."

"Has it ever been suggested to you that I should be investigated?"

"No, sir."

"Do you have any knowledge at all about any investigations of myself being discussed as a possibility?"

"No, sir."

Bonaventure then asked Maddox and Wysocki the same
questions and got the same responses. He told Momot and
Terry that their names had not come up during his discussion
with the tipster.

"I wouldn't even insult you with suggesting that you or
Mr. Momot were in any way even mentioned," he said. "Do
you understand that?"

"Judge, I understand that," Terry responded. "And I appreciate the court's comments because, quite frankly, I've
known the court for a long time . . . I have nothing but respect for this court. I can look you in the eye, take a poly-
graph, whatever you want. That has never been a directive
from me to Mr. Thomas. Mr. Thomas and I have never discussed such a situation."

After further conversation, Terry added: "We're also not unmindful of the fact that Your Honor is going to be doing the sentencing. From a realistic point of view, the last thing I'm going to do in representing a client is authorize a direct investigation on a judge, even if it was for the purpose of getting it out in the media . . . So I have no hesitation in telling you neither Mr. Thomas nor I have ever talked about that."

Terry said he recalled Frank Tabish not being happy about one of the judge's decisions.

"And I can remember what I told him," he explained. "I said, 'You know you have to live with the judge's decision. You respect him for the decision, even if you disagree. There are other courts.' And that was the totality of the conversation."

But Bonaventure continued to press the lawyers and the investigators.

"It's just incomprehensible to me that this could happen, that somebody would investigate me to influence my decision, because there would be felonies committed here. I don't know if Frank Tabish is aware of this. Maybe he should be aware of it—if he's even thinking about it."

Momot suggested that maybe others not in the room had hatched a plot against the judge.

"I can say, besides Mr. Terry, I think I've known the court the longest in this jurisdiction. And I would take it as a personal affront if that was ever brought to my attention."

That gave Bonaventure an opening to inquire about William Fuller, who probably had spent more than $1 million by that time on Murphy's defense.

"You know, I haven't talked to the man in—I don't know how long," Momot said. "And you know, I think he talks primarily with Mr. Scotti in California, to be honest with you."

"Well, again, I don't even necessarily believe any of this is true," Bonaventure replied. "I just thought it was incumbent upon me to bring this to everybody's attention in a sealed condition. We could all surmise, surmise and surmise.

But I mean, it's not coming from you. It's coming from somebody like Frank Tabish, like Bill Fuller. Somebody like that that doesn't like what's happening here . . . if they do it, there are going to be serious consequences."

Then the judge suggested that such an inquiry could have been initiated by someone outside the authority of Momot and Terry. And once more, Terry told the judge he would never allow something like that to happen if it came to his attention.

"But there are other people involved in this case that I have no control over. John has no control over," Terry said.

Bonaventure concluded the secret hearing by saying, "I hope it stops now . . . a word could be brought to these people that if something like this is going to be perpetrated, it's going to have dire consequences."

Terry asked the judge if he minded whether he talked to Tabish's father about it.

"No, I have no problem with you discussing it with Frank Tabish," Bonaventure said. "In fact, it would probably be a good thing that you do it, to prevent him from doing something stupid."

"Correct," Terry replied.

"And the same with maybe Fuller, if he has any ideas. But that's, you know, that's something that you'll have to determine."

Bonaventure then told the parties present that he would keep a transcript of the hearing sealed. Terry later reported to the judge that Frank Tabish denied hiring an investigator. Momot separately reported that Fuller did not respond to his inquiries.

Days later, despite his serious conversation with the key parties in the defense camp, Bonaventure got another tip that a defense investigator had gone to the clerk's office and discovered that the judge did not have his required oath of office and bond on file from his 1996 reelection. The judge heard that the defense was going to try to use that to get him off the case before he ruled on the motions to dismiss. But it turned out the clerk's office had merely misplaced the items.

On September 8, Bonaventure announced his ruling on live television. To no one's surprise, he refused to grant Murphy and Tabish a new trial. He quoted a U.S. Supreme Court decision that said the defendants were entitled to a fair trial but not a perfect one. The sentencing was a week away.

CHAPTER 34

•••••••••••••••••

The Sentencing

•••••••••••••••••

IN HIS AUGUST 8 pre-sentence report, veteran probation officer George Johnson held back no punches when evaluating Sandy Murphy.

Before coming to his conclusions, Johnson had pored through the voluminous records in the Binion murder case and interviewed Murphy, her family and Ted Binion's family.

He said Murphy, on top of her 1995 arrest for drunken driving, had acknowledged past cocaine and marijuana use. Murphy reported that she was introduced to cocaine by Binion in October 1996 and ended up using marijuana on a regular basis in 1998.

"She has sought no formal counseling to address her abuse," Johnson wrote in his sealed, fifteen-page report.

The probation officer had harsher words for Murphy's role in Binion's September 17, 1998, death.

"The defendant's involvement in the commission of the instant offense is horrific and strikes at the very core of trust between significant others and intimate relationships," Johnson said. "Through the defendant's greed, immaturity and knowledge of the victim's shortcomings, she and her codefendant plotted an elaborate scheme to terminate the victim's life, swap him for a younger boyfriend and escape with the decedent's assets.

"The defendant has exhibited an iniquitous desire to rob her benefactor of his riches and his life while she presented a ruse of a caring, loving and trusted friend."

Johnson said Jack Binion had told him the family was convinced that Murphy and Rick Tabish had killed his brother, "not for passion, but instead for pure greed." The family, Johnson added, felt strongly that the two defendants should receive the maximum penalty possible. An emotional letter from Bonnie Binion, expressing her sorrow over the loss of her father, was attached to Johnson's report.

In the handwritten letter, Bonnie, who didn't always enjoy a friendly relationship with her father, said his death came one month after her eighteenth birthday and just three weeks into her first semester in college.

"Losing a parent in any circumstance is difficult, but when it's compounded by murder, a trial and the media, it's unbearable," Bonnie wrote. "I don't go a day without wanting to pick up the phone and call him. Every birthday and holiday is overcast by the hole I feel without him. Someday, when I get married, how can I enjoy walking down the aisle without him? How can I explain someone as colorful as my dad to my children and do him justice?

"My most vivid and happy memories are overshadowed by the vision of him in a casket I had to pick out. I'm haunted by the images of his corpse that were plastered on TV by the media and shown over and over in court. I worry, did he suffer? Was he afraid? How betrayed he must have felt. I had to hear over and over the excruciating details of his last moments."

Bonnie said her pain was compounded by defense lawyers constantly attacking her father.

"The trial should have been some sort of catharsis for me. At least that's what everyone told me," she wrote. "But it was hardly true. To see six weeks of my father, the victim, put on trial, and sit silently was, well, unexplainable. To see defense attorneys take cheap shots at my father and my family, I felt so helpless."

She said she had suffered a variety of physical problems from the stress of the past two years.

"I was a wreck full of anxiety," she continued. "I didn't leave home hardly ever. I didn't get dressed. I was sick all the time. I went to doctor after doctor plagued with stomach problems, chronic headaches, lost weight, nervousness, sleep problems, you name it. Stress was eating me up . . .

"Every time I tried to just grieve alone and move on, I had some obligation or some media or legal reminder that dragged me under."

Bonnie said she was "filled with anger and betrayal, fear and pity.

"It is harder every day knowing he's gone," she concluded. "I love him so much. I still need a father, and no one can replace him. I feel so robbed. Two people did this, took the most important person in my life away."

In his sealed, nineteen-page pre-sentence report on Tabish, Johnson described the convicted killer as "no newcomer to the criminal justice system," having been arrested six times with two misdemeanor convictions and one felony conviction.

Johnson said Tabish "denied criminal culpability" in Binion's death.

"He offered innocuous scenarios, which portrayed him as an innocent victim," Johnson wrote.

Those words intrigued Judge Bonaventure, who on September 11, four days before the sentencing, asked Johnson to explain in more detail Tabish's state of mind following his conviction.

In a two-page supplemental report, Johnson told the judge that Tabish had tried to "dissuade this officer from the truth." Tabish, he said, offered "numerous excuses" for his arrests in Montana, claiming they were the result of a "small-town police force that had targeted him." Tabish also called his 1987 conviction for possessing cocaine a "big mistake" on the part of authorities.

And Tabish denied torturing Leo Casey, saying the incident was a "big misunderstanding" and the result of an overzealous prosecutor.

"The defendant also stated that his involvement with Sandra Murphy was simply him trying to help a person in a bad situation and that his mistake was to come to her aid on the day the victim [died]," Johnson wrote. "He stated that if he would have continued on to the airport instead of responding to Murphy's phone call, he would not be in the mess he finds himself in now. He presented himself as a victim of his good nature and his desire to help Ms. Murphy.

"Throughout the course of the interview," Johnson added, "[Tabish] did not accept responsibility for any of his past criminal involvement. He portrayed himself as a victim, instant offenses included. Additionally, he stated that he is not a criminal and that the Binion Money Machine as well as David Roger and David Wall are the culprits."

Johnson attached a letter from Casey begging for a stiff prison term for Tabish.

"This is not someone who has just once made a mistake," Casey wrote. "This is a criminal who has chosen this as his way of life . . . He chooses to kidnap, kill, beat, torture, maim, rob, steal or anything else that he may choose to do for his own bloodthirsty, evil greed and then begs the court for leniency."

Casey said Tabish had robbed him of his health. He told Johnson he has nerve damage in his neck and suffers from blurred vision, migraine headaches and dizzy spells.

With Johnson's reports in hand, Bonaventure went into the September 15 sentencing prepared to hand out more jail time to Murphy and Tabish on the remaining charges. Prosecutors were hoping Bonaventure would add five more years for Murphy and ten for Tabish on top of the twenty years recommended for each by the jury. Instead, after listening to pleas from the two defendants one last time, the judge met the prosecutors halfway. He handed out sentences that would keep Murphy in prison for a minimum of twenty-two years, and Tabish behind bars for at least twenty-five years.

Once more, on live local and national television, the courtroom was packed with reporters, spectators and family members of the defendants and the victim. And once more, both Murphy and Tabish proclaimed their innocence.

"I believe that I was wrongly convicted," a tearful Murphy told the judge in a soft voice from her seat at the defense table. "It's hard to look guilty when you're innocent."

She again professed her love for Binion while a sneering Bonnie Binion listened reluctantly from the first row of the courtroom.

"I didn't have to hurt Teddy. I would never hurt Teddy," the twenty-eight-year-old Murphy said. "I don't want to ask the court for anything because I didn't do anything wrong, and I shouldn't even be here."

Tabish stood up and told the judge there was no "evil plot" to kill Binion.

"It didn't happen," he said. "You don't do things like that."

He said he was hoping for a new trial so that he could take the witness stand and testify.

"I'm here to face the charges," he said. "I accept my conviction. I pray to God I get a new trial and I get to talk."

Tabish concluded his remarks in an upbeat fashion.

"I want my parents to hold their head up," he said. "I want everybody who knows Rick Tabish to hold their head up because today is a good day."

Bonaventure was not moved by the words of the defendants.

"Here it is almost two years to the day of Mr. Binion's murder, and we all wish we were not here today," Bonaventure said. "Unfortunately, due to the cowardly acts of the defendants, we are. The many lives they have ruined will never be the same."

Murphy, her now-natural brown hair in a ponytail, looked down at the defense table in a sullen mood as the judge spoke. Tabish sat with an empty look on his face, gazing straight ahead. In the first row, Bonnie, surrounded by her boyfriend and family, began to shed some tears.

Bonaventure referred to the "heart-wrenching letter" he had received from Bonnie.

"The court can do many things," Bonaventure said. "Unfortunately, it cannot heal Bonnie's hurt. Mr. Tabish and Ms. Murphy, by murdering this young lady's father, you forever stole her innocence and peace of mind. Bonnie asks for justice.

"This court asks that Bonnie accept that none of us can help the things that life has done to us and not let your grief and pain harden your heart and steal your soul forever. If you allow that to happen, the defendants will have succeeded in also taking your life."

Bonaventure said greed played a key role in the murder scheme.

"However, what most concerns this court in the defendants' actions is the disregard of Mr. Binion's trust; for it is clear that Mr. Binion was truly in love with the defendant Ms. Murphy and that he had befriended Mr. Tabish. What a horrendous image this court envisions when it conjures up the picture of a man who so completely entrusts his confidences to his loved one, to only then be a victim of her ultimate betrayal.

"It is a sad irony of Ted Binion's life that whatever caused him to devote his love to Ms. Murphy also started the spiral of his demise. The disdain that our society has for individuals who gain the trust of others only to cause them harm is far greater than the aversion we have for criminals who carry out their crimes upon complete strangers."

Bonaventure then looked at Tabish and called him a "con man, one who gains the trust of others only to then betray them for your own personal gain.

"Additionally, what is most striking to this court is that you come from a family of some prominence and stability," he said. "In fact, you yourself were making a decent, fair and honest living, one which most people would be content with having. It was a life that you decided to give up to satisfy the most primal of your desires.

"There is no justification that you could bring this court for your actions, as you are here by your own choice. Your lack of remorse and your ramblings as to the guilt of others are clearly an indication that you have not yet acquired the ability to take responsibility for your own actions."

Next, Bonaventure turned his attention to Murphy.

"Ms. Murphy, your involvement in these crimes is horrific and strikes at the very core of trust between significant others," he said. "Through your greed and betrayal, you plotted an elaborate scheme to kill Mr. Binion and steal his money, as well as swap him for a younger boyfriend . . . You presented yourself as a caring and loving girlfriend only to lure your victim into a trap, which ultimately cost him his life.

"The court has witnessed firsthand your disdain for the laws of our society and particularly of this jurisdiction. No record could perpetuate your scowl of resentment or bland indifference toward these proceedings that this court has witnessed. Your attitude reflects that of one who shows little respect for these proceedings and of this system of law.

"The public must be protected from individuals like yourself, for you do not display the telltale signs of a criminal actor," the judge said. "Your feigned innocence permeated this court, as if you are oblivious to the predicament you are in. Your facade is of no concern, as you are to receive just punishment for your offenses.

"You chose to steal that which is not yours, and now you must live with the aftermath. You chose to betray and kill your lover, and now you must live with the consequences. It is this court's hope that after your period of incarceration, you will have awakened from the Alice in Wonderland dreamlike state you have attempted to portray in this courtroom and will have finally gained the understanding of what the law intends to do when certain lines are crossed and broken."

Before he adjourned, Bonaventure also had a few words to say to the Las Vegas community, which had been glued to every development in the case for the past two years.

"As this case has garnered much media attention in this community and around the world, this court is cognizant of the fact that this community was very much affected by this case and its outcome," he said. "Now that the case has been resolved, it is hoped that Las Vegas will also find a sense of closure and return to more important matters that affect this great community. Justice, though due the accused, is due the accuser also. Justice has been served. This case is closed."

EPILOGUE

....

The Aftermath

....

THREE WEEKS AFTER the sentencing of Sandy Murphy and Rick Tabish, District Judge Joseph Bonaventure raised his left arm at the bench and in his best Italian accent yelled an enthusiastic *"Finito!"*

His excitement, before a crowded courtroom and live television cameras, came at the conclusion of the sentencing of the four remaining defendants accused of lesser crimes in the Ted Binion murder case.

After more than two years, the case that had captivated Las Vegans and a good part of the nation was finally over. All that was left was the lengthy appeals process in the higher courts.

Bonaventure accepted pleas from David Mattsen, Michael Milot, Steven Wadkins and John Joseph. All four, as a result of a generous offer from prosecutors, pleaded no contest to gross misdemeanor charges with no jail time attached. Mattsen and Milot pleaded to conspiracy to commit grand larceny stemming from the September 19, 1998, theft of Binion's $6 million silver fortune in Pahrump. Wadkins and Joseph pleaded to conspiracy to commit extortion in the July 28, 1998, torture of Leo Casey at the Jean sand pit.

Having convicted Murphy and Tabish, the main players in the conspiracy against Binion, prosecutors had made it clear they wanted to deal with the remaining defendants. They didn't want to spend more taxpayer money on additional trials, and they didn't want those cases to create new appellate issues for Murphy and Tabish.

As part of their plea agreements, Bonaventure ordered all four defendants to pay a $2,000 fine or serve 200 hours of community service. Milot, Wadkins and Joseph opted for the fine. Mattsen, who weeks earlier had proclaimed that the notoriety over the Binion case had left him "penniless," chose community service. He agreed to break horses for the Bureau of Land Management.

Mattsen had provided one last bit of drama to the case a week before his sentencing, when he led prosecutors and Binion's estate lawyers on an unsuccessful treasure hunt at Binion's 125-acre ranch in Pahrump. Mattsen claimed that Binion had told him where he had buried millions in diamonds and double eagle gold coins. On the morning of Saturday, September 30, with media helicopters hovering above and reporters and photographers waiting at the gates of the ranch, Mattsen took investigators to the site of the would-be treasure. Several hours later, after nothing had been found, the dig was called off.

While prosecutors were looking for buried treasure, Murphy's eighty-four-year-old benefactor, William Fuller, hired Alan Dershowitz to help John Momot with her appeal. Fuller also persuaded Thomas Pitaro, a highly regarded Las Vegas lawyer and close Momot friend, to work on the appeal. Pitaro had been brought into the murder trial at the end to help Momot with some of the defense's medical experts. He also represented Wadkins.

Momot still remained convinced that Murphy was innocent.

"To this day, none of the jurors can articulate how Sandy participated in this alleged murder," he said. "No one can say how she forced him to ingest drugs. There is no physical evidence linking her to Ted's death."

Murphy and Tabish would have to continue their fight from their cells in the tough Nevada prison system, where they became assimilated into a population of 10,000 inmates.

Bonnie Binion, at the age of twenty, heartbroken and three semesters behind in her studies in college, decided she no longer wanted to make Las Vegas her home. She put her father's house up for sale and moved in temporarily with her mother, Doris, in Dallas.

Binion's $55 million estate, with help from the Nevada Supreme Court, took steps to settle his affairs, fulfilling one of his last wishes by moving in court for a judgment to cut Murphy out of his will.

The estate also distributed the $100,000 reward to seven people who had played key roles in the case.

Four people each received $20,000: Deana Perry, Steven Kurt Gratzer, Jeannine Pierce and Bobbi Frazer. Mary Montoya-Gascoigne was given $10,000 and Thomas Loveday and Christopher Hendrick each got $5,000.

Gratzer was arrested in Missoula on felony drug charges just days after he had received his share of the reward. Police there seized methamphetamine, cocaine and $4,100 in cash from him.

Tom Dillard became a hot property at the courthouse, finding himself a ton of new clients, and David Roger, David Wall and James Buczek all moved on to their next cases.

Becky Behnen returned to focusing her energy on running the family's Horseshoe Club.

As for Judge Bonaventure, it was back to business as usual for him, too, but not before being singled out by the Italian-American community as the man of the year.

After the sentencing of the remaining defendants, Bonaventure took time to look back at the biggest case of his twenty-two years on the bench.

He said he was pleased that a verdict had been reached.

"It was a very complex case. I think this jury was a very educated jury. They just took a long time and wanted to do the right thing. I was relieved when they came back with a decision."

His law clerk, Al Lasso, who was with the judge every step of the way and helped write his thoughtful decisions, said he was proud of how Bonaventure had conducted himself.

"The judge didn't cave in to any pressure," Lasso said. "There was pressure from every source, but the judge was fair and impartial no matter what the pressure. He ran the trial the way he runs every trial."

Bonaventure said he went into the case well prepared.

"I knew a lot about the case even before the arraignment. It was like a circus, but I decided right from the beginning that I'm not going to change the way I am. I'm too old to change."

Bonaventure also decided he wasn't going to play to the cameras during the trial.

"I just treated this case the same as I do every murder case, but more thoroughly," he said. "I researched it more thoroughly. I made sure every point was correct. I wanted to do the best job I could."

When it was over, most Las Vegans had praise for the way Bonaventure had conducted the case.

"I got lots of calls and letters from people who said they wished I had handled the O. J. Simpson case," Bonaventure recalled. "Everybody's faith in judgment was restored. It was a nice feeling."

Roger said he received the same kind of response from the community.

"They told me that as a result of the O. J. case, they felt that justice came to the highest bidder—that if a criminal defendant has enough money to hire the experts, hire the big attorneys, they're going to get off. They thought the O. J. case was an atrocity. But because of the Binion case, they said their faith in the criminal justice system had been restored."

From the very beginning of the case, Roger said, Murphy and Tabish talked about hiring Dershowitz and their dream team.

"I think they thought that they could buy their way out of this mess," he said. "They paid a lot of money for attorneys. They paid a lot of money for experts."

It turned the case into the biggest real-life drama in Las Vegas in years.

"This was an incredible case," Roger said. "Most people don't have the interest in watching a court proceeding because it's usually so dry. But this case was so fascinating. It had so many twists and turns and was so circumstantial, and there was a tremendous cast of characters. People were glued to the TV set, both in Las Vegas and throughout the United States.

"I think people really got an insight into what happens inside a courtroom. They got an insight into what our criminal justice system is all about."